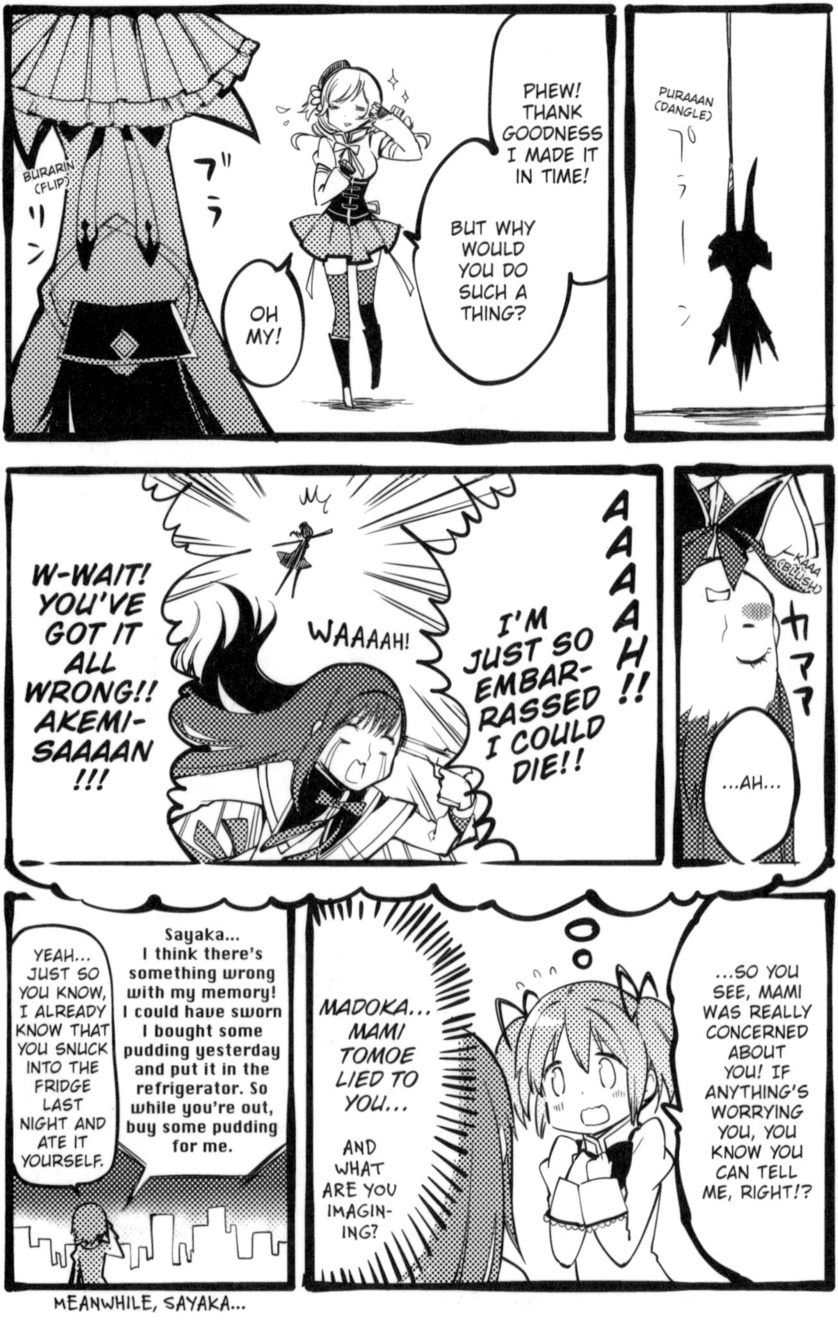
PURAAAN (DANGLE)
プラーン
PHEW! THANK GOODNESS I MADE IT IN TIME!
BUT WHY WOULD YOU DO SUCH A THING?
OH MY!
ブラ
BURARIN (FLIP)
リン
KAAA (BLUSH)
カァァ
...AH...
AAAAAH!!
I'M JUST SO EMBARRASSED I COULD DIE!!
WAAAAH!
W-WAIT! YOU'VE GOT IT ALL WRONG!! AKEMI-SAAAAN!!!
...SO YOU SEE, MAMI WAS REALLY CONCERNED ABOUT YOU! IF ANYTHING'S WORRYING YOU, YOU KNOW YOU CAN TELL ME, RIGHT!?
MADOKA... MAMI TOMOE LIED TO YOU...
AND WHAT ARE YOU IMAGINING?
Sayaka... I think there's something wrong with my memory! I could have sworn I bought some pudding yesterday and put it in the refrigerator. So while you're out, buy some pudding for me.
YEAH... JUST SO YOU KNOW, I ALREADY KNOW THAT YOU SNUCK INTO THE FRIDGE LAST NIGHT AND ATE IT YOURSELF.
MEANWHILE, SAYAKA...

US $13.00 CAN $15.50

ISBN 978-0-316-30939-4

51300

9 780316 309394

E A N

OLDER TEEN
OT
LV

Yen Press

Homura discovers that she has been trapped in an illusory space all along.
Though she resolves to find and put a stop to the culprit behind the illusion,
her friends' apparent happiness in this false reality makes Homura wonder if
she has more to lose than gain by putting an end to it.

The manga adaptation of the record-breaking hit *Puella Magi Madoka Magica:
The Movie -Rebellion-* film continues on!

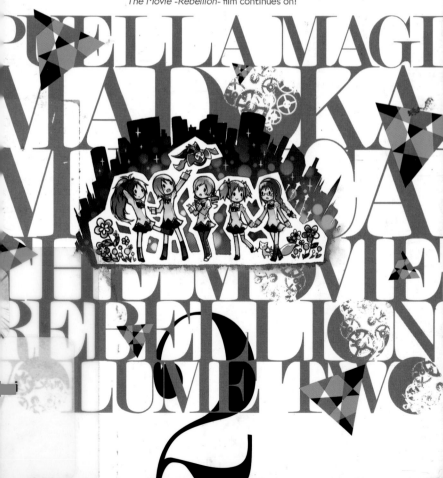

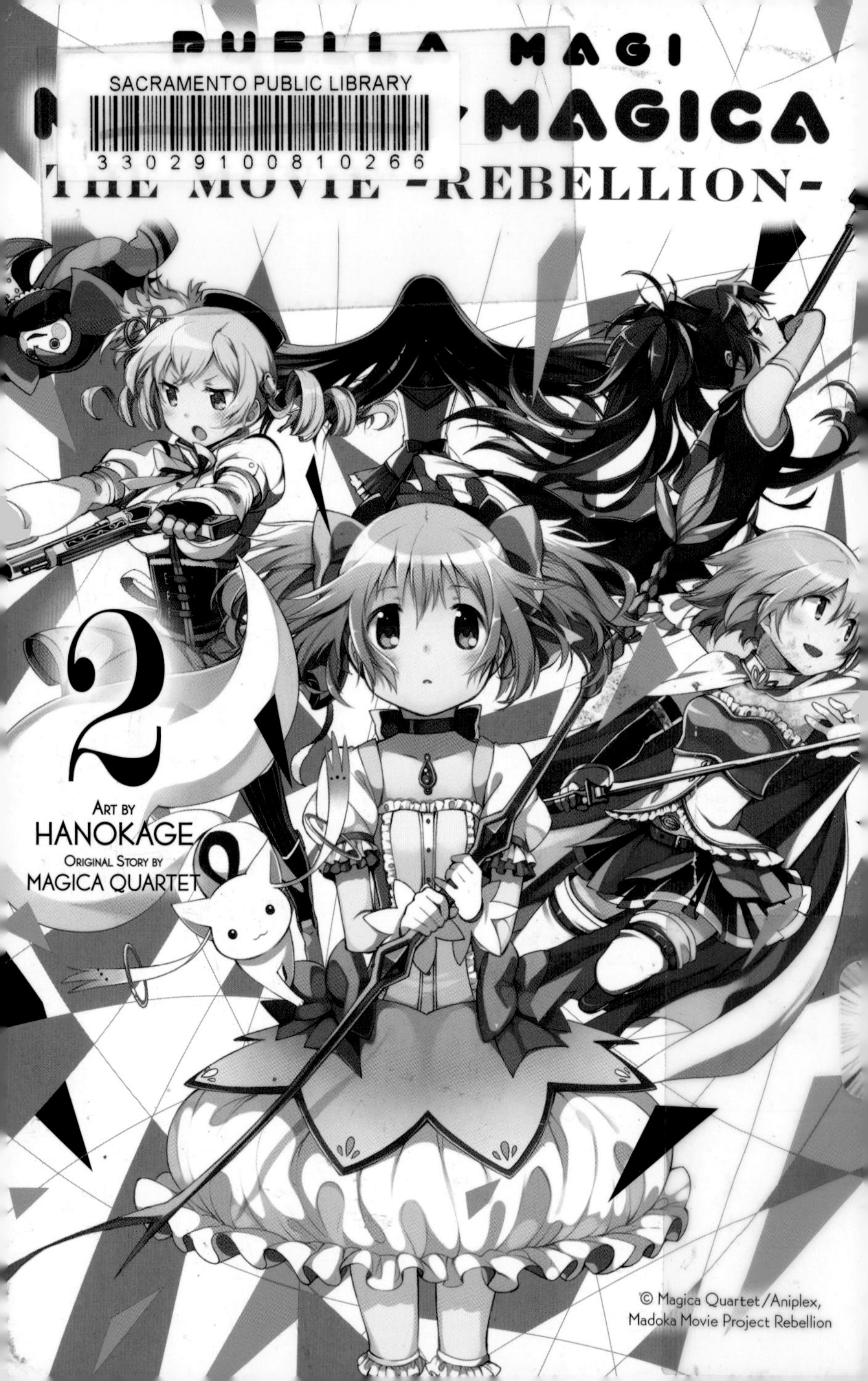

MAGI
MAGICA
THE MOVIE -REBELLION-
2
ART BY
HANOKAGE
ORIGINAL STORY BY
MAGICA QUARTET
© Magica Quartet/Aniplex,
Madoka Movie Project Rebellion

MOVIE EDITION Mitakihara Suspense Theater

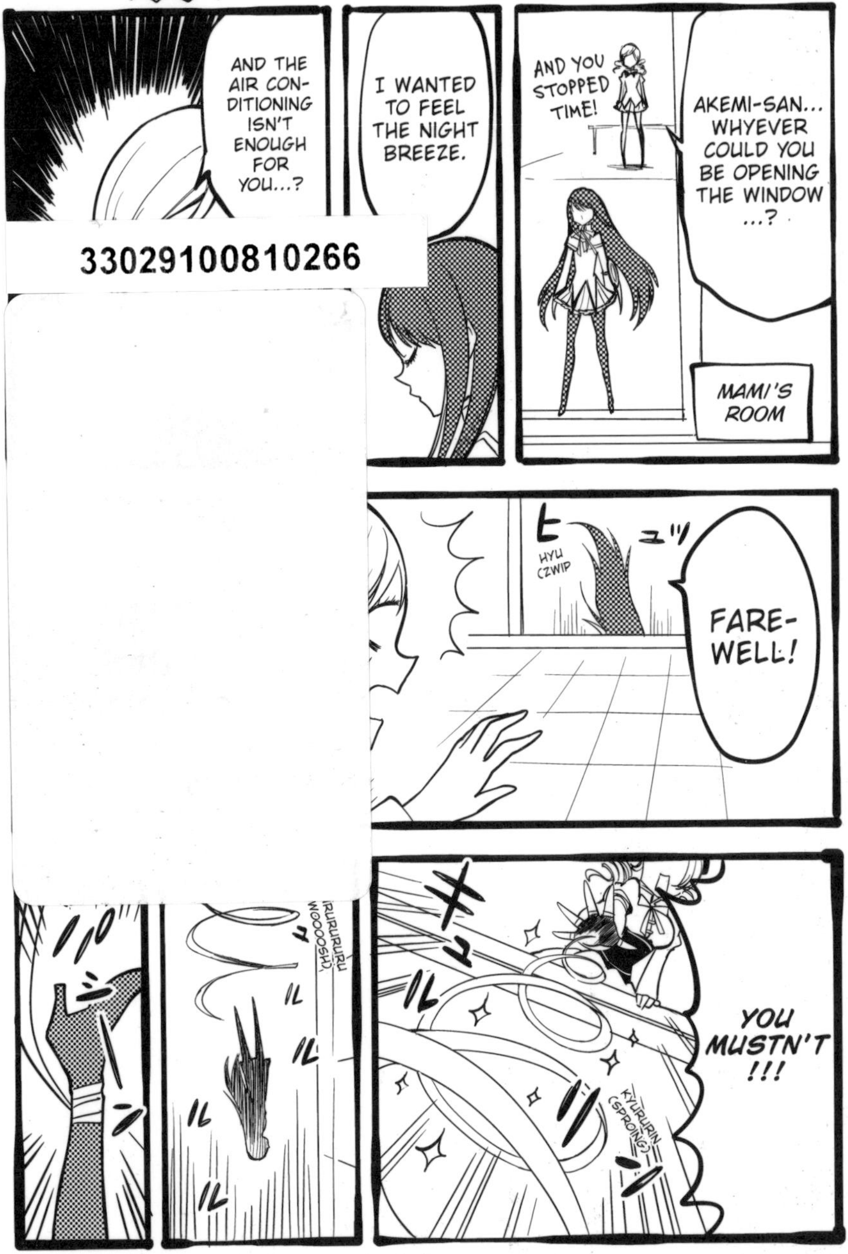
AKEMI-SAN... WHYEVER COULD YOU BE OPENING THE WINDOW ...?
AND YOU STOPPED TIME!
MAMI'S ROOM
I WANTED TO FEEL THE NIGHT BREEZE.
AND THE AIR CON-DITIONING ISN'T ENOUGH FOR YOU...?
FARE-WELL!
HYU CZWIP
YOU MUSTN'T !!!
KYURURIN (SPROING)
KYURURURU (WOOOOSH)

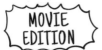

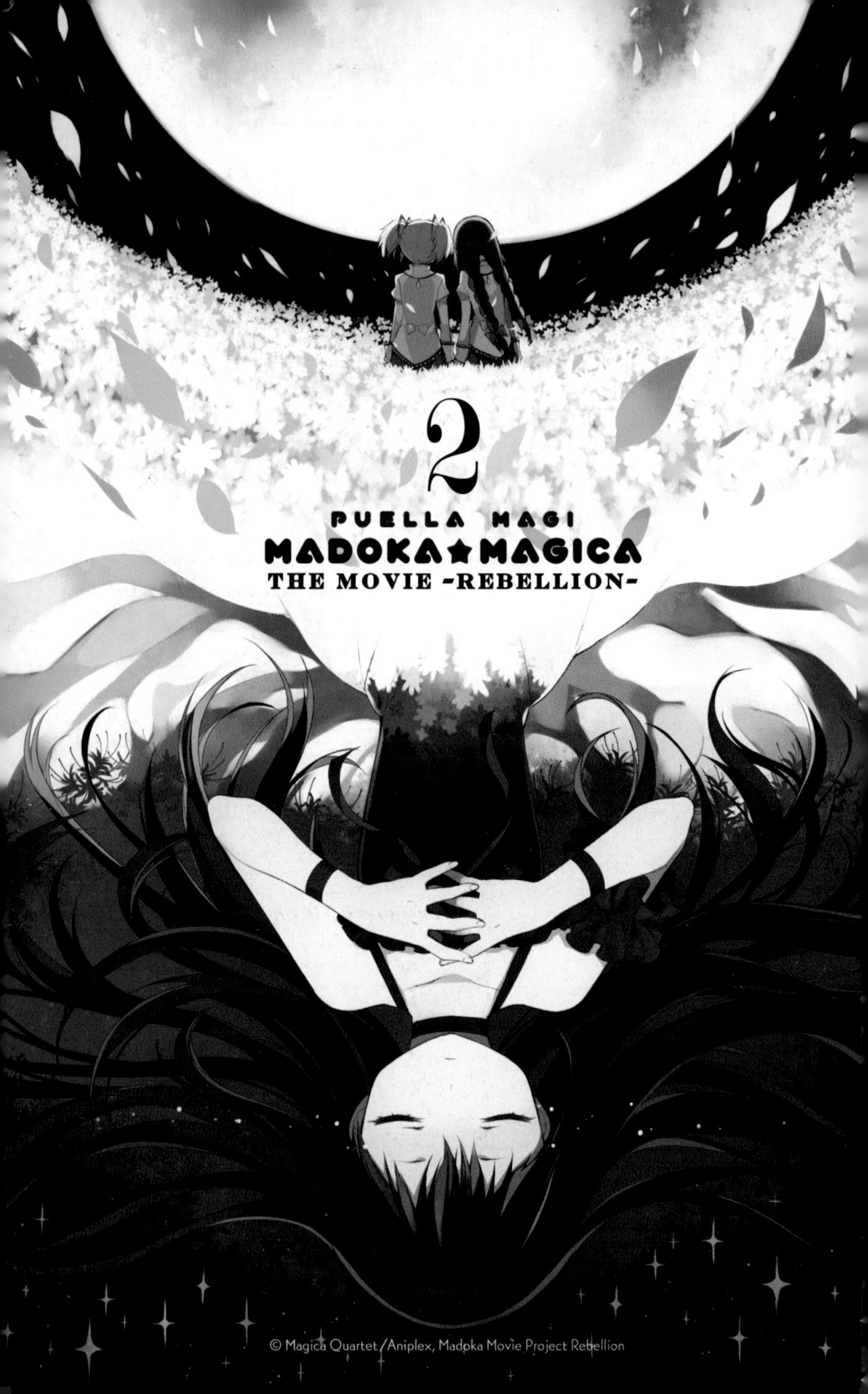
2
PUELLA MAGI
MADOKA☆MAGICA
THE MOVIE -REBELLION-

CONTENTS

PUELLA MAGI MADOKA MAGICA
THE MOVIE -REBELLION-
VOLUME TWO

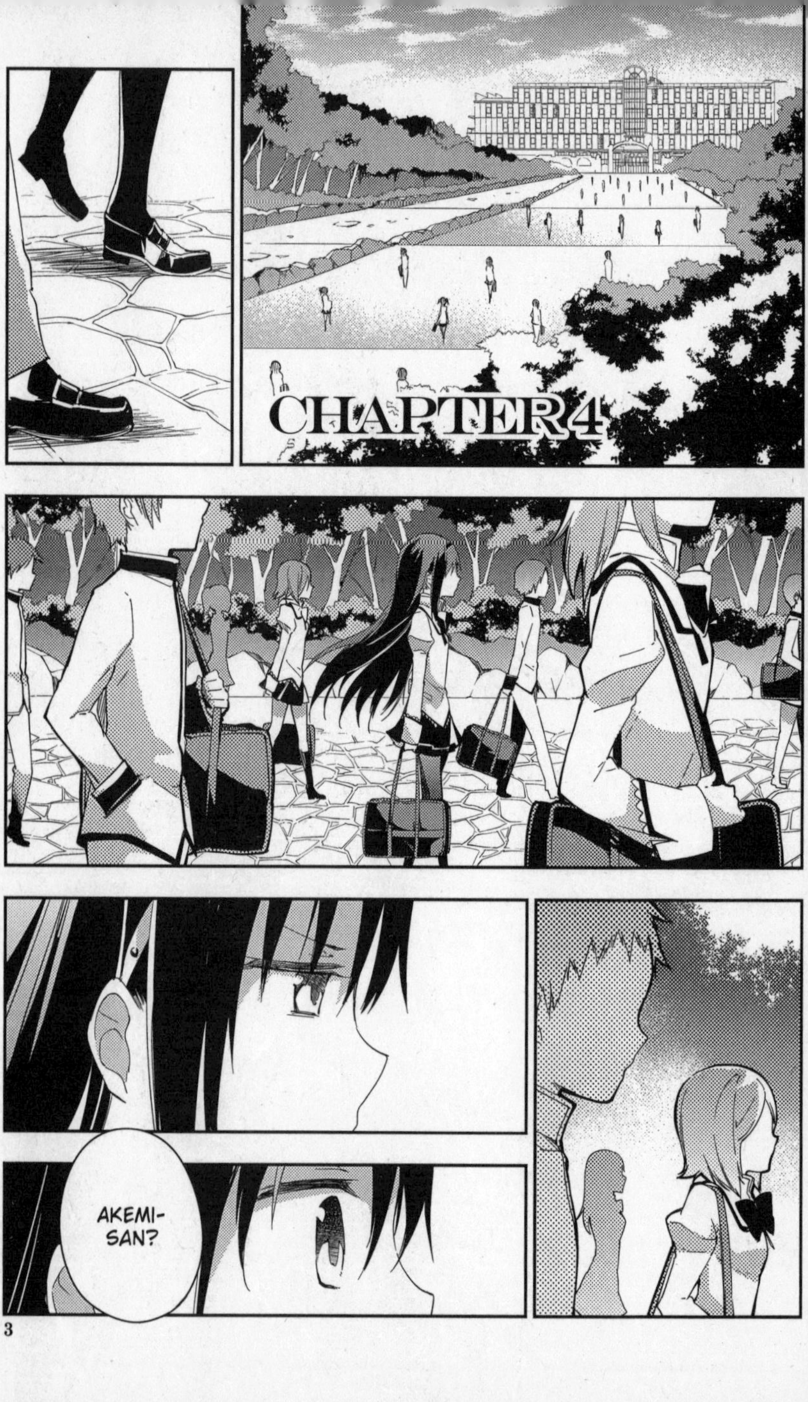
CHAPTER 4
AKEMI-SAN?

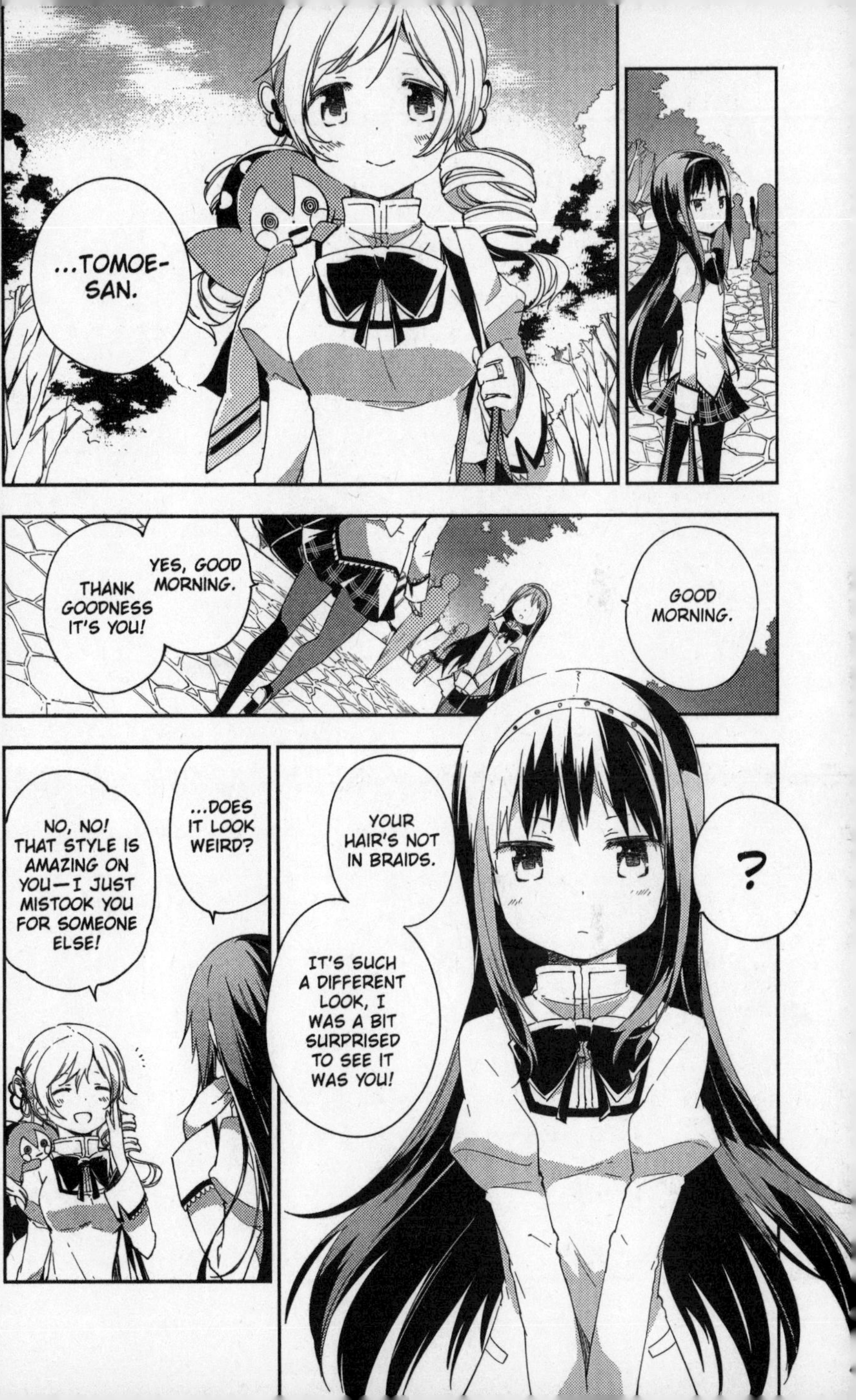
...TOMOE-SAN.
GOOD MORNING.
YES, GOOD MORNING.
THANK GOODNESS IT'S YOU!
?
YOUR HAIR'S NOT IN BRAIDS.
IT'S SUCH A DIFFERENT LOOK, I WAS A BIT SURPRISED TO SEE IT WAS YOU!
...DOES IT LOOK WEIRD?
NO, NO! THAT STYLE IS AMAZING ON YOU—I JUST MISTOOK YOU FOR SOMEONE ELSE!

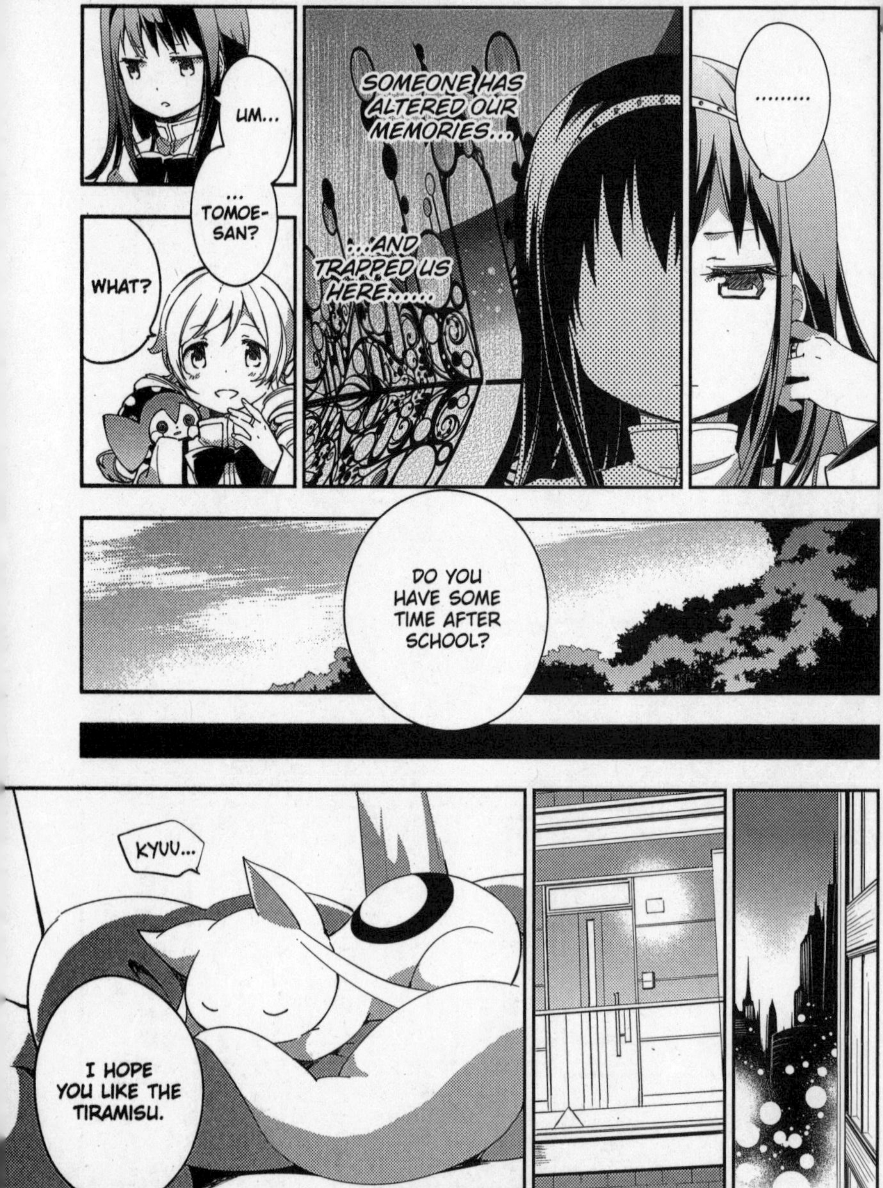
....
SOMEONE HAS ALTERED OUR MEMORIES...
...AND TRAPPED US HERE......
UM...
... TOMOE-SAN?
WHAT?
DO YOU HAVE SOME TIME AFTER SCHOOL?
KYUU...
I HOPE YOU LIKE THE TIRAMISU.

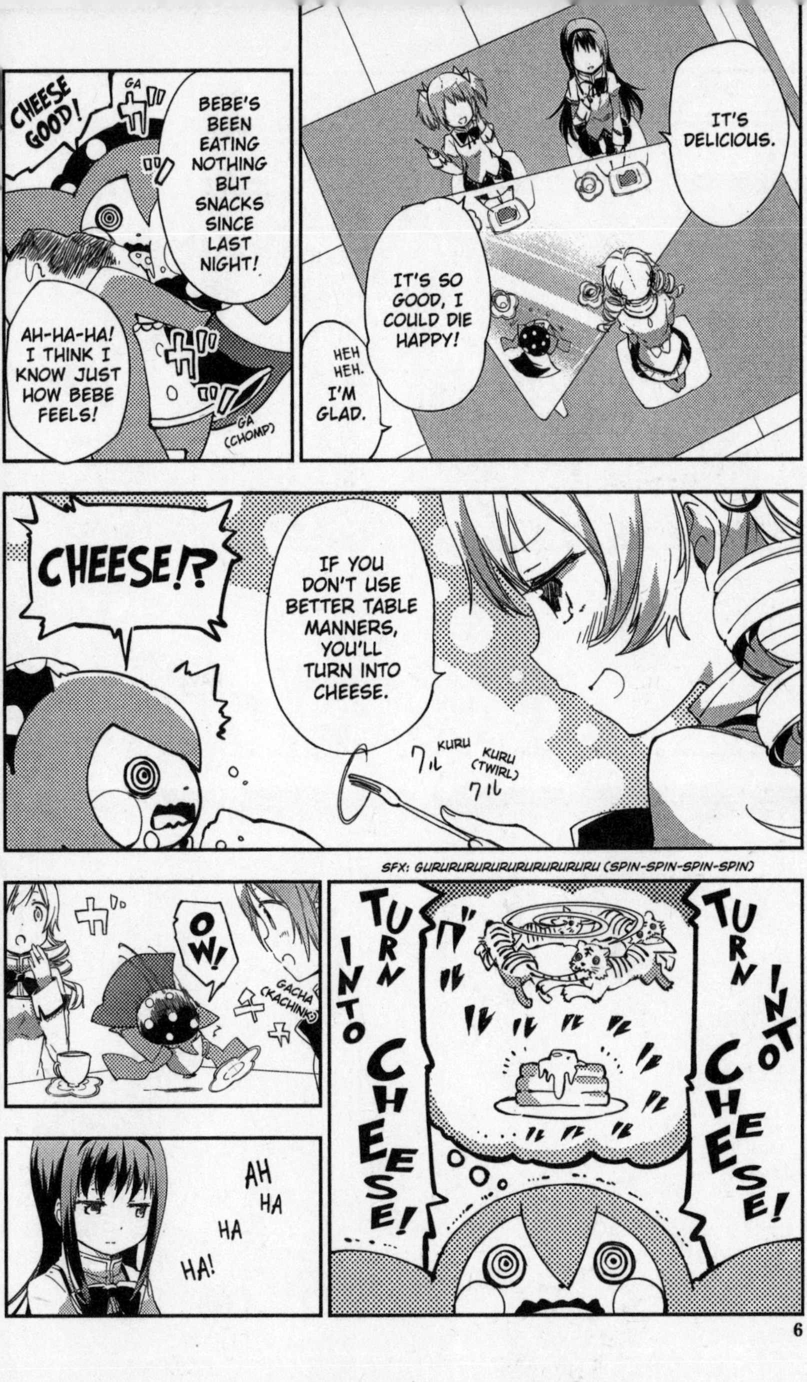
IT'S DELICIOUS.
IT'S SO GOOD, I COULD DIE HAPPY!
HEH HEH. I'M GLAD.
BEBE'S BEEN EATING NOTHING BUT SNACKS SINCE LAST NIGHT!
CHEESE GOOD!
GA
AH-HA-HA! I THINK I KNOW JUST HOW BEBE FEELS!
GA (CHOMP)
IF YOU DON'T USE BETTER TABLE MANNERS, YOU'LL TURN INTO CHEESE.
KURU KURU (TWIRL)
CHEESE!?
SFX: GURURURURURURURURURURU (SPIN-SPIN-SPIN-SPIN)
TURN INTO CHEESE!
TURN INTO CHEESE!
OW!
GACHA (KACHINK)
AH HA HA HA!

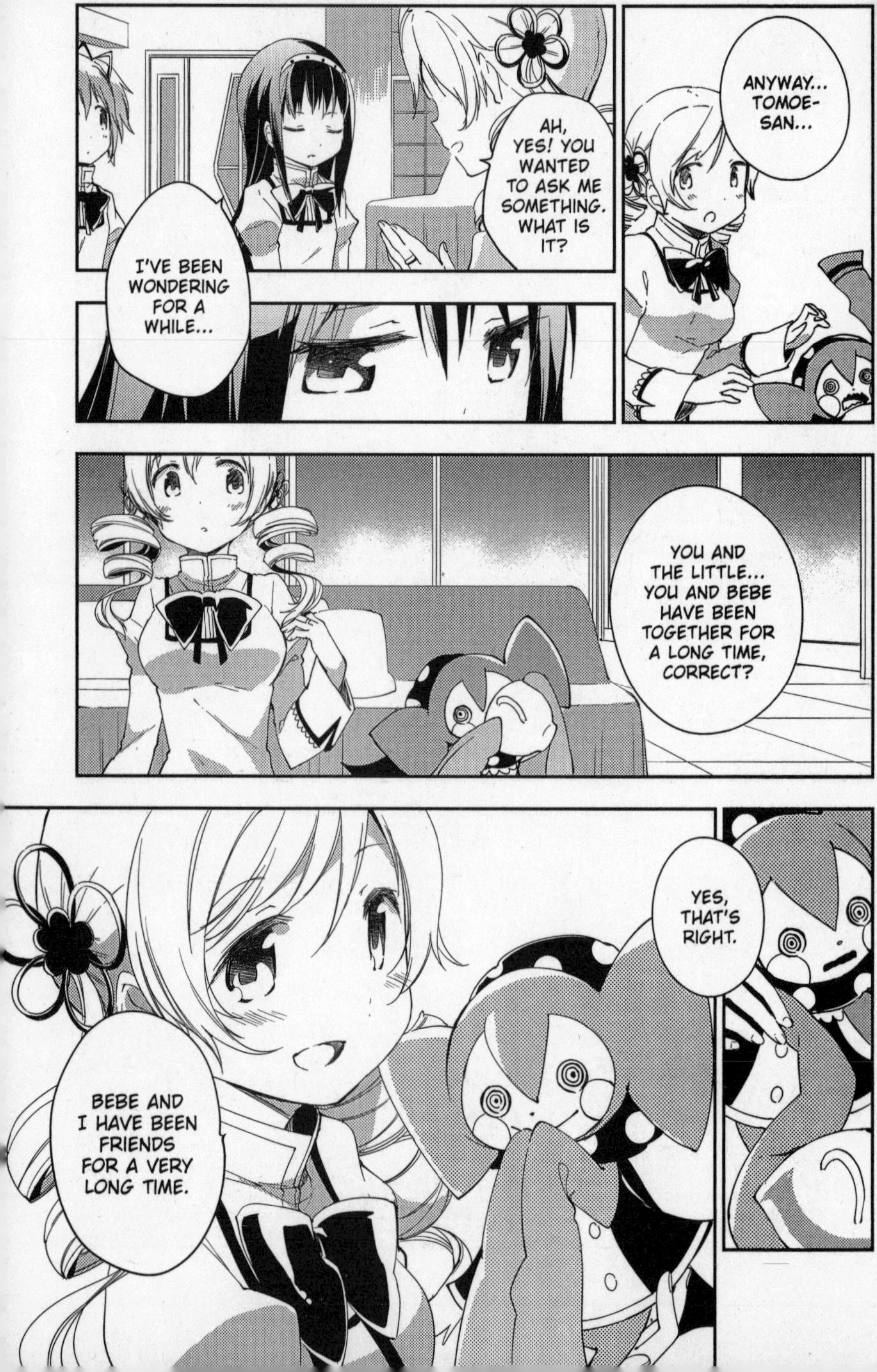
ANYWAY... TOMOE-SAN...
AH, YES! YOU WANTED TO ASK ME SOMETHING. WHAT IS IT?
I'VE BEEN WONDERING FOR A WHILE...
YOU AND THE LITTLE... YOU AND BEBE HAVE BEEN TOGETHER FOR A LONG TIME, CORRECT?
YES, THAT'S RIGHT.
BEBE AND I HAVE BEEN FRIENDS FOR A VERY LONG TIME.

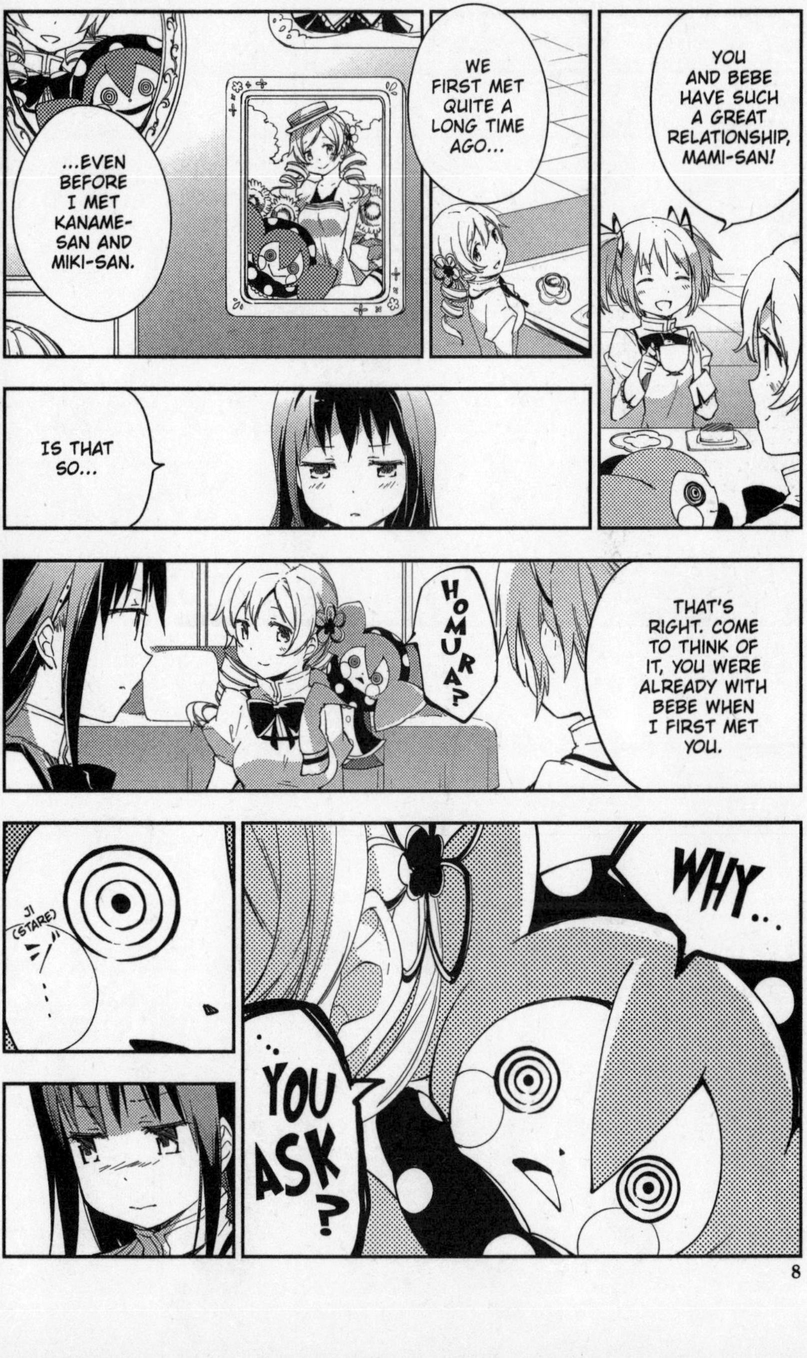
YOU AND BEBE HAVE SUCH A GREAT RELATIONSHIP, MAMI-SAN!
WE FIRST MET QUITE A LONG TIME AGO...
...EVEN BEFORE I MET KANAME-SAN AND MIKI-SAN.
IS THAT SO...
THAT'S RIGHT. COME TO THINK OF IT, YOU WERE ALREADY WITH BEBE WHEN I FIRST MET YOU.
HOMURA?
WHY...
...YOU ASK?
JI (STARE)
...

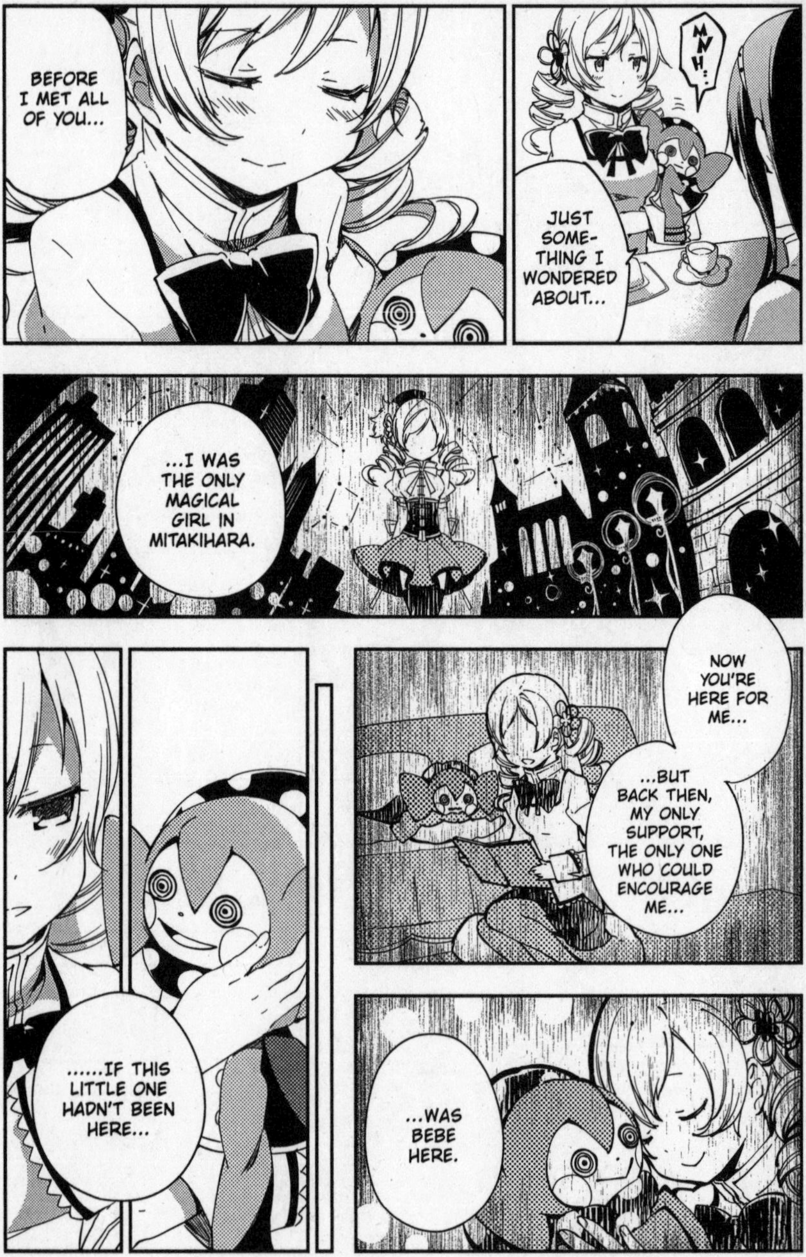
MNH!?
JUST SOMETHING I WONDERED ABOUT...
BEFORE I MET ALL OF YOU...
...I WAS THE ONLY MAGICAL GIRL IN MITAKIHARA.
NOW YOU'RE HERE FOR ME...
...BUT BACK THEN, MY ONLY SUPPORT, THE ONLY ONE WHO COULD ENCOURAGE ME...
...WAS BEBE HERE.
......IF THIS LITTLE ONE HADN'T BEEN HERE...

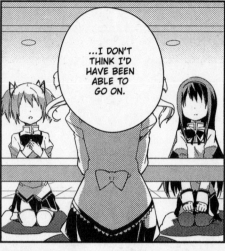

...I DON'T THINK I'D HAVE BEEN ABLE TO GO ON.
MAMI-SAN, NO...
TOMOE-SAN... YOU ARE STRONGER AND MORE RESILIENT THAN YOU THINK.
THANK YOU.
YES, THERE WAS A TIME WHEN I WANTED TO ACT THE RELIABLE SENPAI FOR YOUNGER MAGICAL GIRLS.
BUT...
...NOW THAT KANAME-SAN AND MIKI-SAN HAVE SO MUCH EXPERIENCE...
...AND SAKURA-SAN AND AKEMI-SAN HAVE JOINED OUR TEAM...

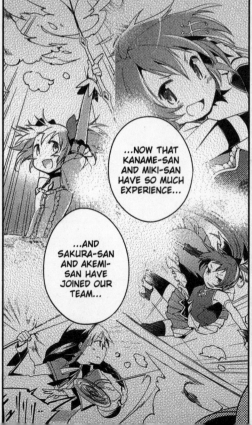

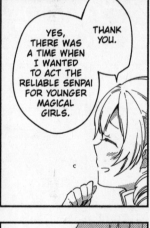

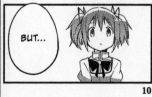

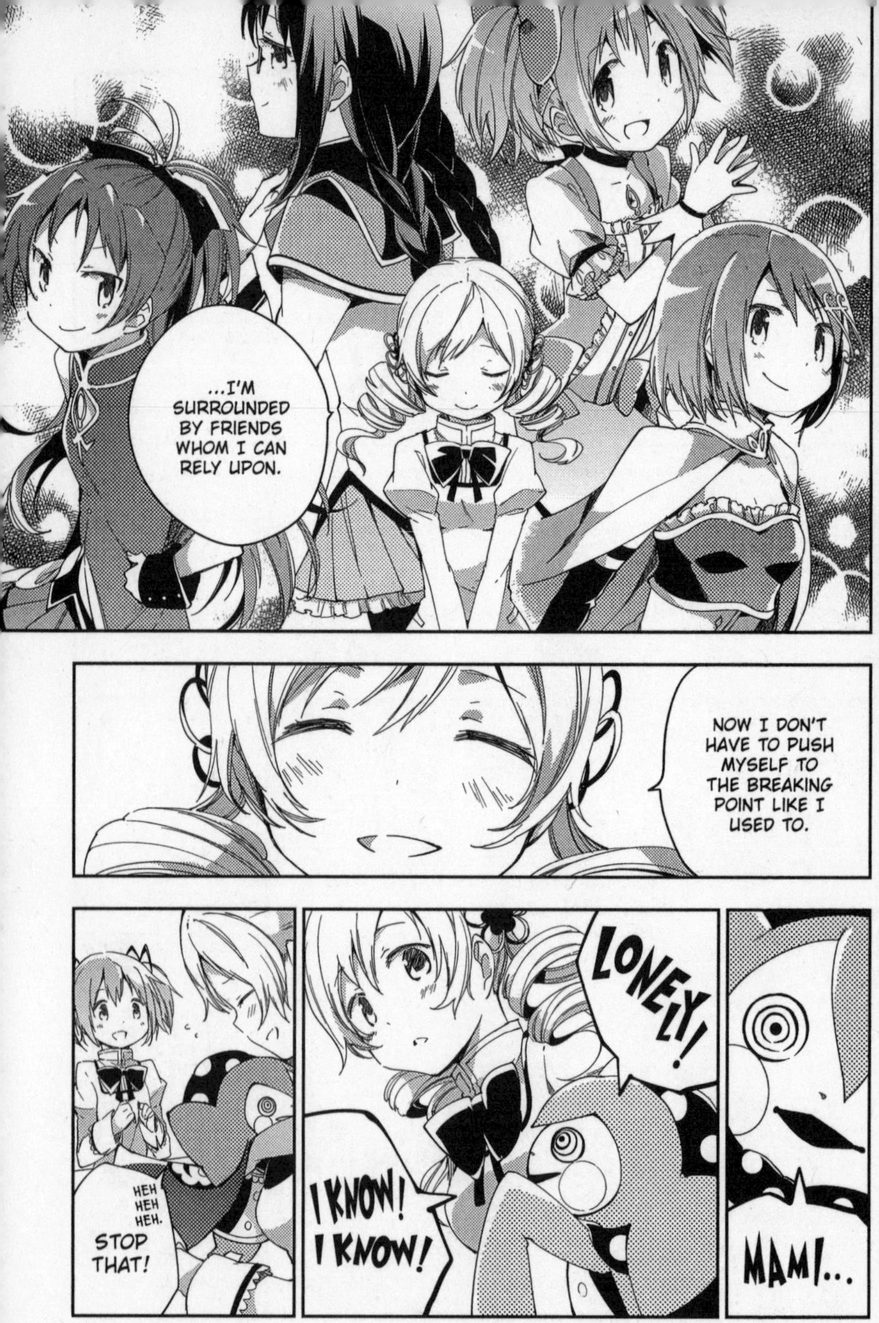
...I'M SURROUNDED BY FRIENDS WHOM I CAN RELY UPON.
NOW I DON'T HAVE TO PUSH MYSELF TO THE BREAKING POINT LIKE I USED TO.
MAMI...
LONELY!
I KNOW! I KNOW!
HEH HEH HEH.
STOP THAT!

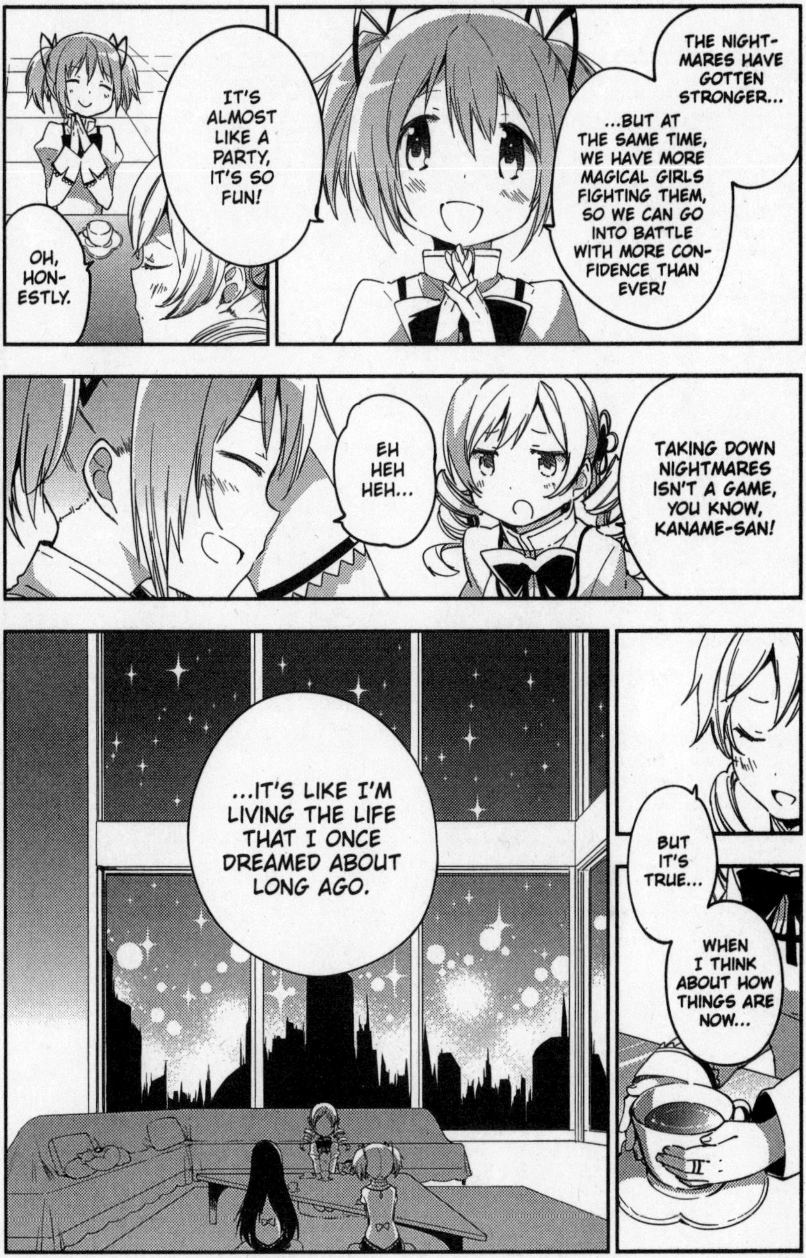
THE NIGHTMARES HAVE GOTTEN STRONGER...
...BUT AT THE SAME TIME, WE HAVE MORE MAGICAL GIRLS FIGHTING THEM, SO WE CAN GO INTO BATTLE WITH MORE CONFIDENCE THAN EVER!
IT'S ALMOST LIKE A PARTY, IT'S SO FUN!
OH, HONESTLY.
TAKING DOWN NIGHTMARES ISN'T A GAME, YOU KNOW, KANAME-SAN!
EH HEH HEH...
BUT IT'S TRUE...
WHEN I THINK ABOUT HOW THINGS ARE NOW...
...IT'S LIKE I'M LIVING THE LIFE THAT I ONCE DREAMED ABOUT LONG AGO.

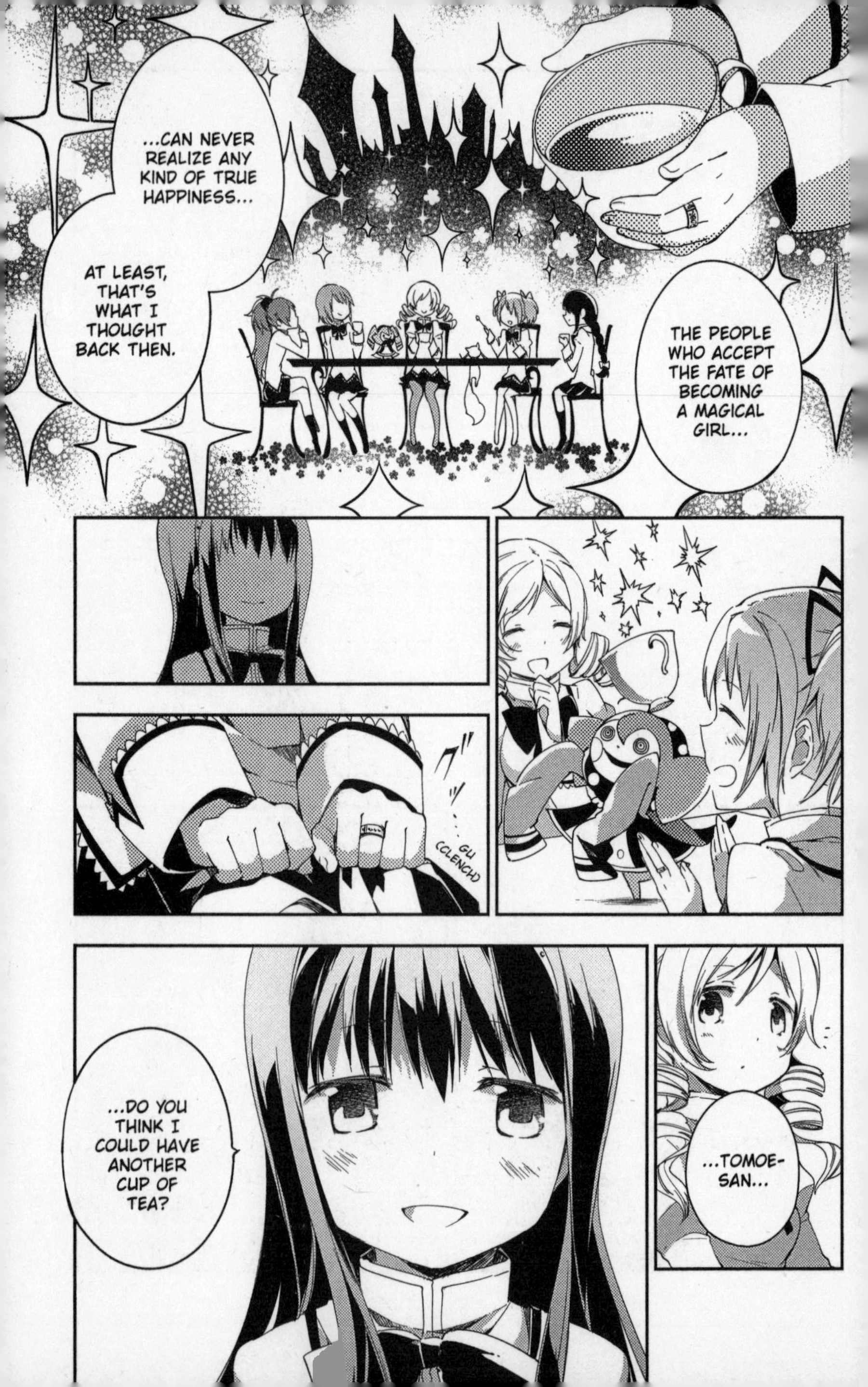
THE PEOPLE WHO ACCEPT THE FATE OF BECOMING A MAGICAL GIRL...
...CAN NEVER REALIZE ANY KIND OF TRUE HAPPINESS...
AT LEAST, THAT'S WHAT I THOUGHT BACK THEN.
GU (CLENCH)
...TOMOE-SAN...
...DO YOU THINK I COULD HAVE ANOTHER CUP OF TEA?

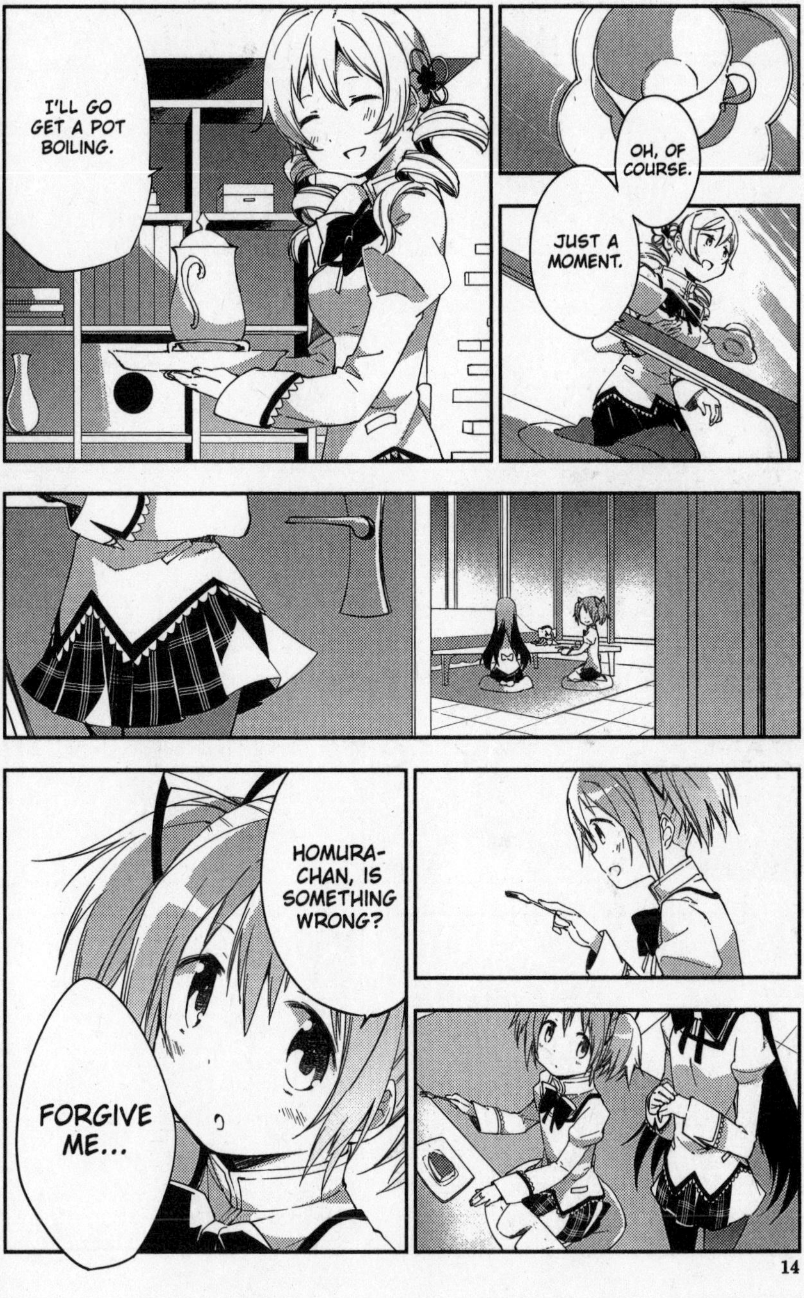
OH, OF COURSE.
JUST A MOMENT.
I'LL GO GET A POT BOILING.
HOMURA-CHAN, IS SOMETHING WRONG?
FORGIVE ME...

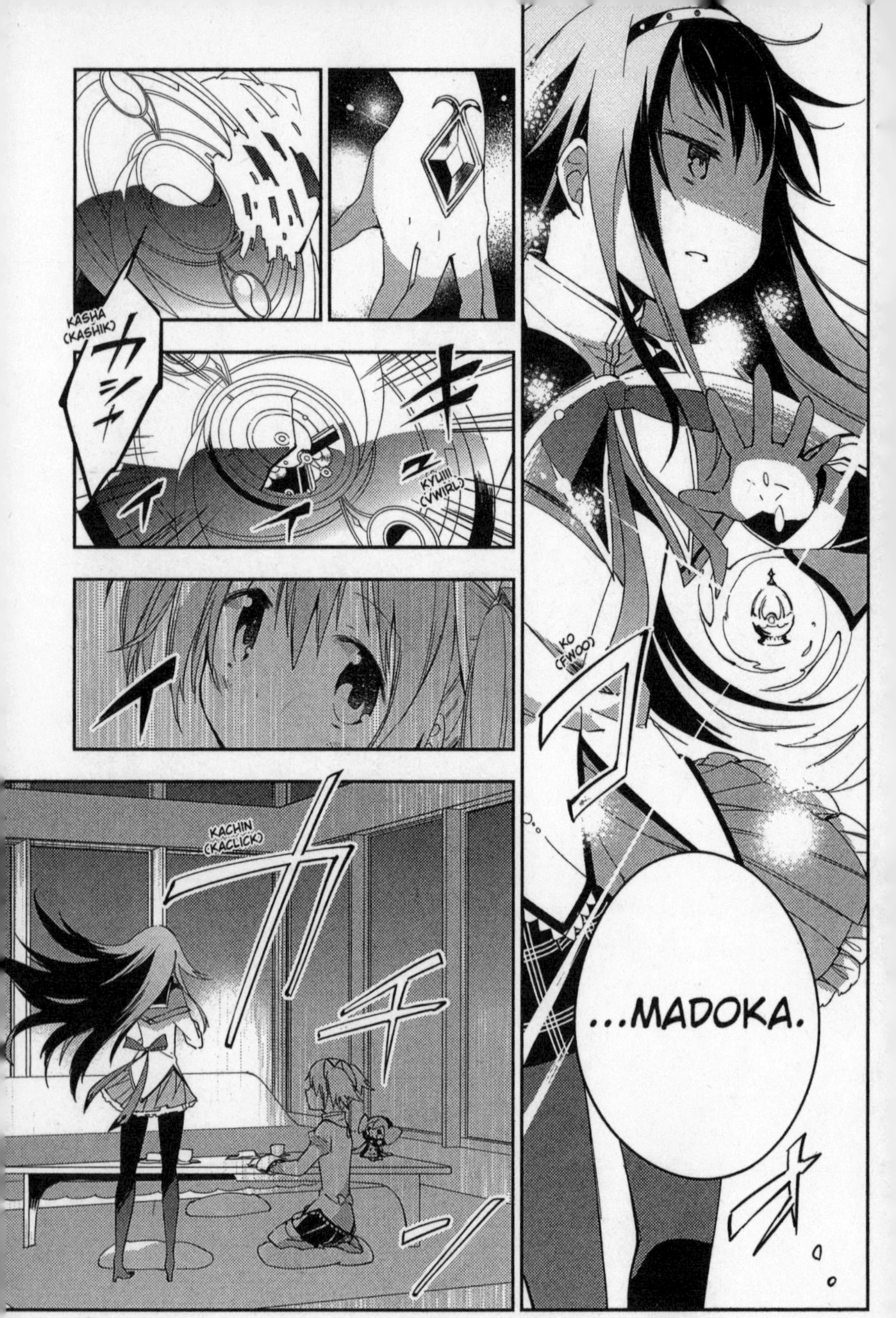
KO (FWOO)
...MADOKA.
KYUIII (VWIRL)
KASHA (KASHIK)
KACHIN (KACLICK)

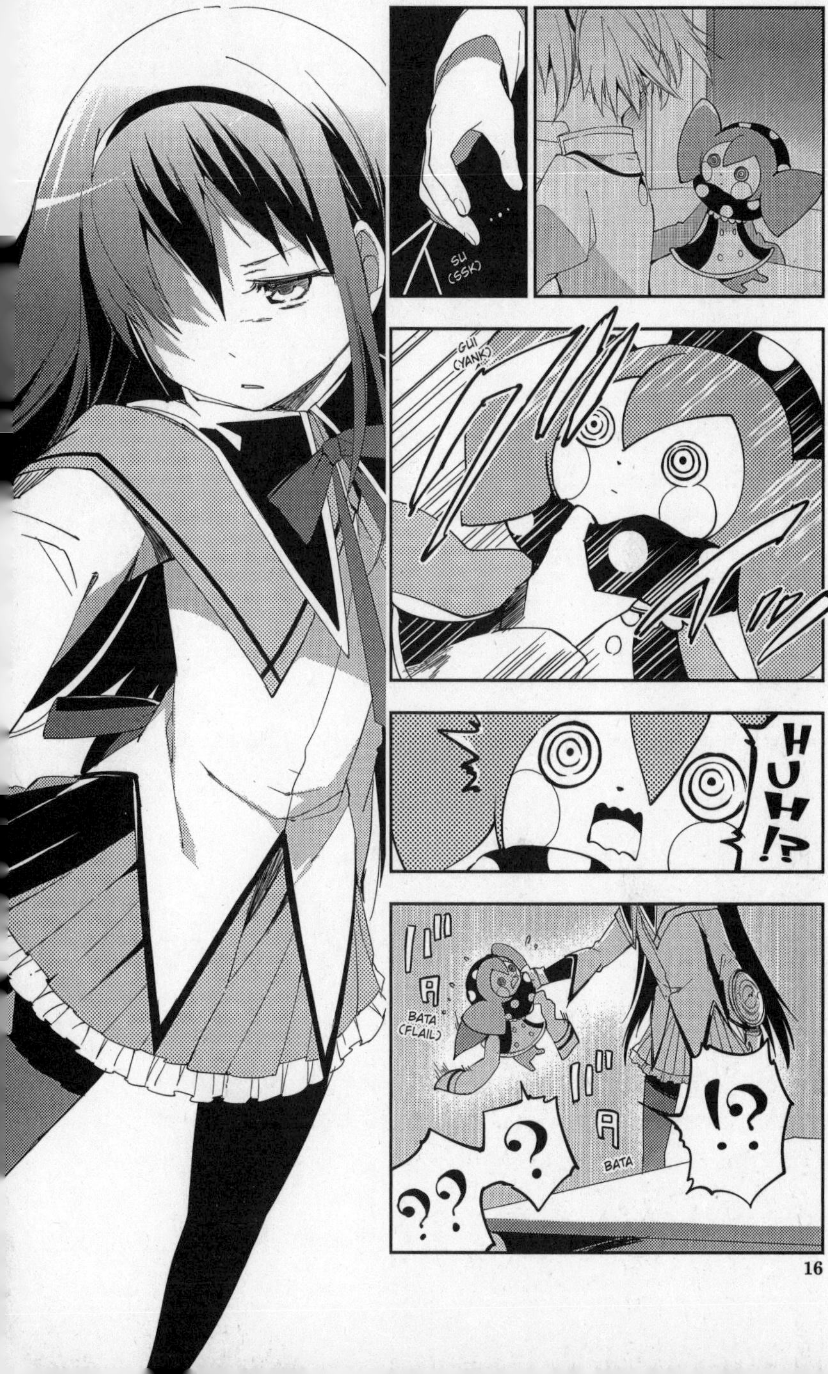
SU (SSK)
GUI (YANK)
HUH!?
BATA (FLAIL)
BATA
!?
?
??

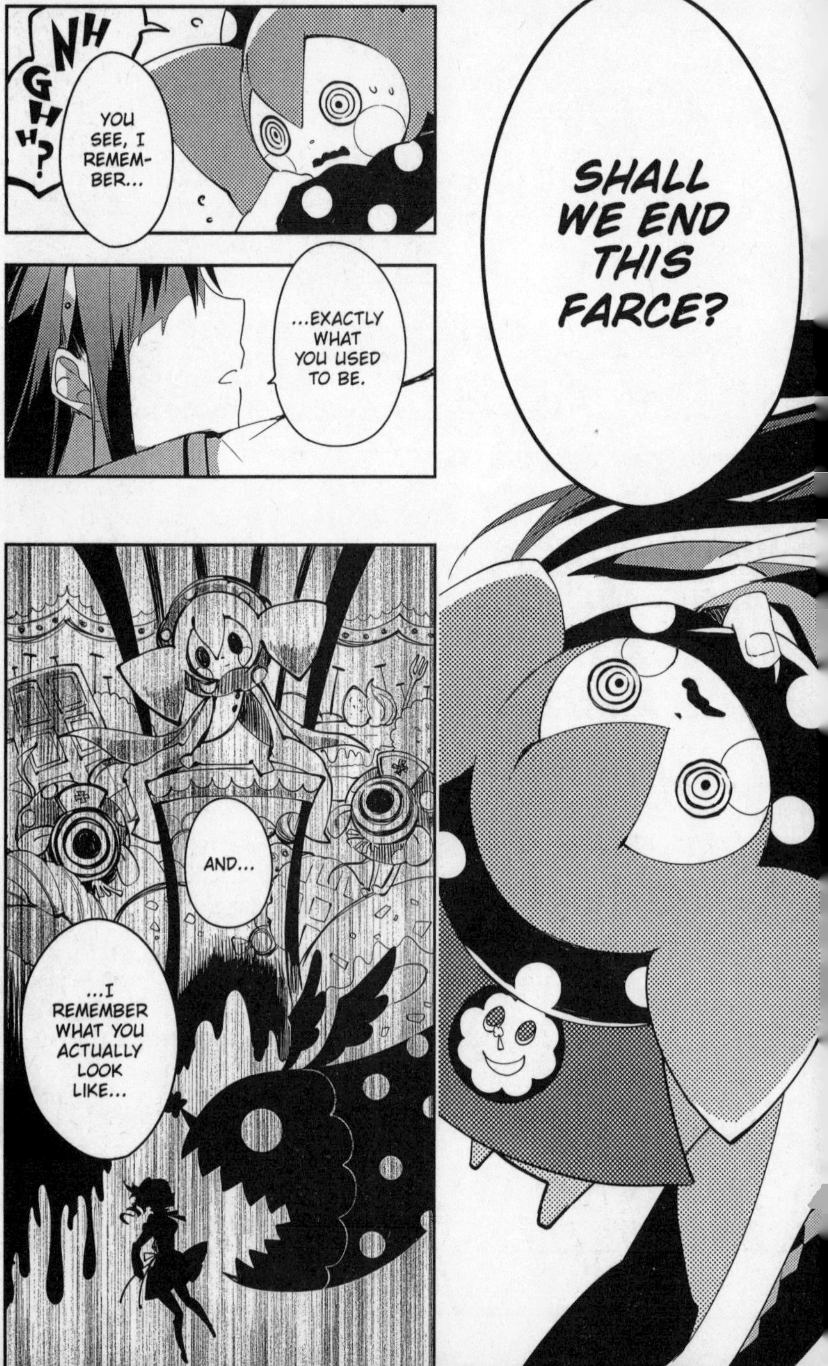
SHALL WE END THIS FARCE?
HNGHH?
YOU SEE, I REMEMBER...
...EXACTLY WHAT YOU USED TO BE.
AND...
...I REMEMBER WHAT YOU ACTUALLY LOOK LIKE...

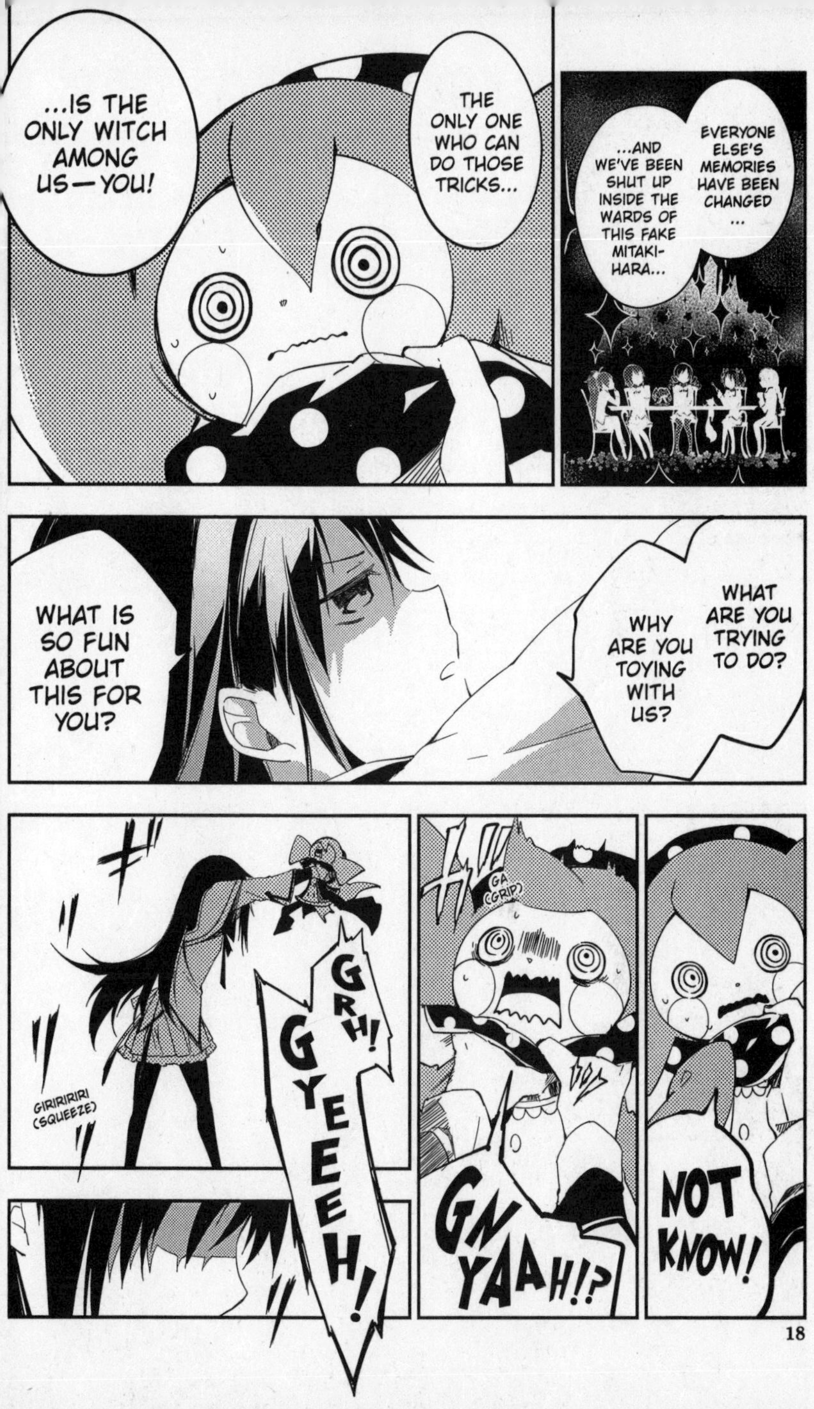
EVERYONE ELSE'S MEMORIES HAVE BEEN CHANGED ...
...AND WE'VE BEEN SHUT UP INSIDE THE WARDS OF THIS FAKE MITAKI-HARA...
THE ONLY ONE WHO CAN DO THOSE TRICKS...
...IS THE ONLY WITCH AMONG US—YOU!
WHAT ARE YOU TRYING TO DO?
WHY ARE YOU TOYING WITH US?
WHAT IS SO FUN ABOUT THIS FOR YOU?
NOT KNOW!
GA (GRIP)
GNYAAH!?
GRH!
GYEEEH!
GIRIRIRIRI (SQUEEZE)

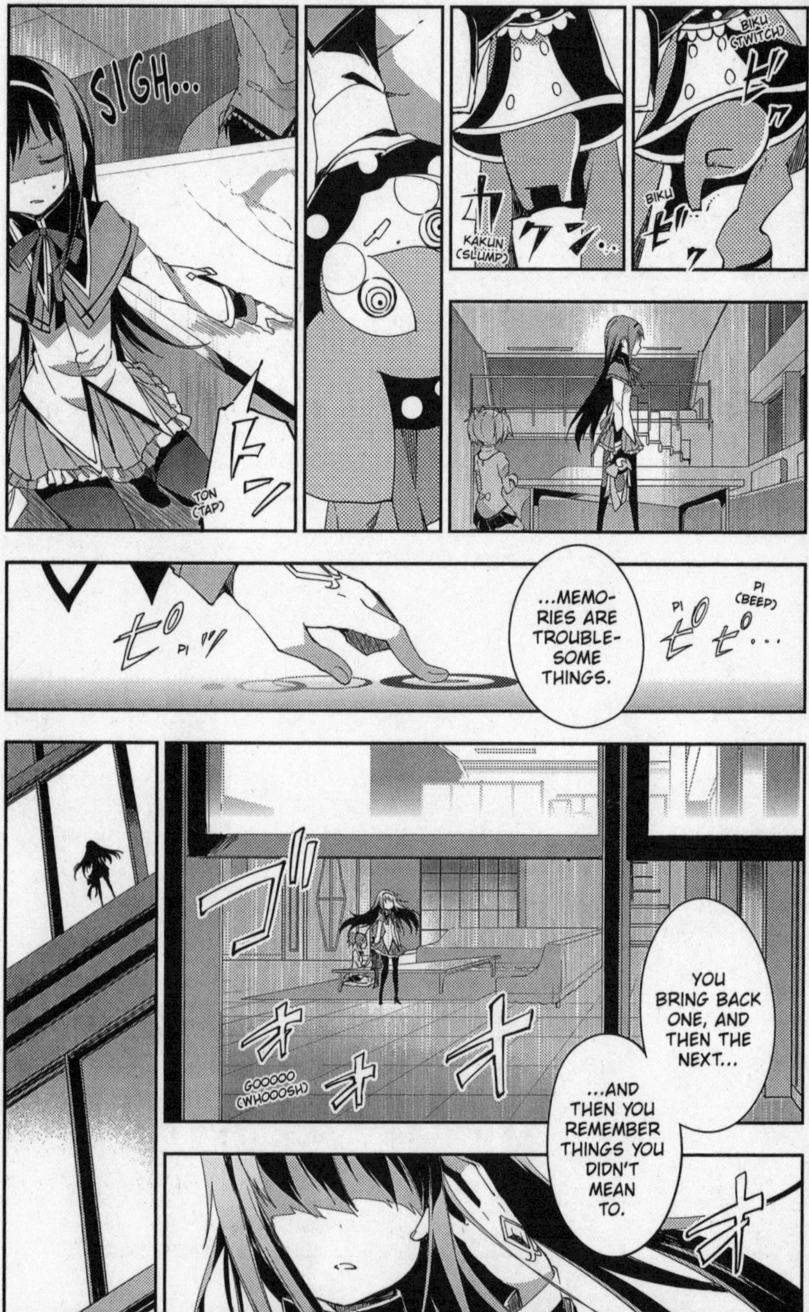
BIKU (TWITCH)
BIKU
KAKUN (SLUMP)
SIGH...
TON (TAP)
PI (BEEP)
PI
...MEMO-RIES ARE TROUBLE-SOME THINGS.
PI
YOU BRING BACK ONE, AND THEN THE NEXT...
...AND THEN YOU REMEMBER THINGS YOU DIDN'T MEAN TO.
GOOOOO (WHOOOSH)

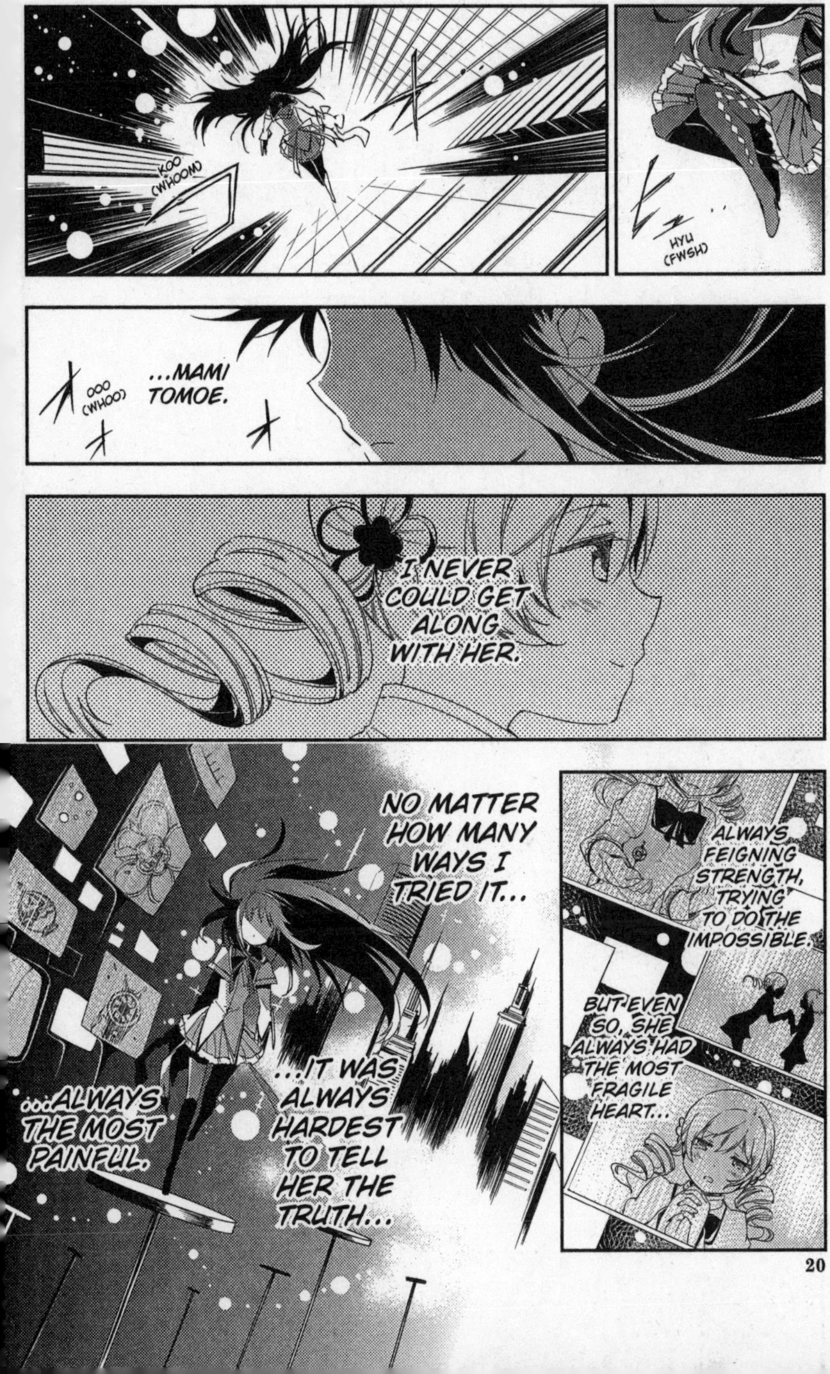
HYU (FWSH)
KOO (WHOOM)
OOO (WHOO)
...MAMI TOMOE.
I NEVER COULD GET ALONG WITH HER.
ALWAYS FEIGNING STRENGTH, TRYING TO DO THE IMPOSSIBLE.
BUT EVEN SO, SHE ALWAYS HAD THE MOST FRAGILE HEART...
NO MATTER HOW MANY WAYS I TRIED IT...
...IT WAS ALWAYS HARDEST TO TELL HER THE TRUTH...
...ALWAYS THE MOST PAINFUL.

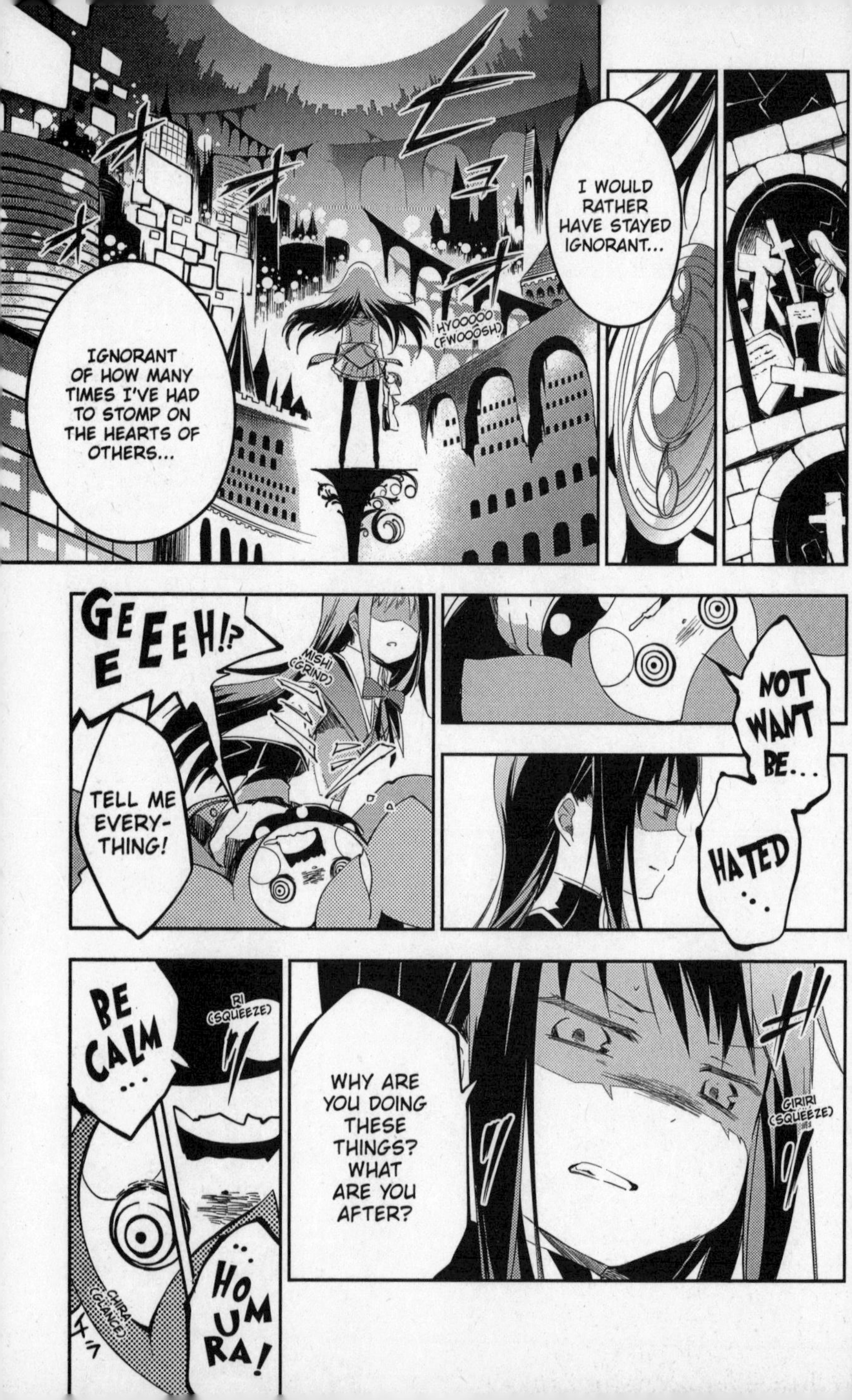
I WOULD RATHER HAVE STAYED IGNORANT...
HYOOOOO (FWOOOSH)
IGNORANT OF HOW MANY TIMES I'VE HAD TO STOMP ON THE HEARTS OF OTHERS...
NOT WANT BE... HATED...
GEEEEH!?
MISHI (GRIND)
TELL ME EVERYTHING!
GIRIRI (SQUEEZE)
WHY ARE YOU DOING THESE THINGS? WHAT ARE YOU AFTER?
BE CALM...
RI (SQUEEZE)
...HOMURA!
CHIRA (GLANCE)

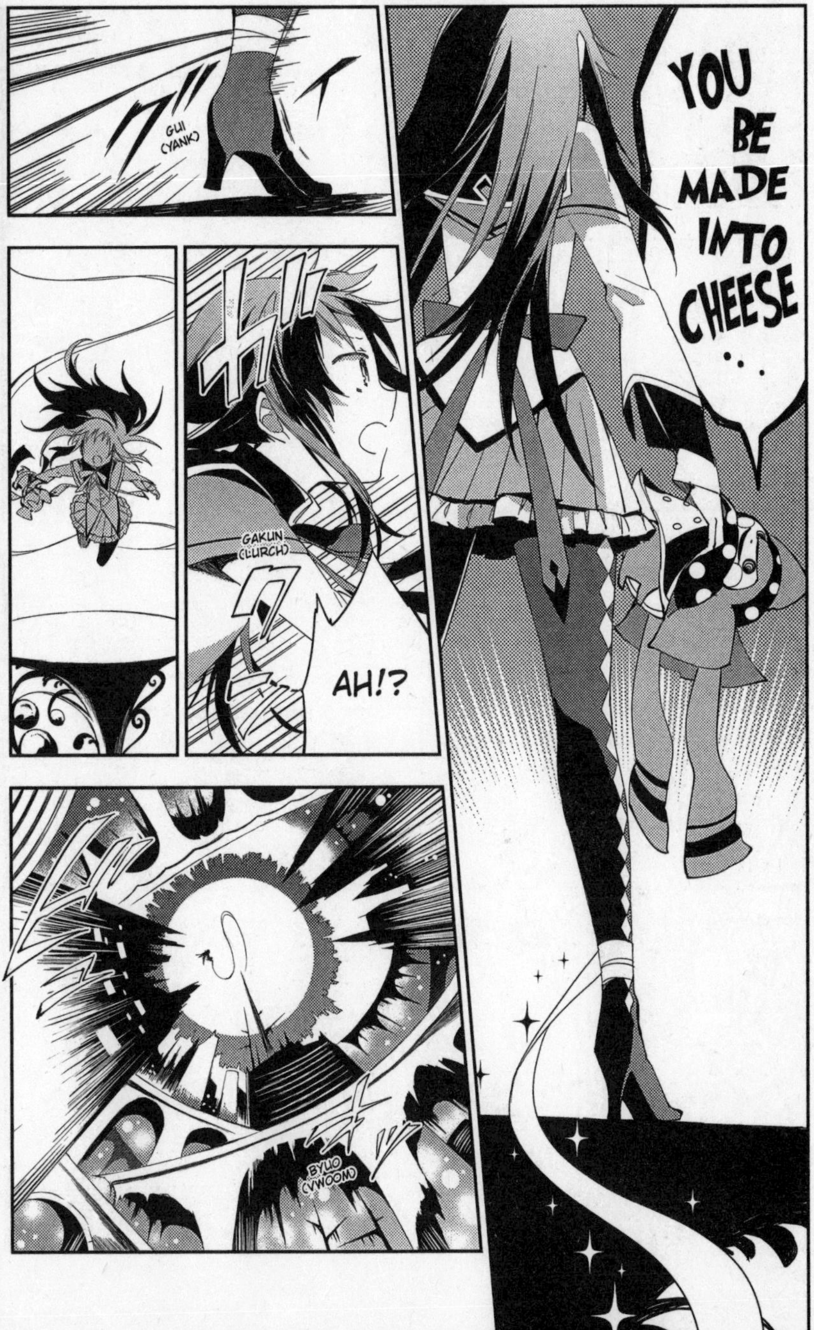
YOU BE MADE INTO CHEESE . . .
GUI (YANK)
GAKUN (LURCH)
AH!?
BYUO (VWOOM)

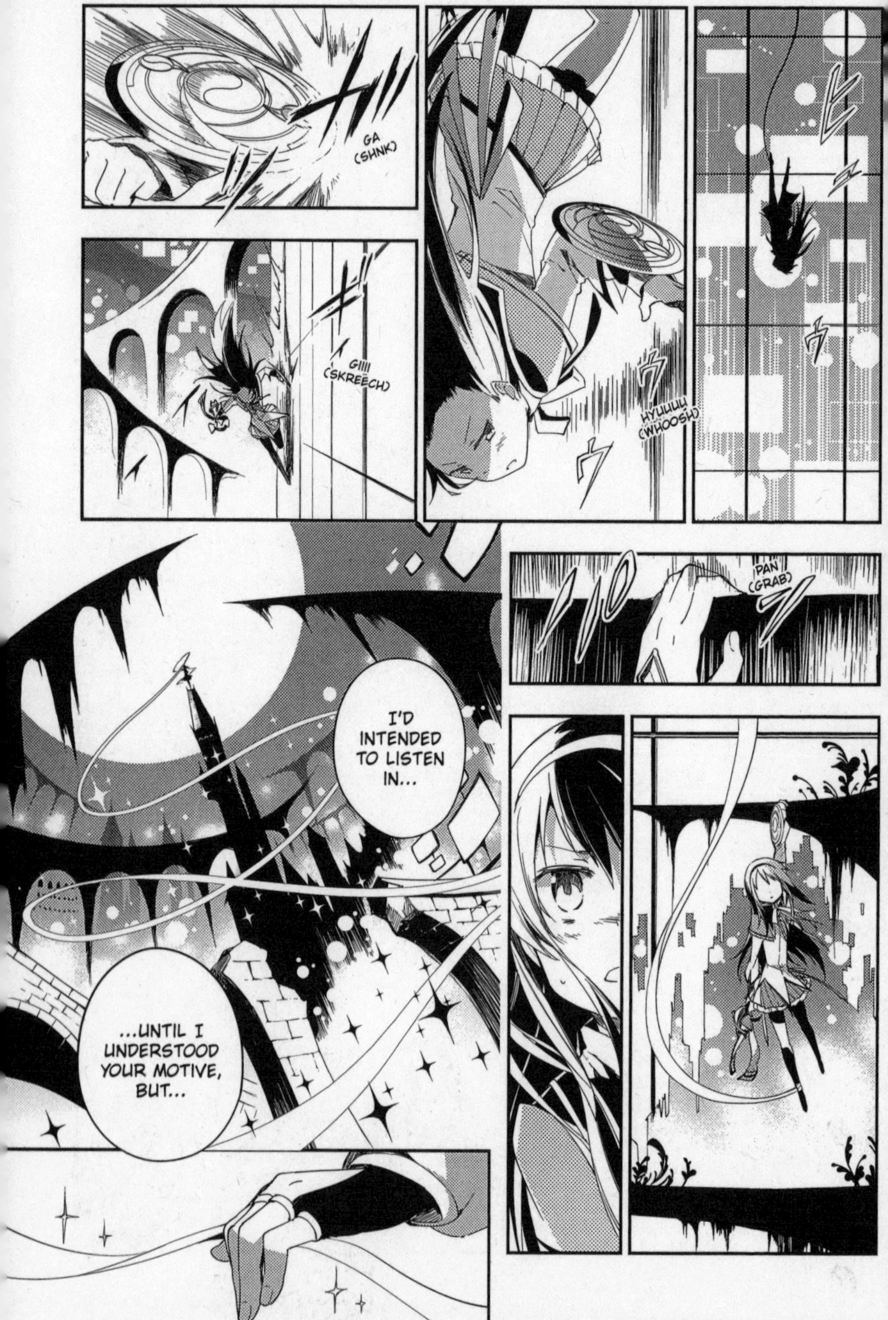
HYUUUU (WHOOSH)
GA (SHNK)
GIIII (SKREECH)
PAN (GRAB)
I'D INTENDED TO LISTEN IN...
...UNTIL I UNDERSTOOD YOUR MOTIVE, BUT...

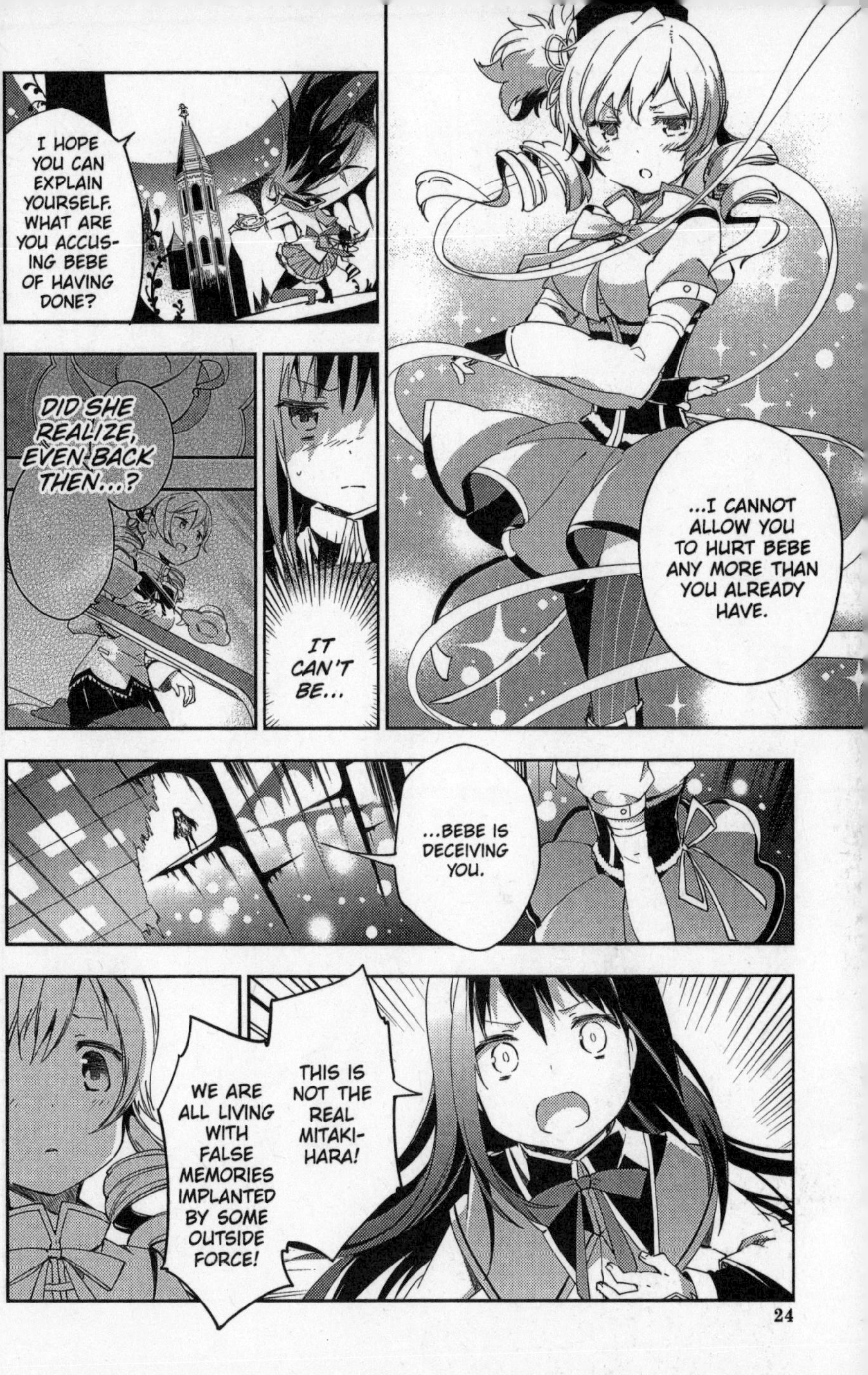
...I CANNOT ALLOW YOU TO HURT BEBE ANY MORE THAN YOU ALREADY HAVE.
I HOPE YOU CAN EXPLAIN YOURSELF. WHAT ARE YOU ACCUS-ING BEBE OF HAVING DONE?
IT CAN'T BE...
DID SHE REALIZE, EVEN BACK THEN...?
...BEBE IS DECEIVING YOU.
THIS IS NOT THE REAL MITAKI-HARA!
WE ARE ALL LIVING WITH FALSE MEMORIES IMPLANTED BY SOME OUTSIDE FORCE!

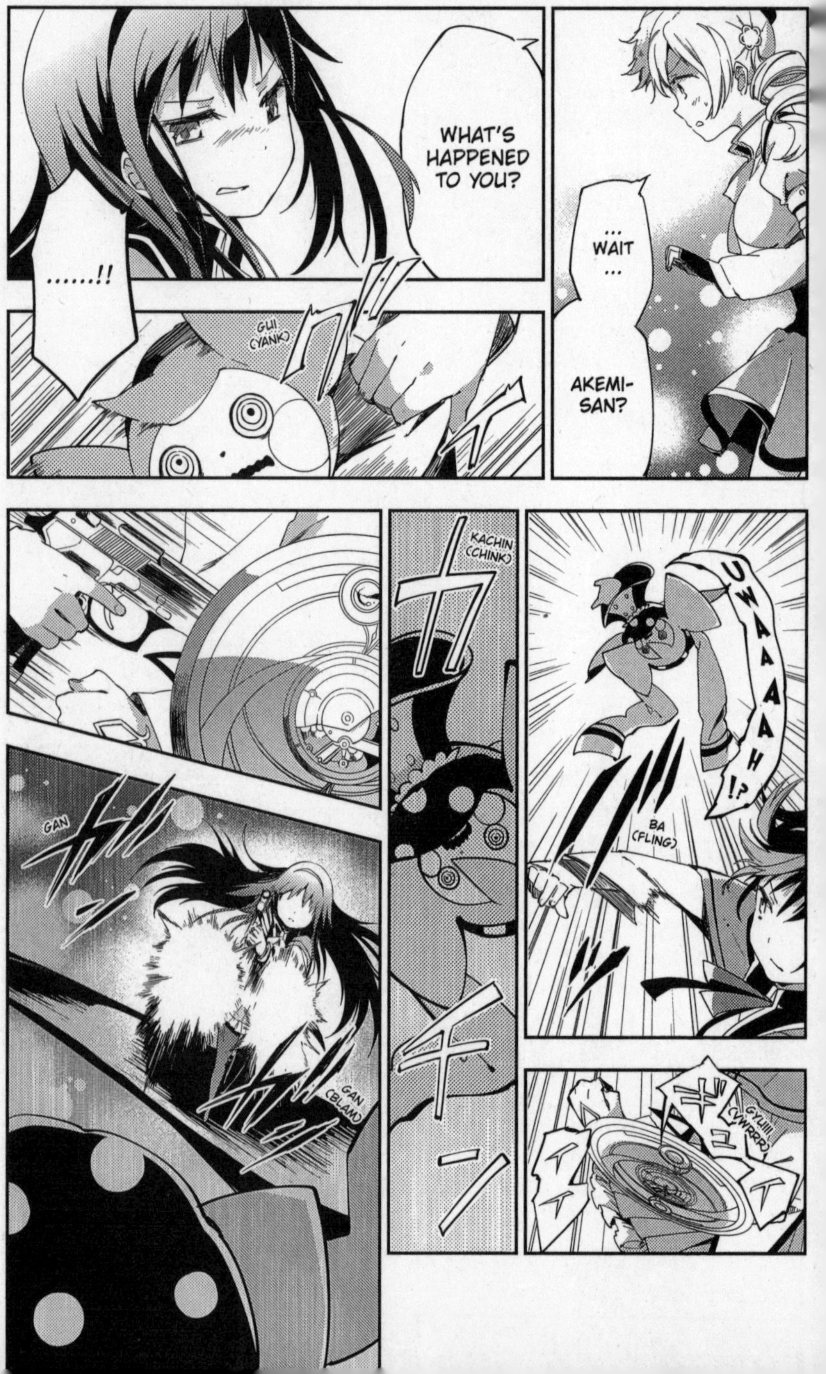
... WAIT ...
AKEMI-SAN?
WHAT'S HAPPENED TO YOU?
......!!
GUI (YANK)
UWAAAAAH!?
BA (FLING)
GYUIII (VWRRR)
KACHIN (CHINK)
GAN
GAN (BLAM)

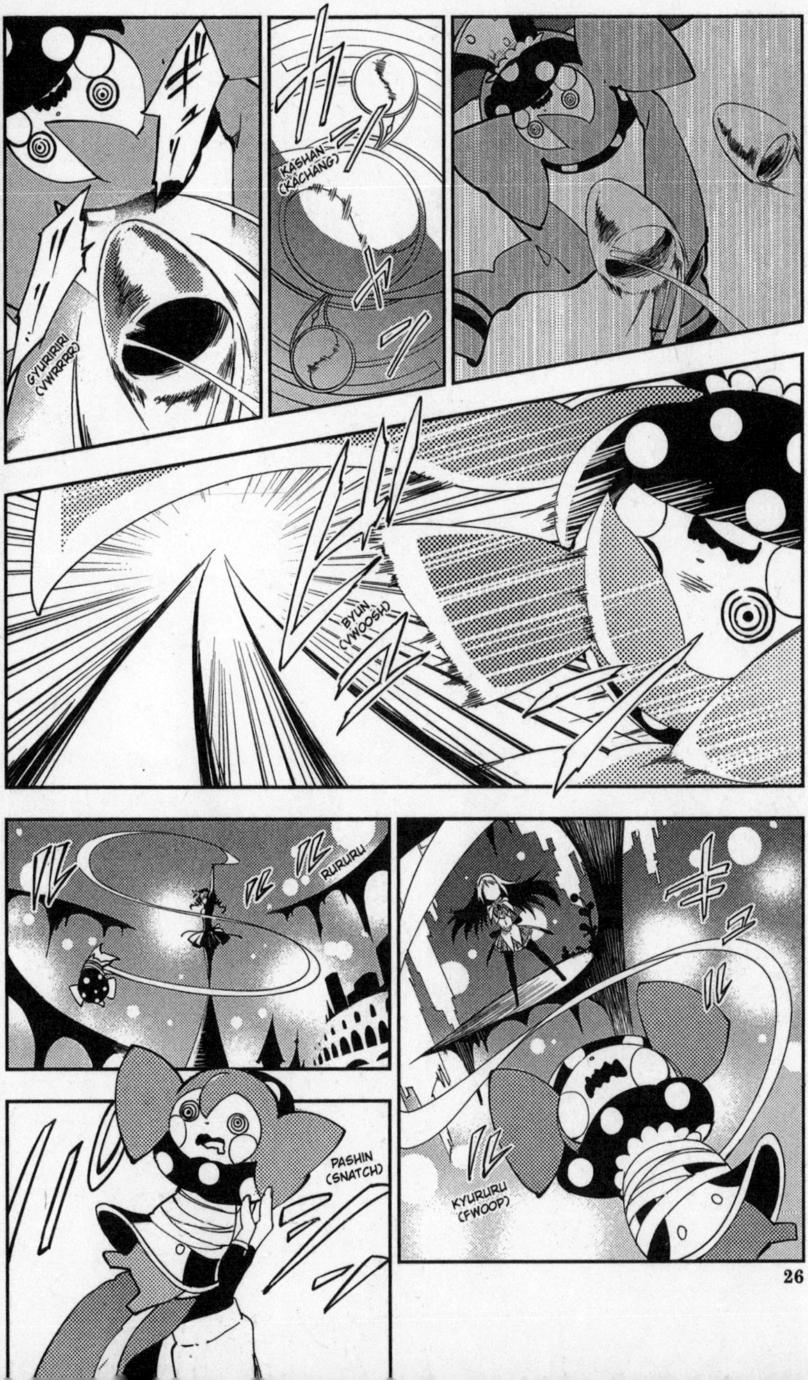
KASHAN (KACHANG)
GYURIRIRI (VWRRRR)
BYUN (VWOOSH)
KYURURU (FWOOP)
RURURU
PASHIN (SNATCH)

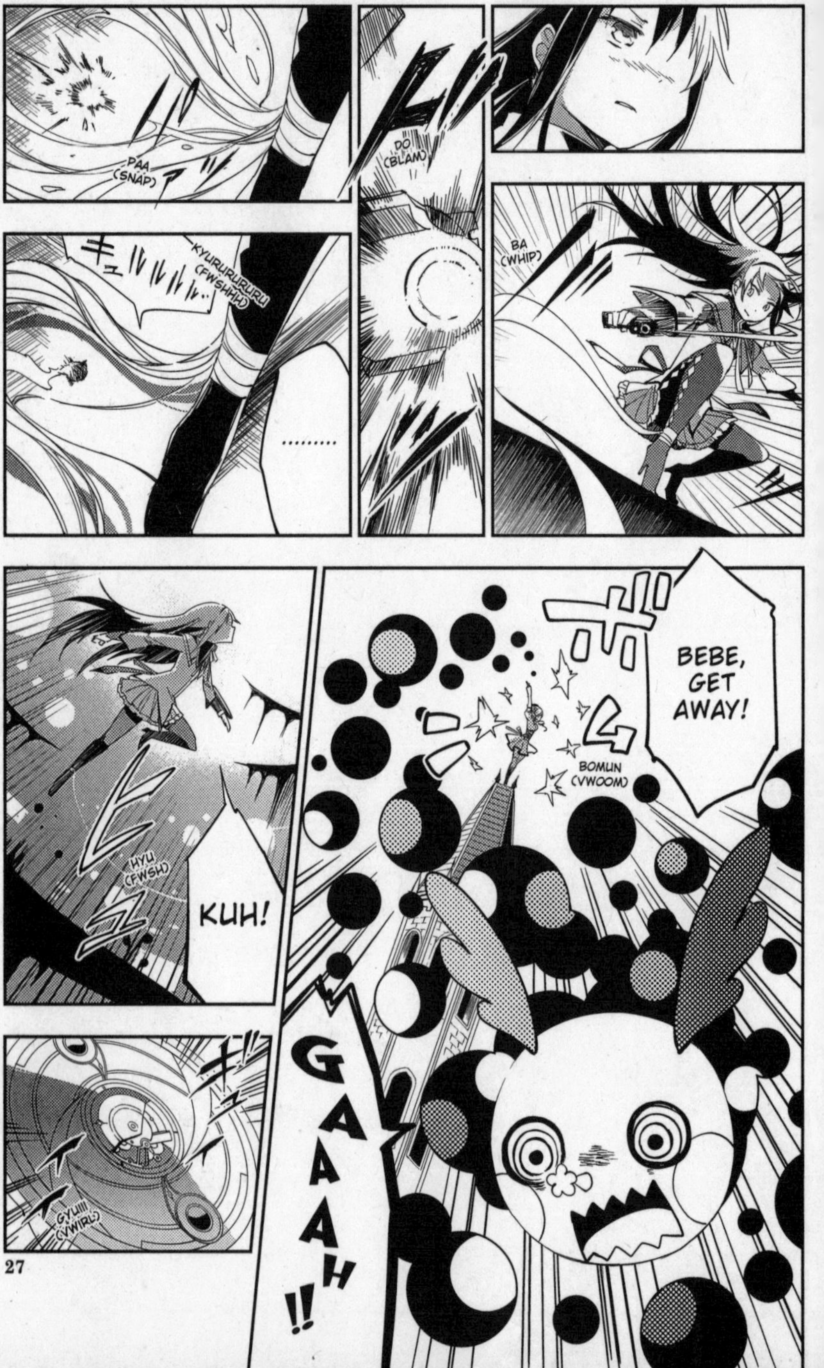
BA
(WHIP)
DO
(BLAM)
PAA
(SNAP)
KYURURURURU
(FWSHHH)
....
BEBE, GET AWAY!
BOMUN
(VWOOM)
GAAAAH!!
HYU
(FWSH)
KUH!
GYUIII
(VWIRL)

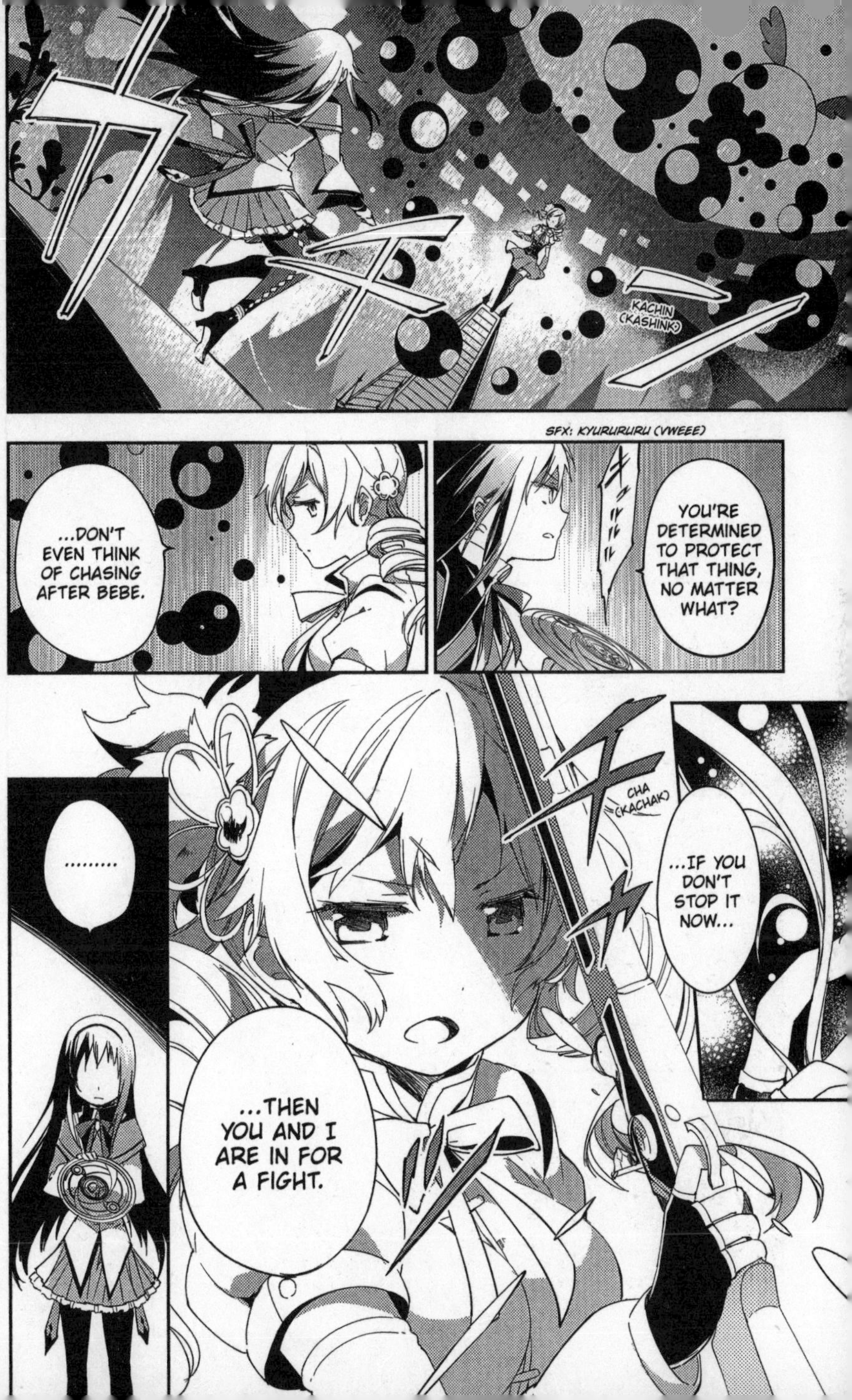
KACHIN (KASHINK)
SFX: KYURURURU (VWEEE)
YOU'RE DETERMINED TO PROTECT THAT THING, NO MATTER WHAT?
...DON'T EVEN THINK OF CHASING AFTER BEBE.
CHA (KACHAK)
...IF YOU DON'T STOP IT NOW...
...THEN YOU AND I ARE IN FOR A FIGHT.
....

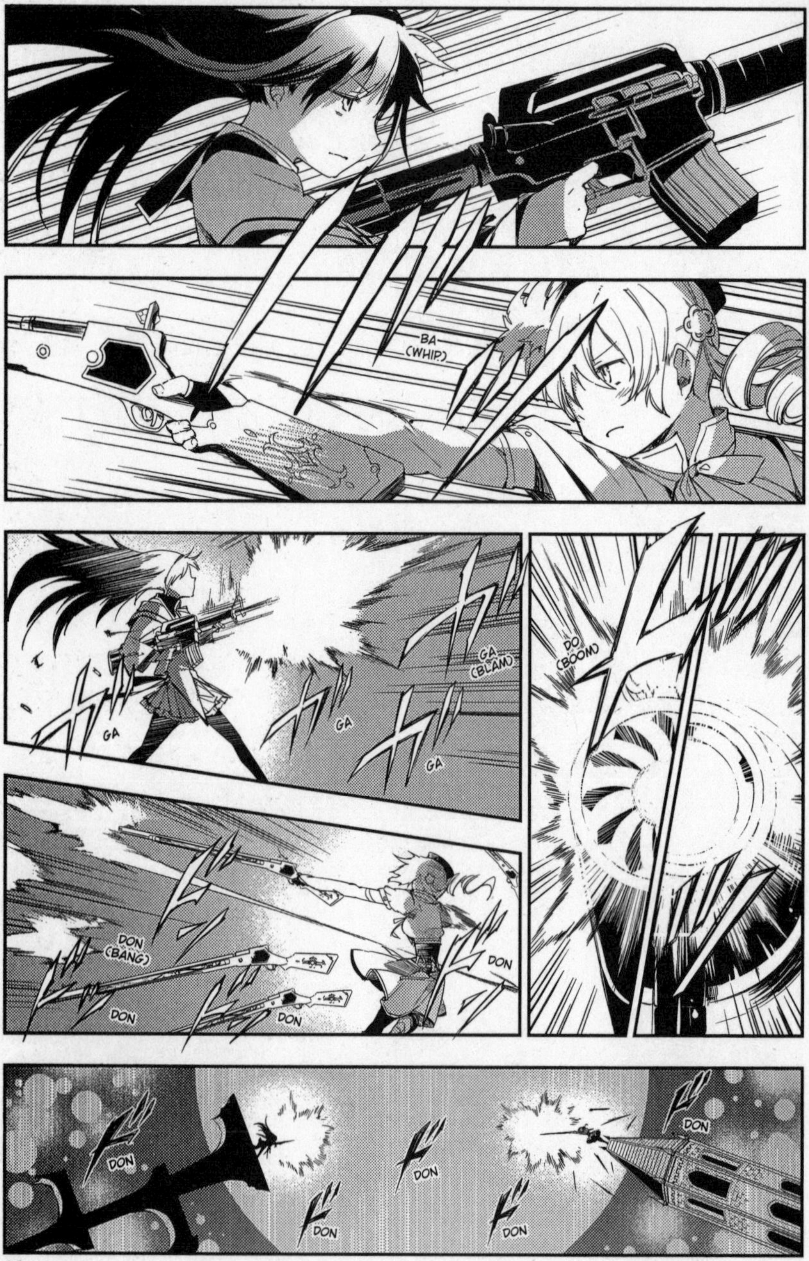
BA
(WHIP)
DO
(BOOM)
GA
(BLAM)
GA
GA
GA
DON
DON
(BANG)
DON
DON
DON
DON
DON
DON
DON

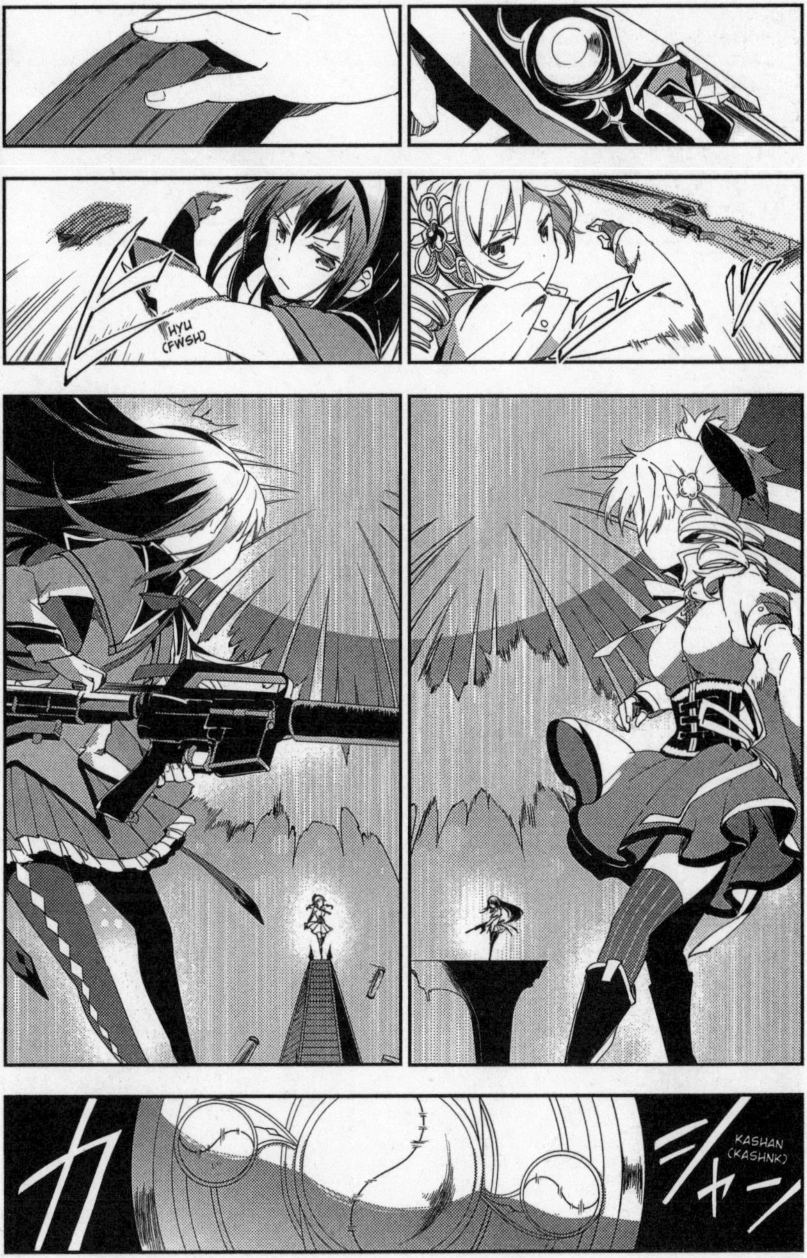
HYU
(FWSH)
KASHAN
(KASHNK)

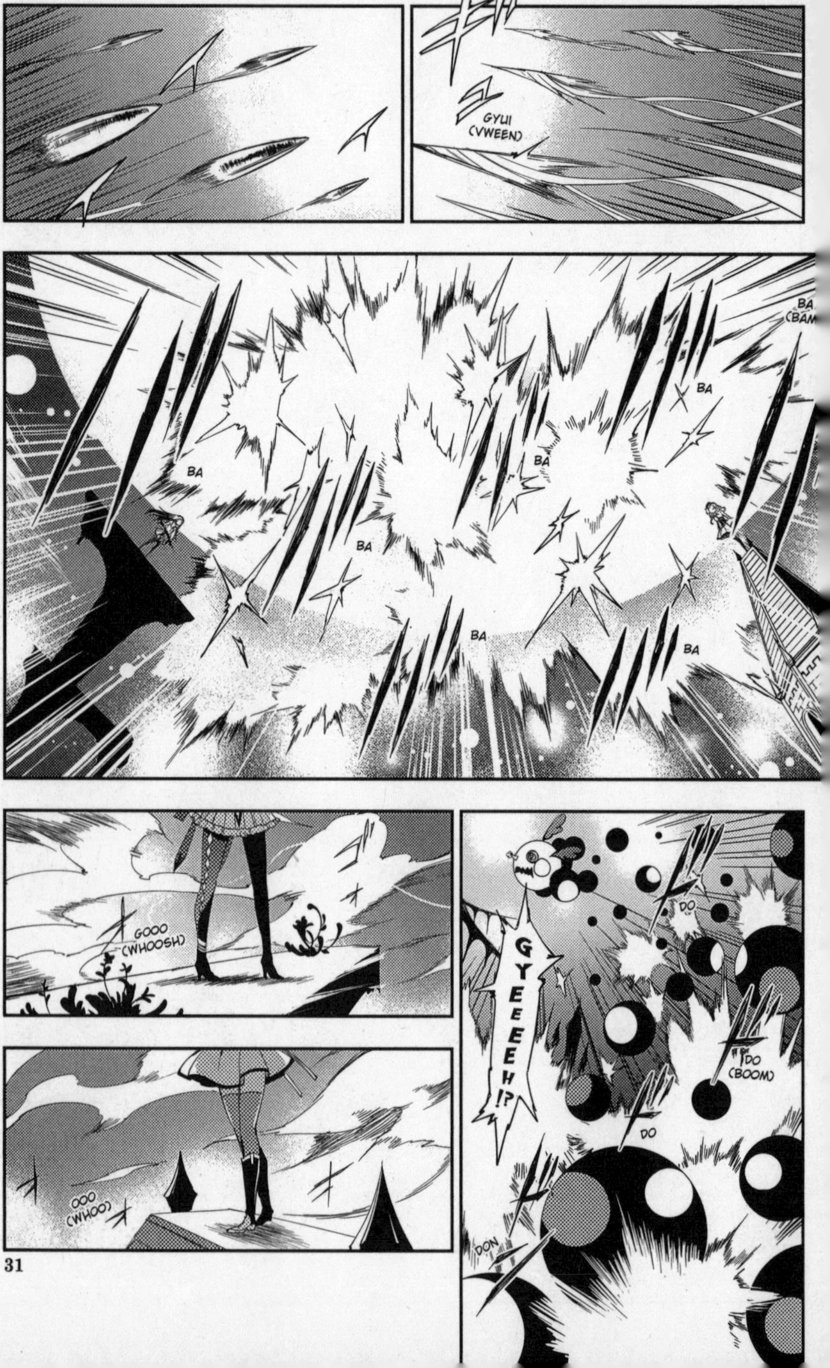
GYUI (VWEEN)
BA (BAM)
BA
BA
BA
BA
BA
BA
GYEEEEEH!?
DO
DO (BOOM)
DO
DON
GOOO (WHOOSH)
OOO (WHOO)

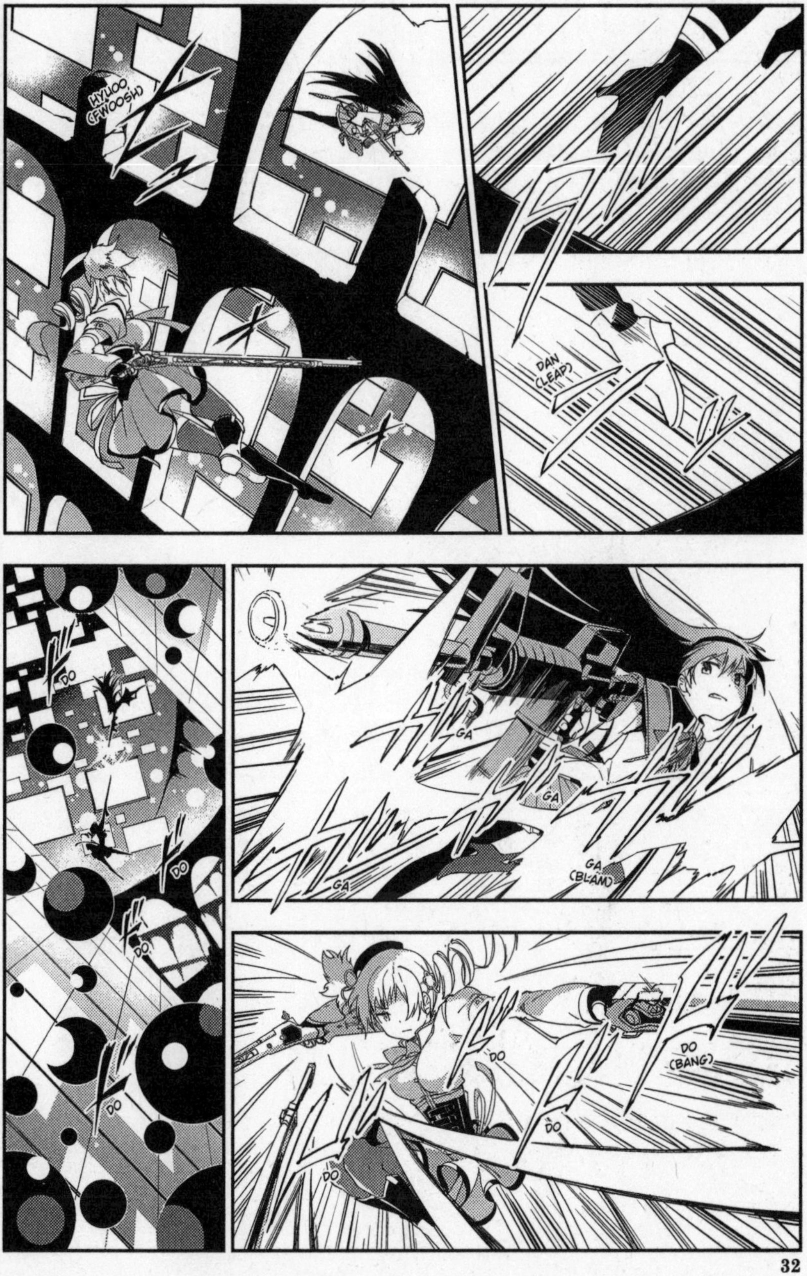
DAN
(LEAP)
HYUOO
(FWOOSH)
GA
GA
GA
(BLAM)
GA
DO
(BANG)
DO
DO
DO
DO
DO
DO
DO

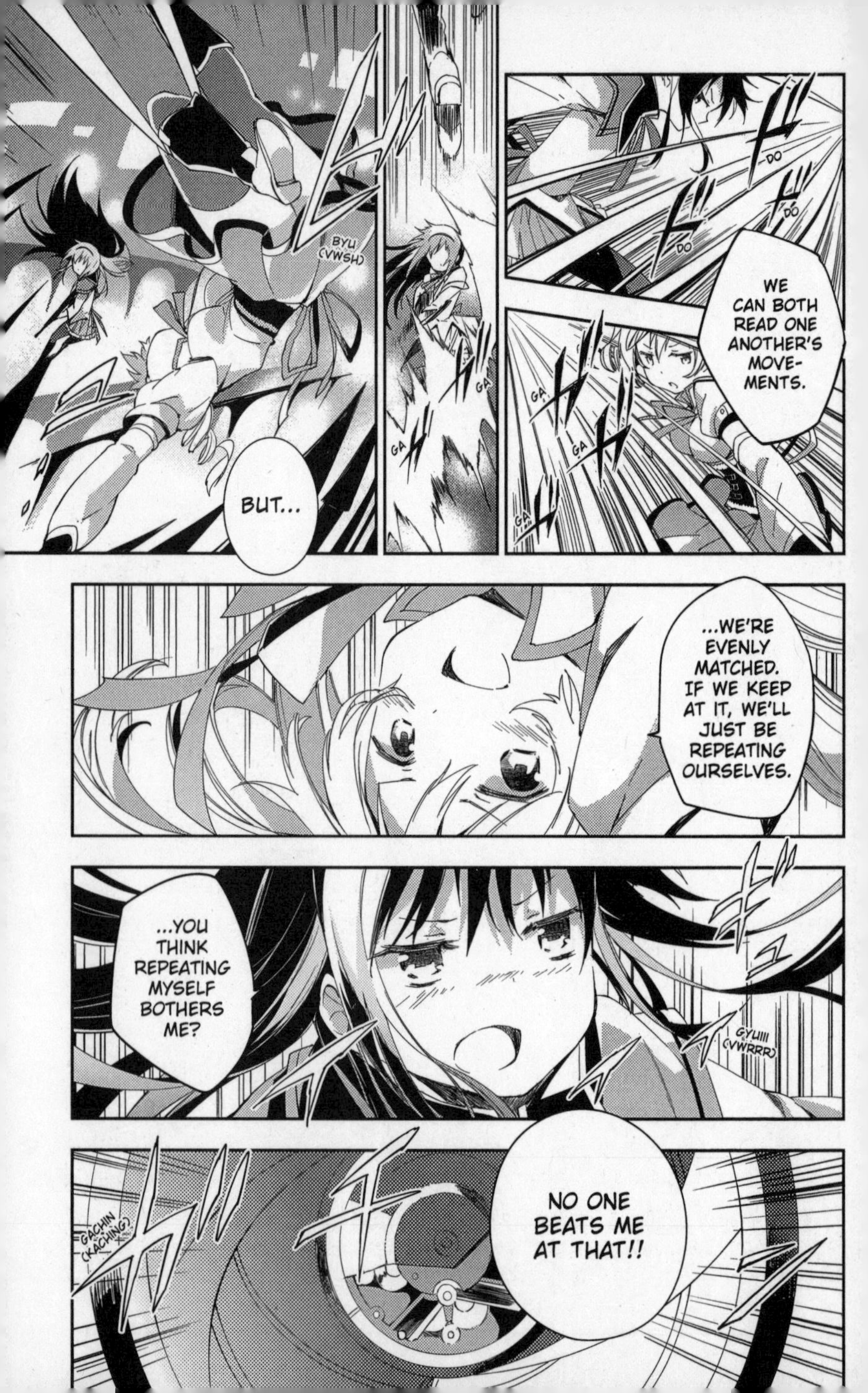
DO
DO
DO
WE CAN BOTH READ ONE ANOTHER'S MOVE-MENTS.
GA
GA
GA
GA
GA
BYU (VWSH)
BUT...
...WE'RE EVENLY MATCHED. IF WE KEEP AT IT, WE'LL JUST BE REPEATING OURSELVES.
...YOU THINK REPEATING MYSELF BOTHERS ME?
GYUIII (VWRRR)
GACHIN (KACHING)
NO ONE BEATS ME AT THAT!!

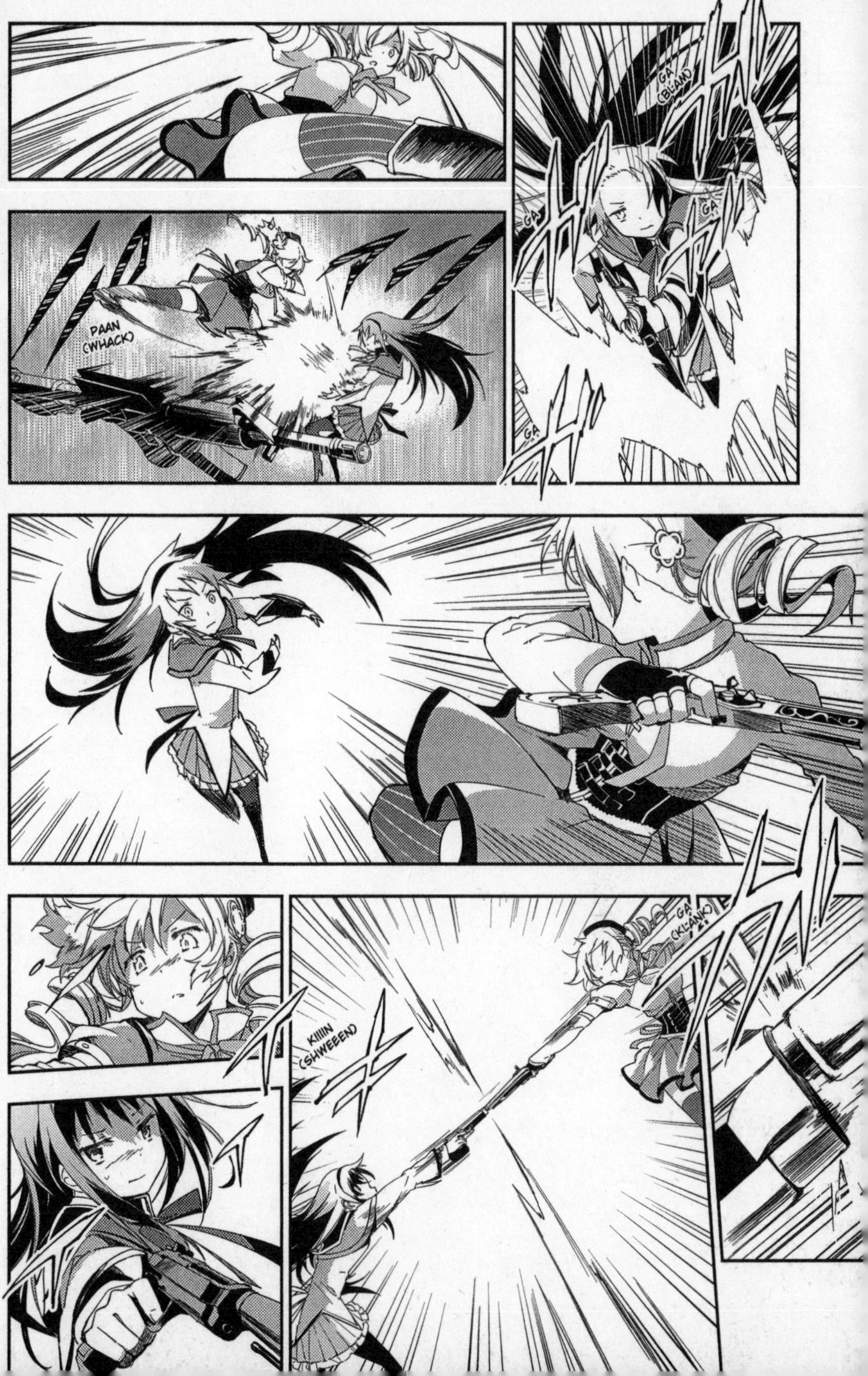
GA (BLAM)
GA
GA
GA
PAAN (WHACK)
GA (KLANK)
KIIIIN (SHWEEEN)

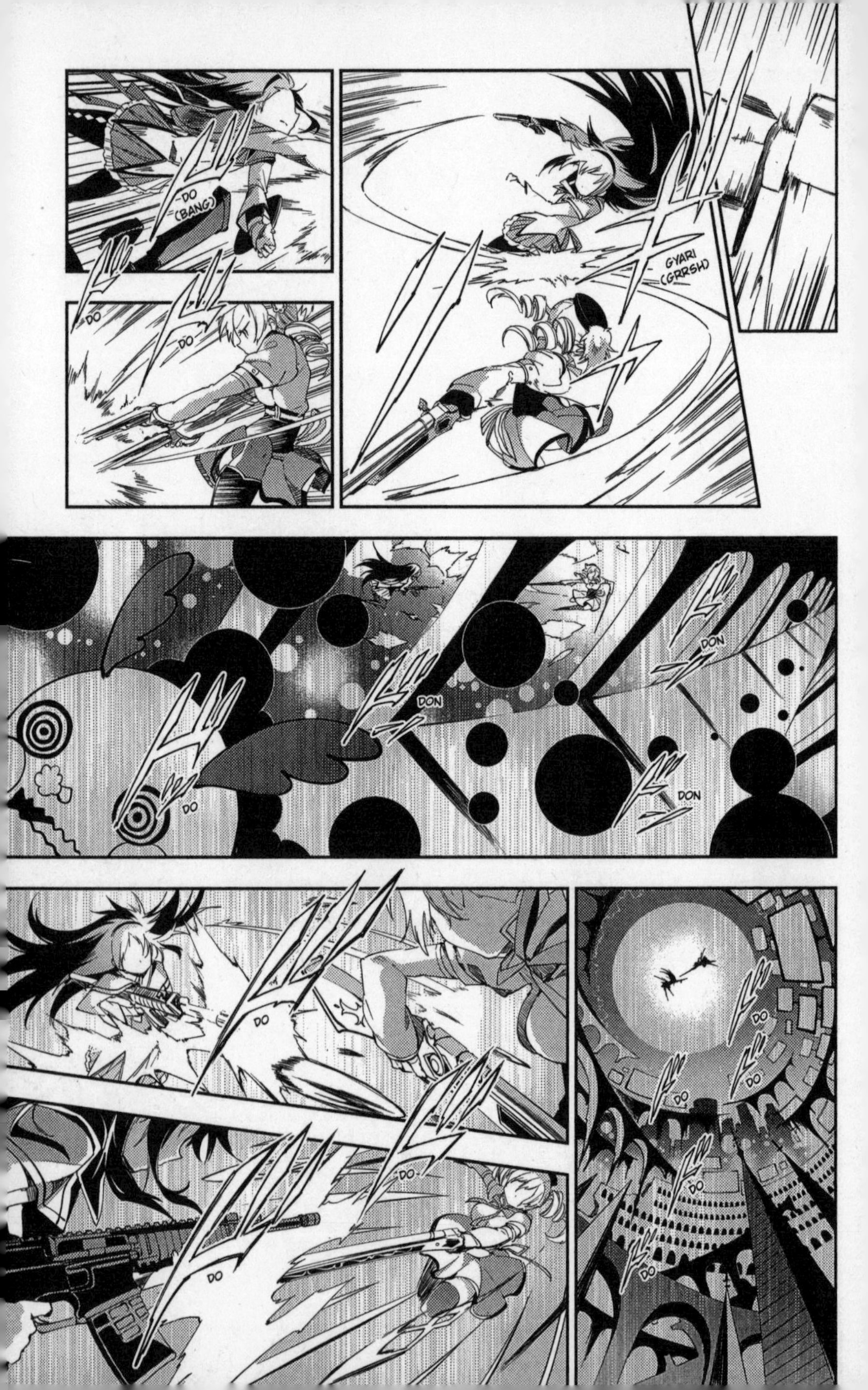
GYARI (GRRSH)
DO (BANG)
DO
DO
DON
DON
DON
DO
DO
DO
DO
DO
DO
DO
DO
DO
DO

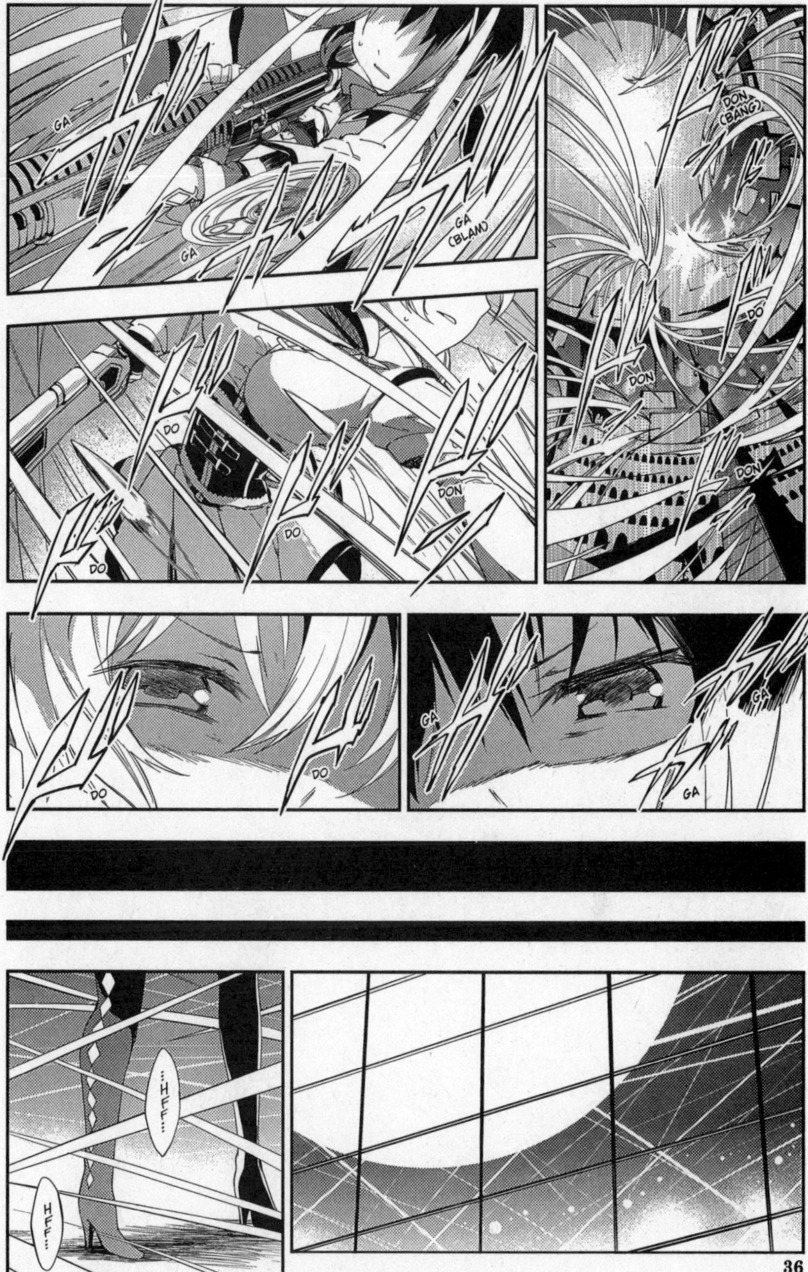
DON
(BANG)
DO
DON
DON
GA
GA
GA
(BLAM)
DO
DON
DO
DO
GA
GA
GA
DO
DO
...HFF...
HFF...

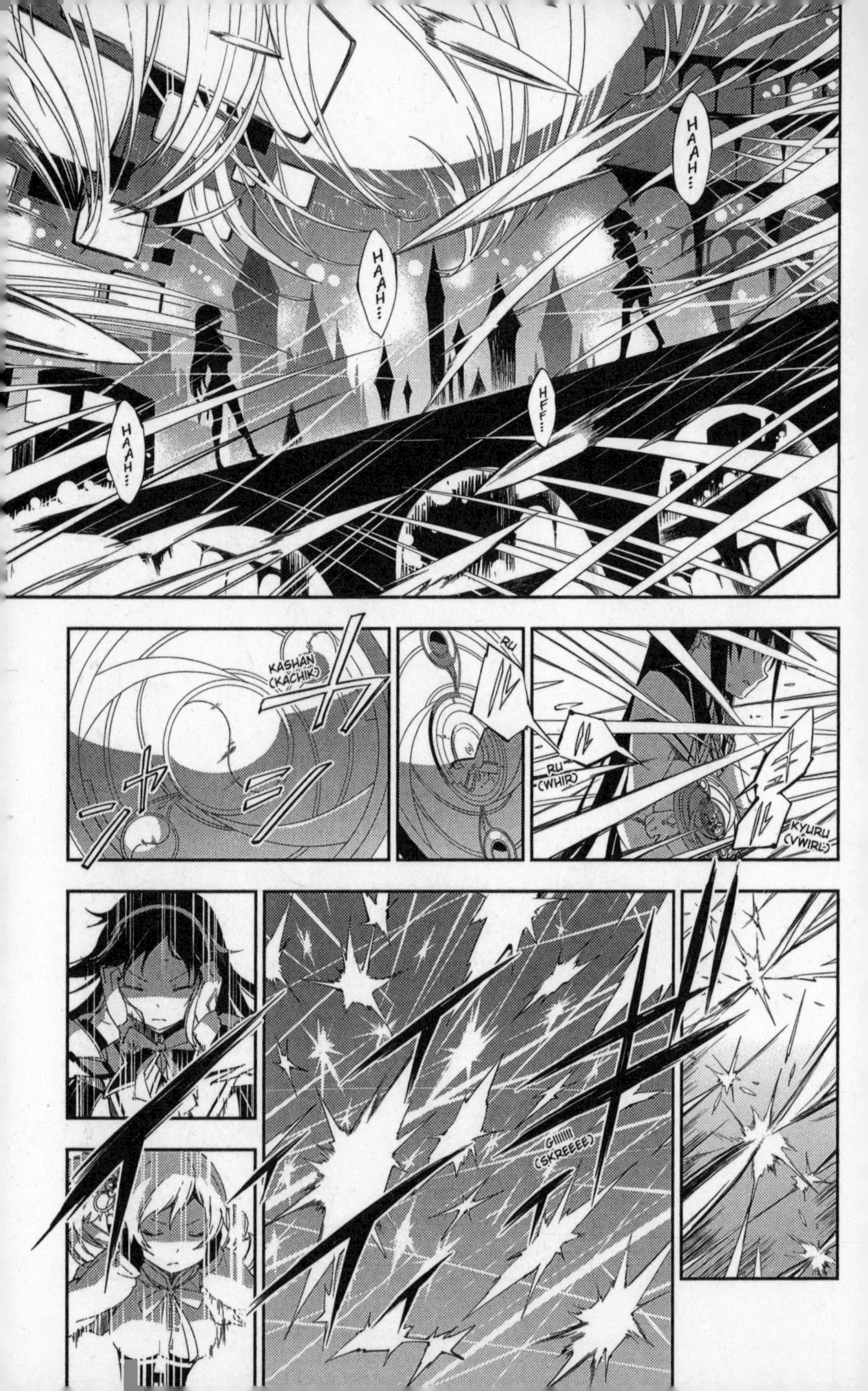
HAAAH...
HFF...
HAAAH...
HAAAH...
RU (WHIR)
KYURU (VWIRL)
RU
KASHAN (KACHIK)
GIIIIII (SKREEEE)

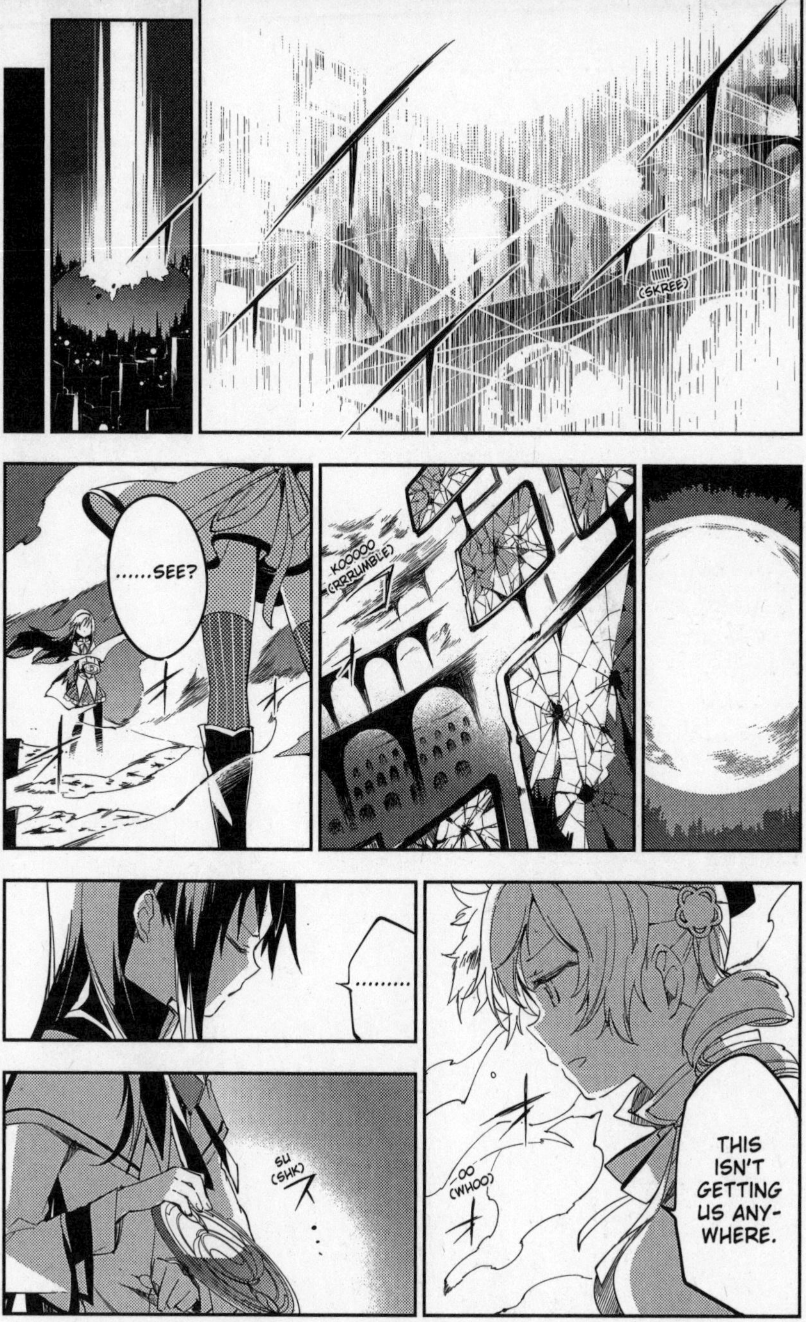
(SKREE)
KOOOOO (RRRUMBLE)
......SEE?
THIS ISN'T GETTING US ANY-WHERE.
OO (WHOO)
....
SU (SHK)

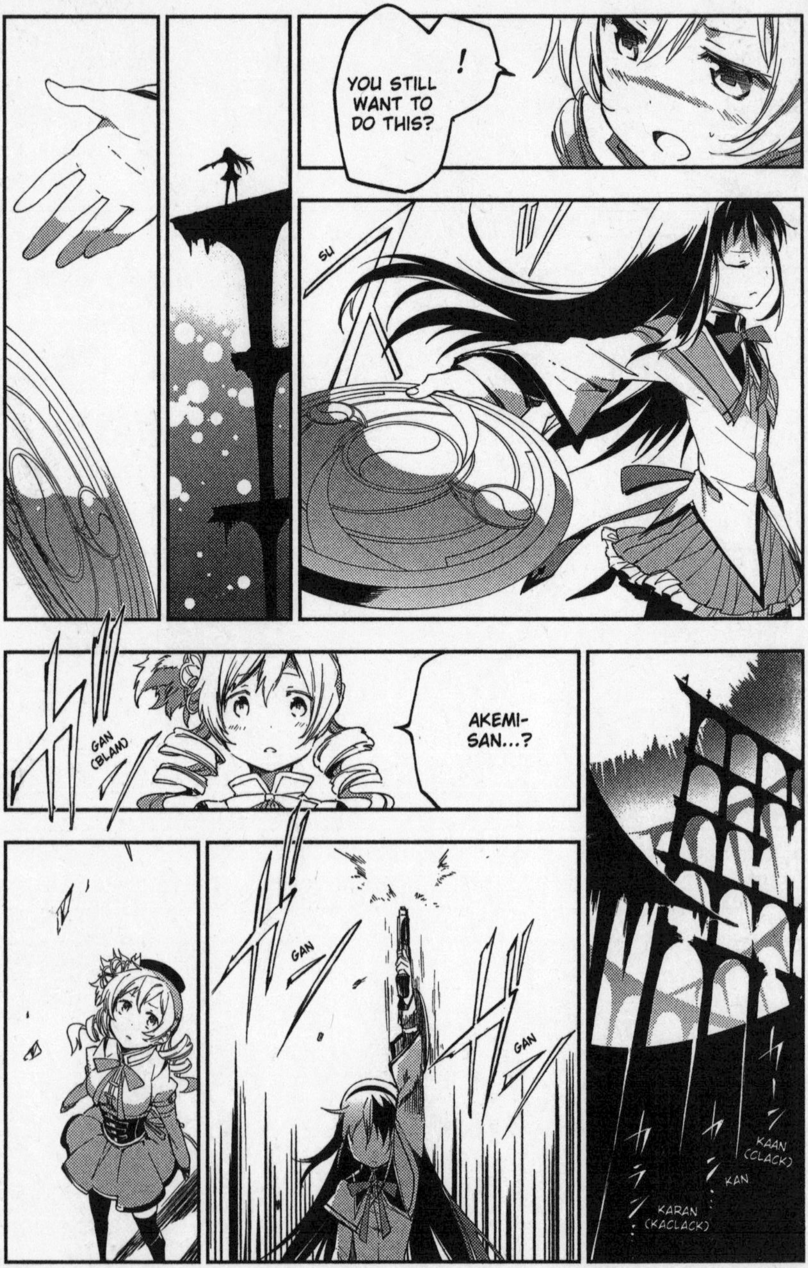
!
YOU STILL WANT TO DO THIS?
SU
KAAN (CLACK)
KAN
KARAN (KACLACK)
AKEMI-SAN...?
GAN (BLAM)
GAN
GAN

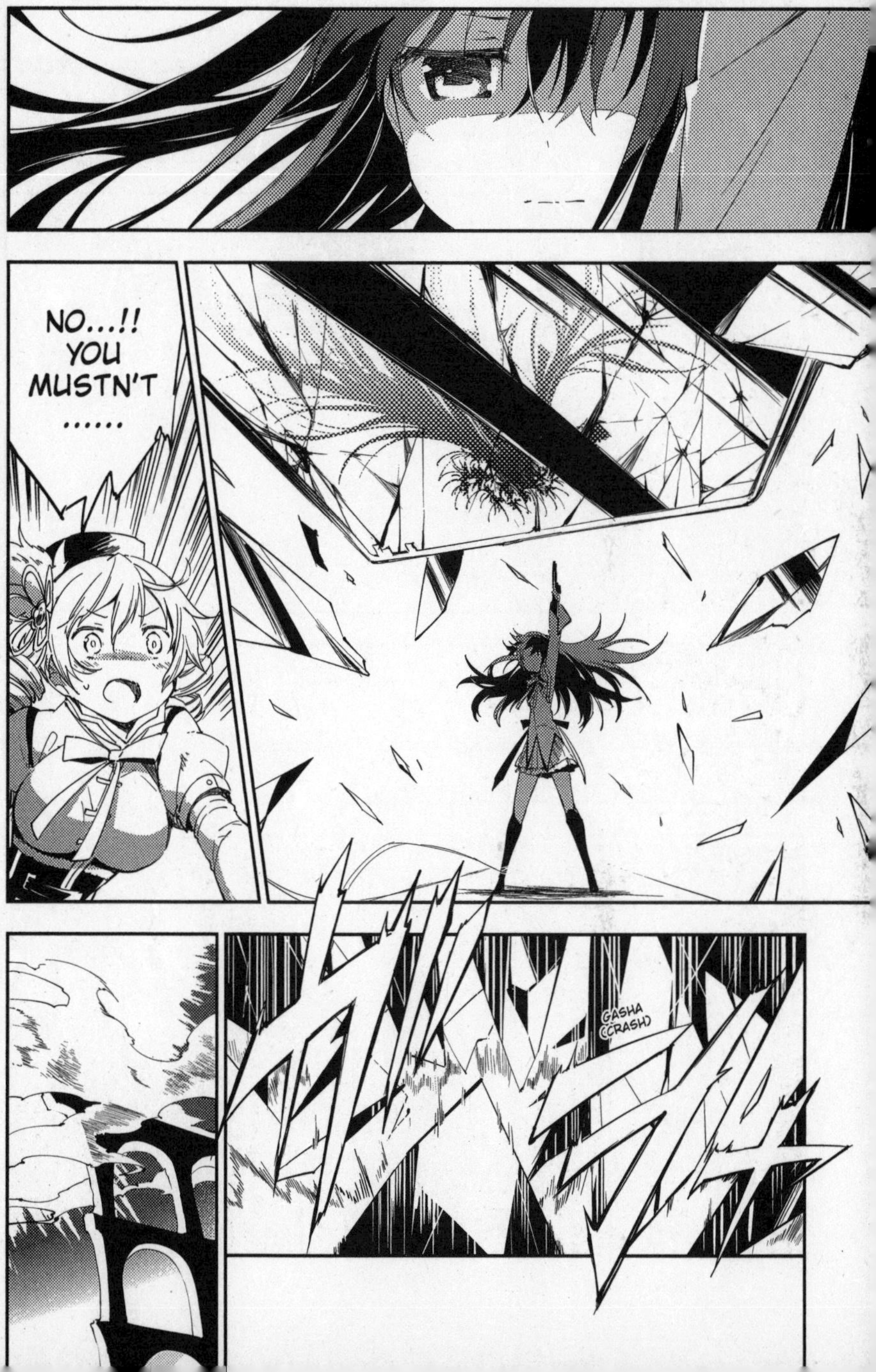
......
NO...!! YOU MUSTN'T ......
GASHA (CRASH)

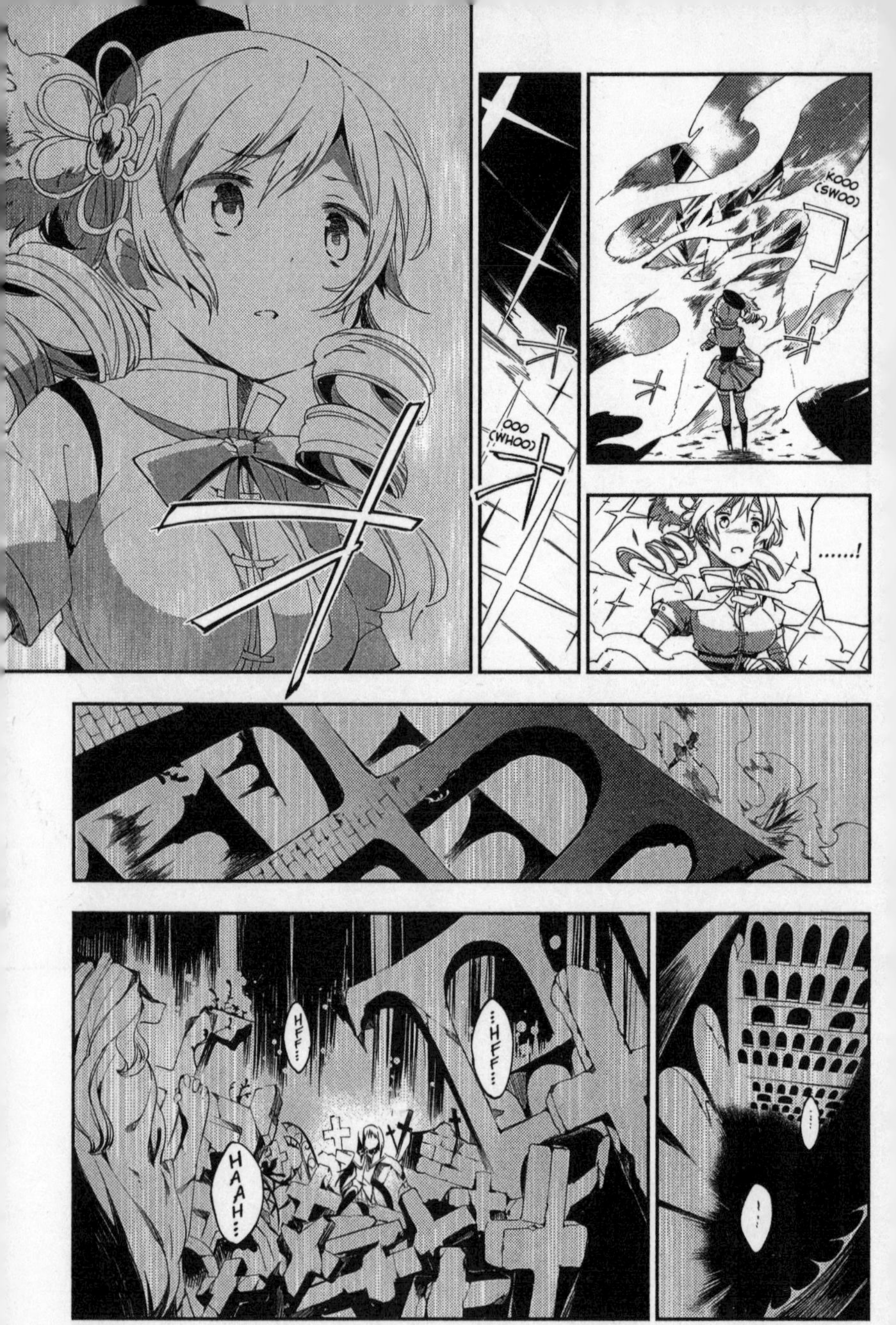
KOOO
(SWOO)
......!
OOO
(WHOO)
...
!...
...HFF...
HFF...
HAAH...

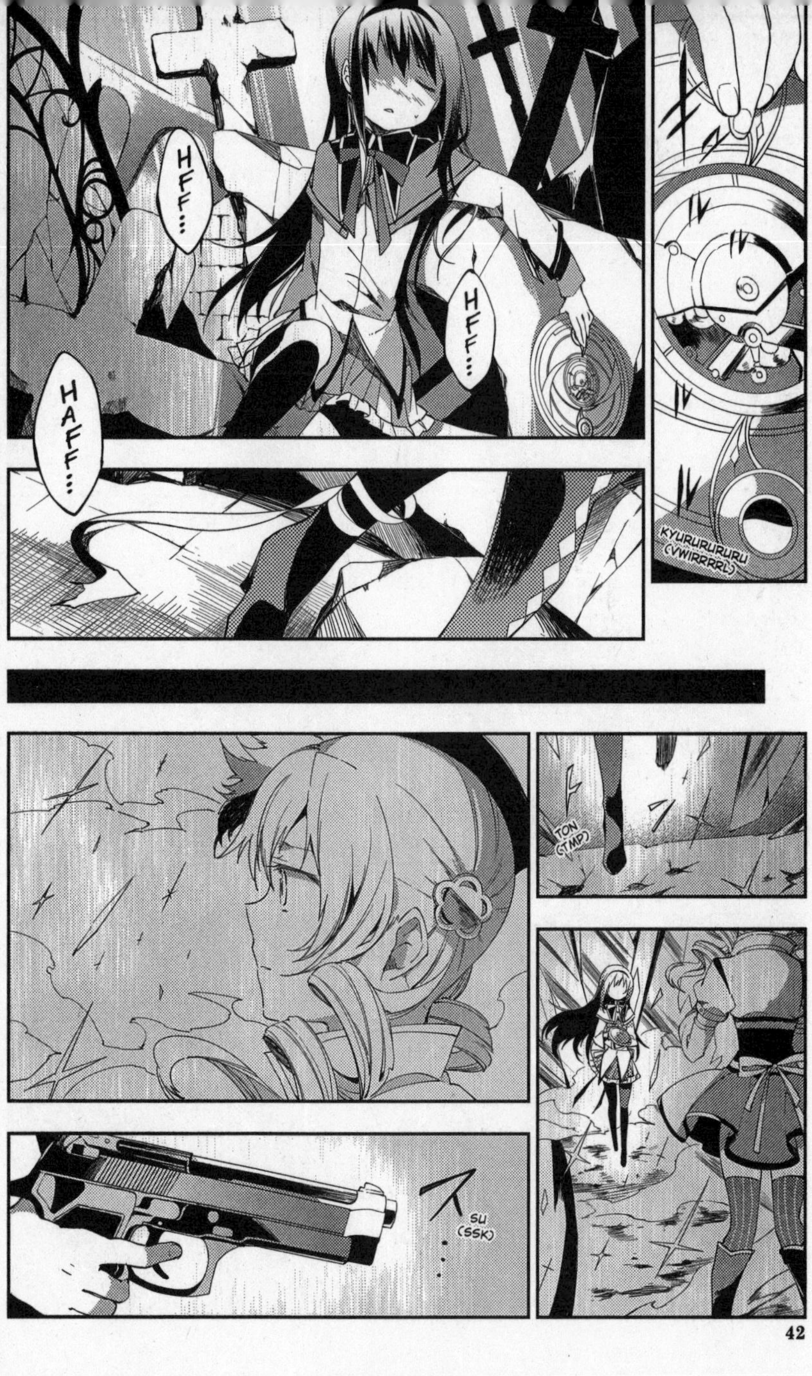
KYURURURURU
(VWIRRRRL)
HFF...
HFF...
HAFF...
TON
(TMP)
SU
(SSK)

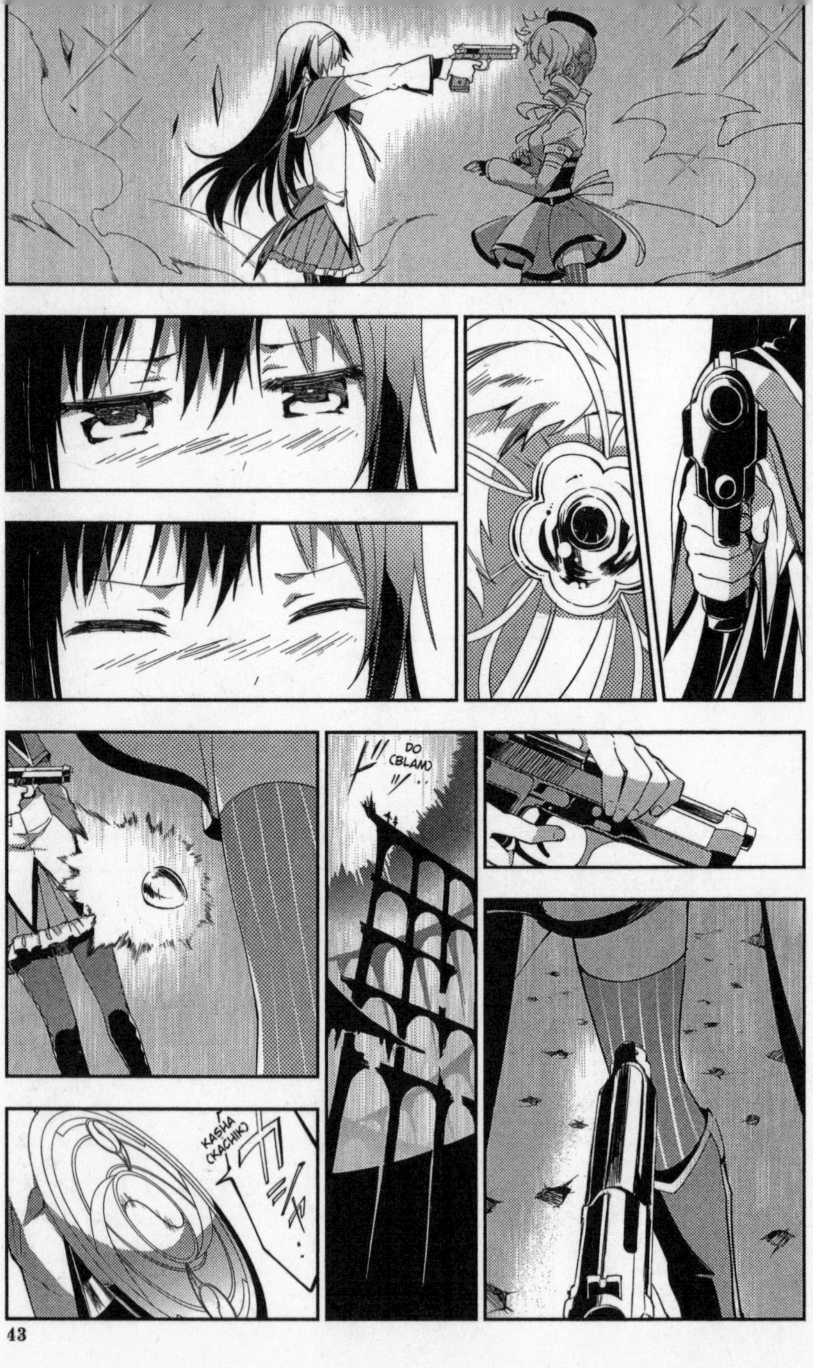
DO (BLAM)
KASHA (KACHIK)

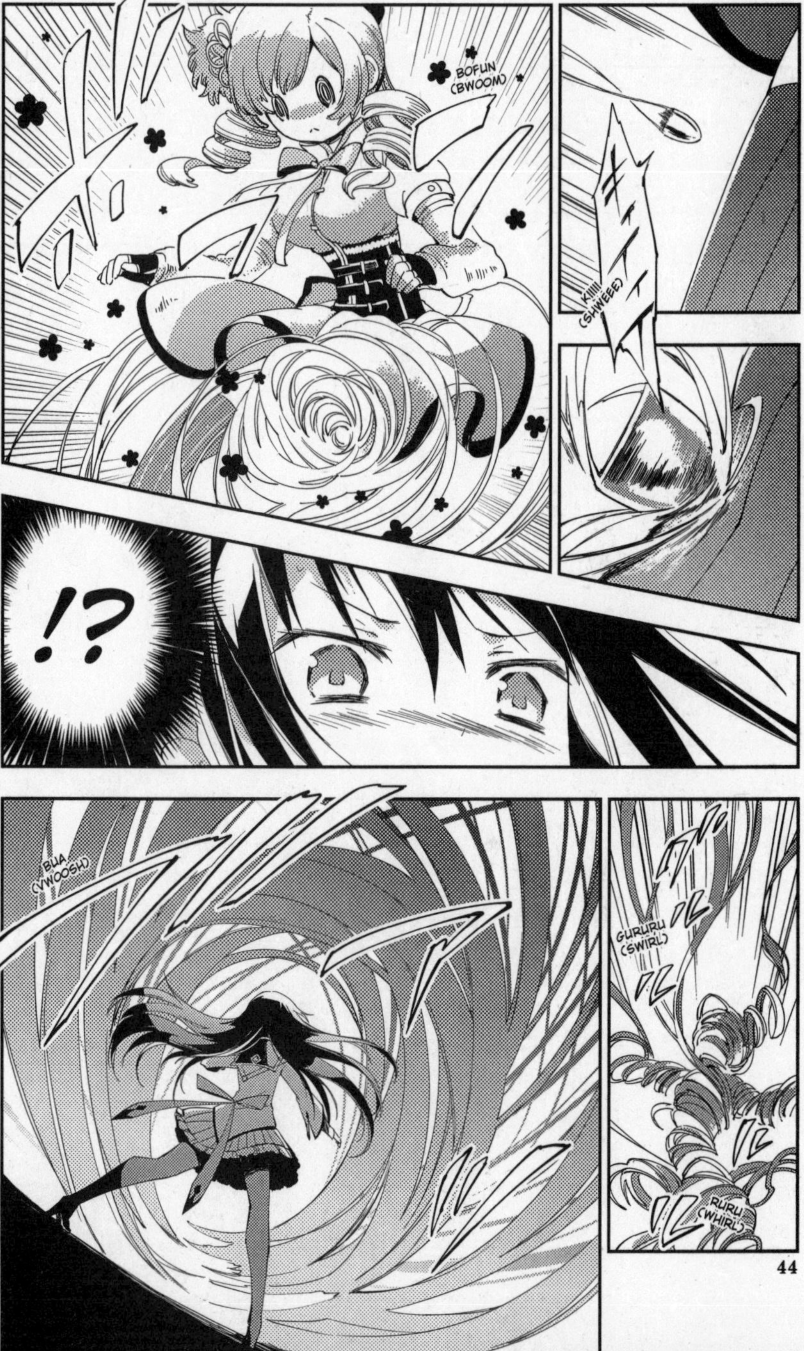
KIIIII (SHWEEE)
BOFUN (BWOOM)
!?
GURURU (SWIRL)
RURU (WHIRL)
BUA (VWOOSH)

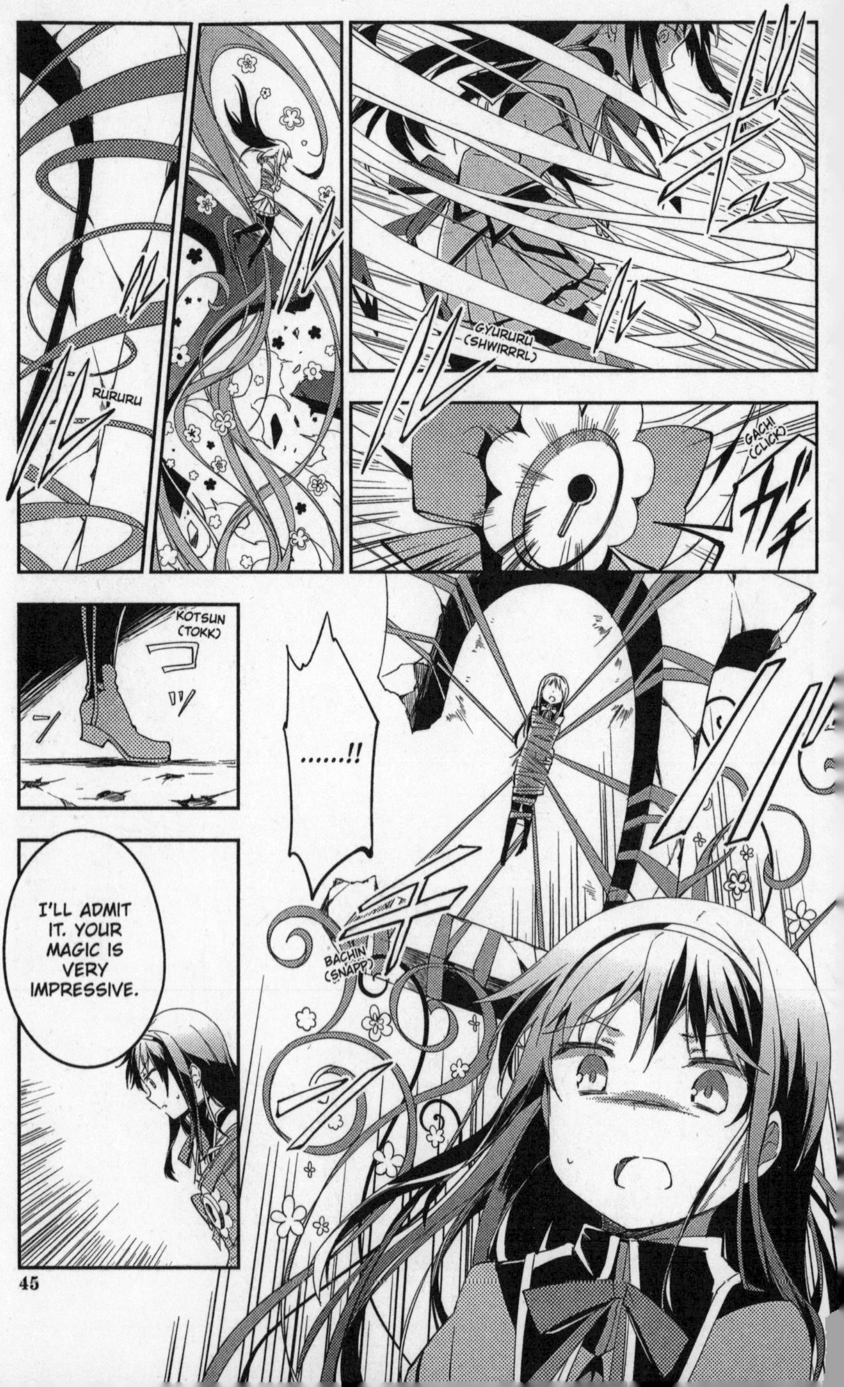
GYURURU (SHWIRRRL)
GACHI (CLICK)
RURURU
......!!
BACHIN (SNAPP)
KOTSUN (TOKK)
I'LL ADMIT IT. YOUR MAGIC IS VERY IMPRESSIVE.

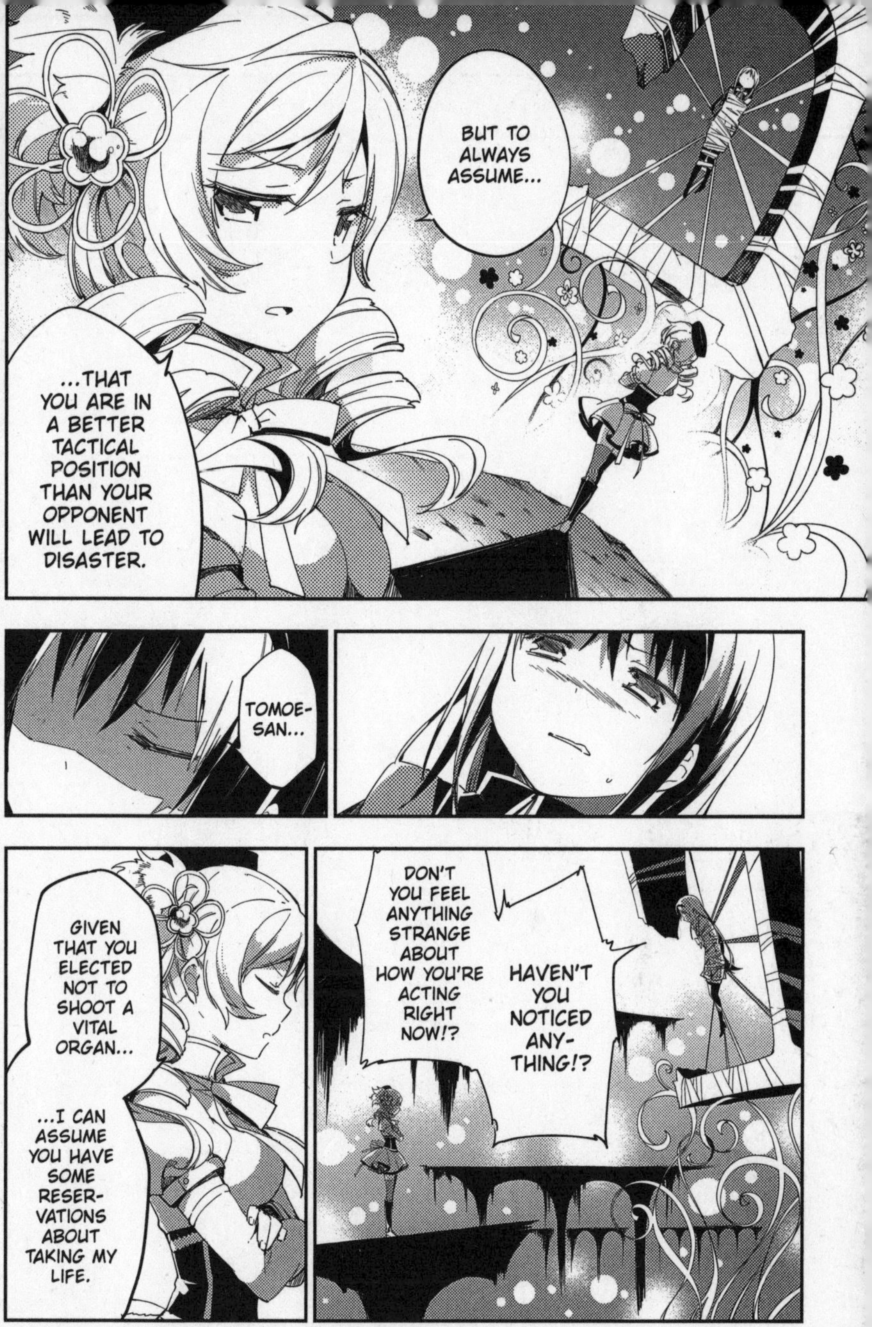
BUT TO ALWAYS ASSUME...
...THAT YOU ARE IN A BETTER TACTICAL POSITION THAN YOUR OPPONENT WILL LEAD TO DISASTER.
TOMOE-SAN...
HAVEN'T YOU NOTICED ANYTHING!?
DON'T YOU FEEL ANYTHING STRANGE ABOUT HOW YOU'RE ACTING RIGHT NOW!?
GIVEN THAT YOU ELECTED NOT TO SHOOT A VITAL ORGAN...
...I CAN ASSUME YOU HAVE SOME RESERVATIONS ABOUT TAKING MY LIFE.

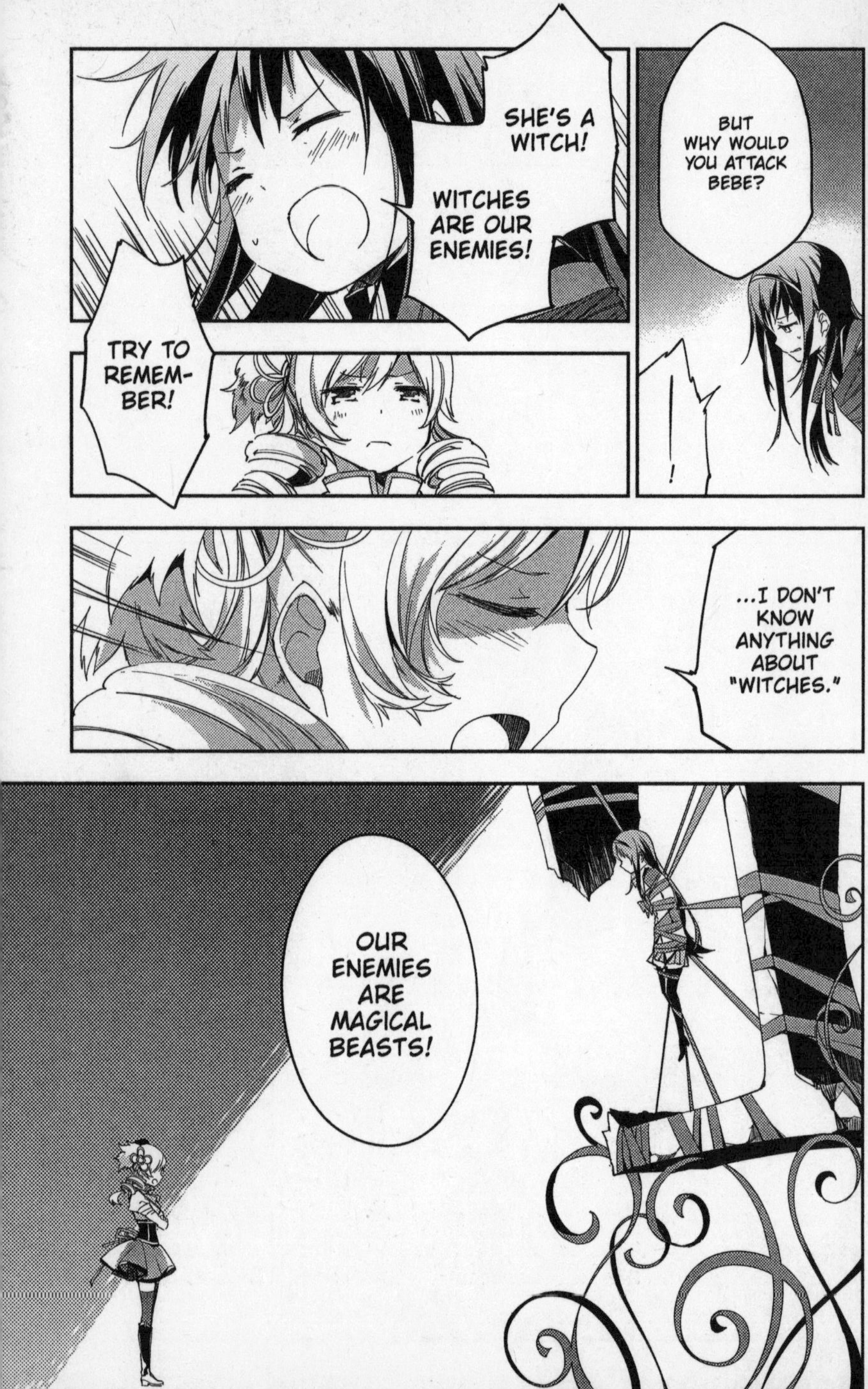
BUT WHY WOULD YOU ATTACK BEBE?
SHE'S A WITCH!
WITCHES ARE OUR ENEMIES!
TRY TO REMEM-BER!
...I DON'T KNOW ANYTHING ABOUT "WITCHES."
OUR ENEMIES ARE MAGICAL BEASTS!

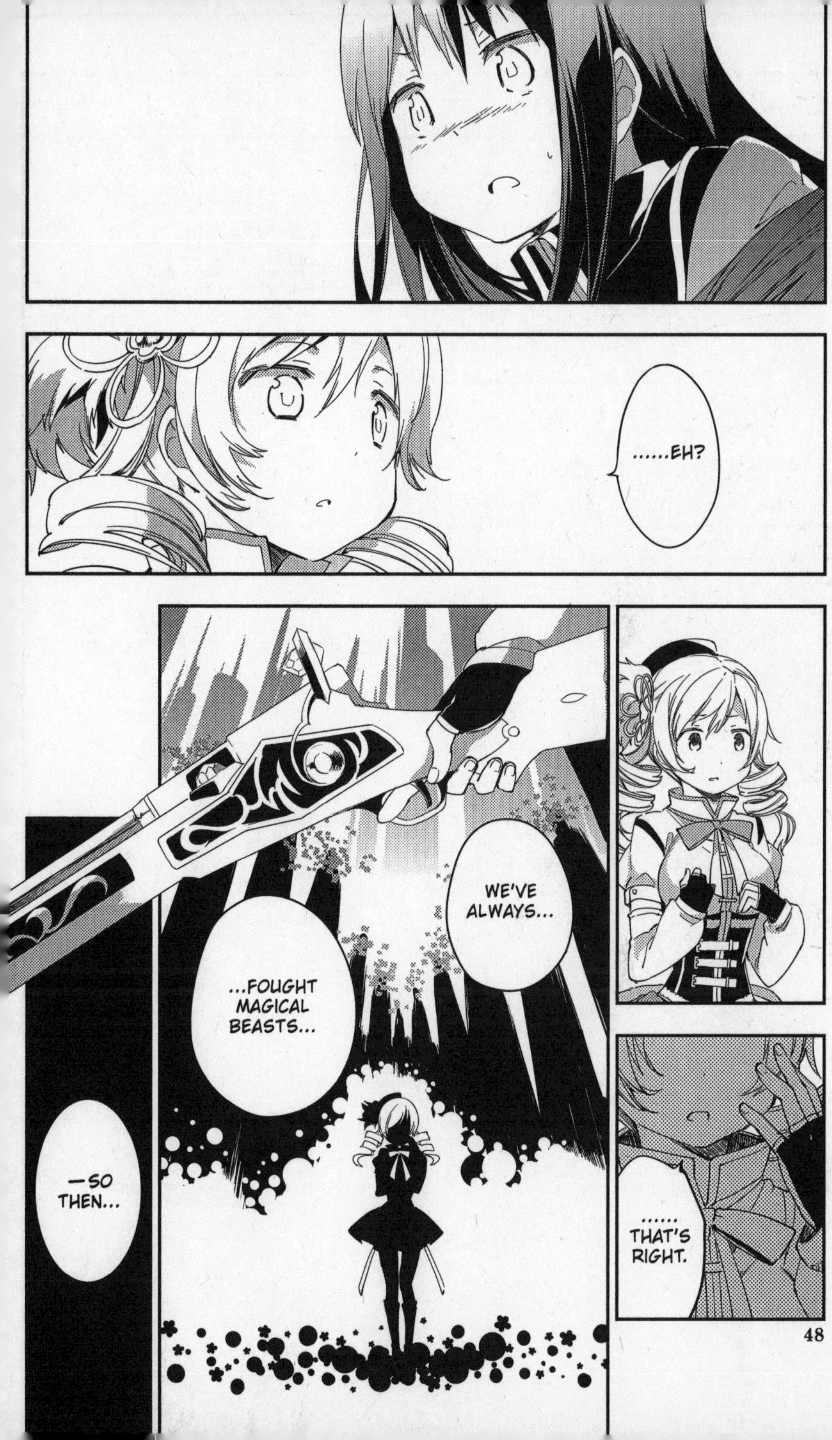
......EH?
......THAT'S RIGHT.
WE'VE ALWAYS...
...FOUGHT MAGICAL BEASTS...
—SO THEN...

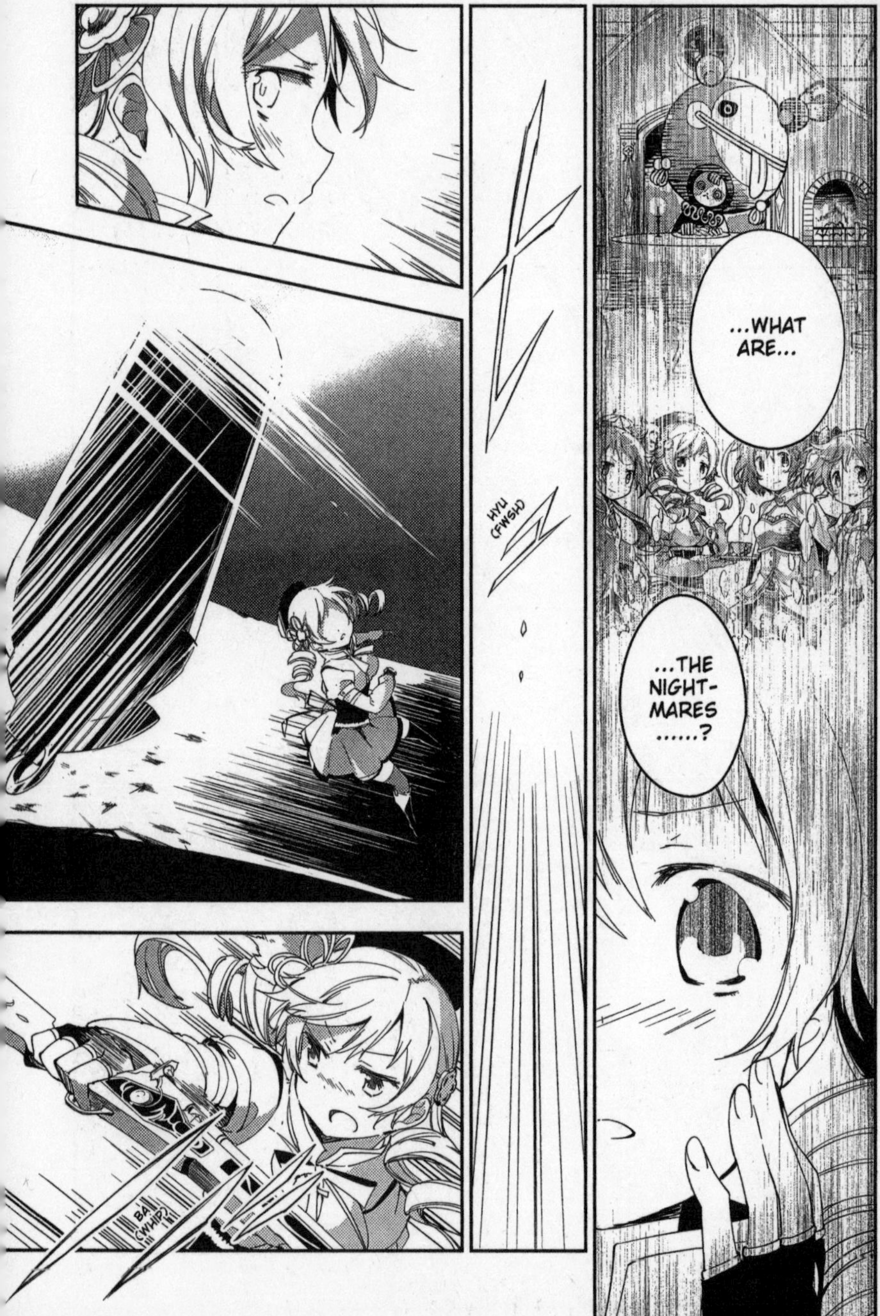
...WHAT ARE...
...THE NIGHT-MARES ......?
HYU (FWSH)
BA (WHIP)

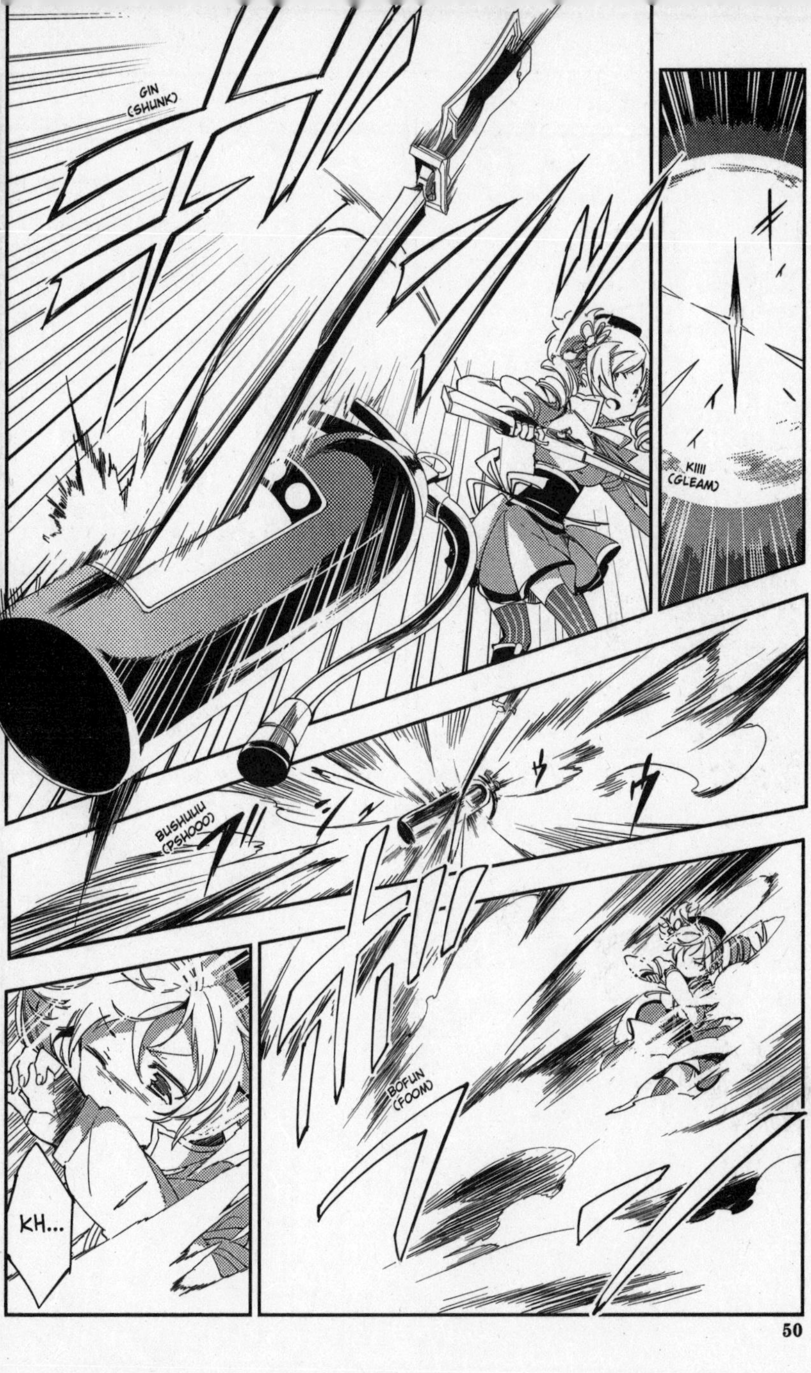
KIIII (GLEAM)
GIN (SHUNK)
BUSHUUU (PSHOOO)
BOFUN (FOOM)
KH...

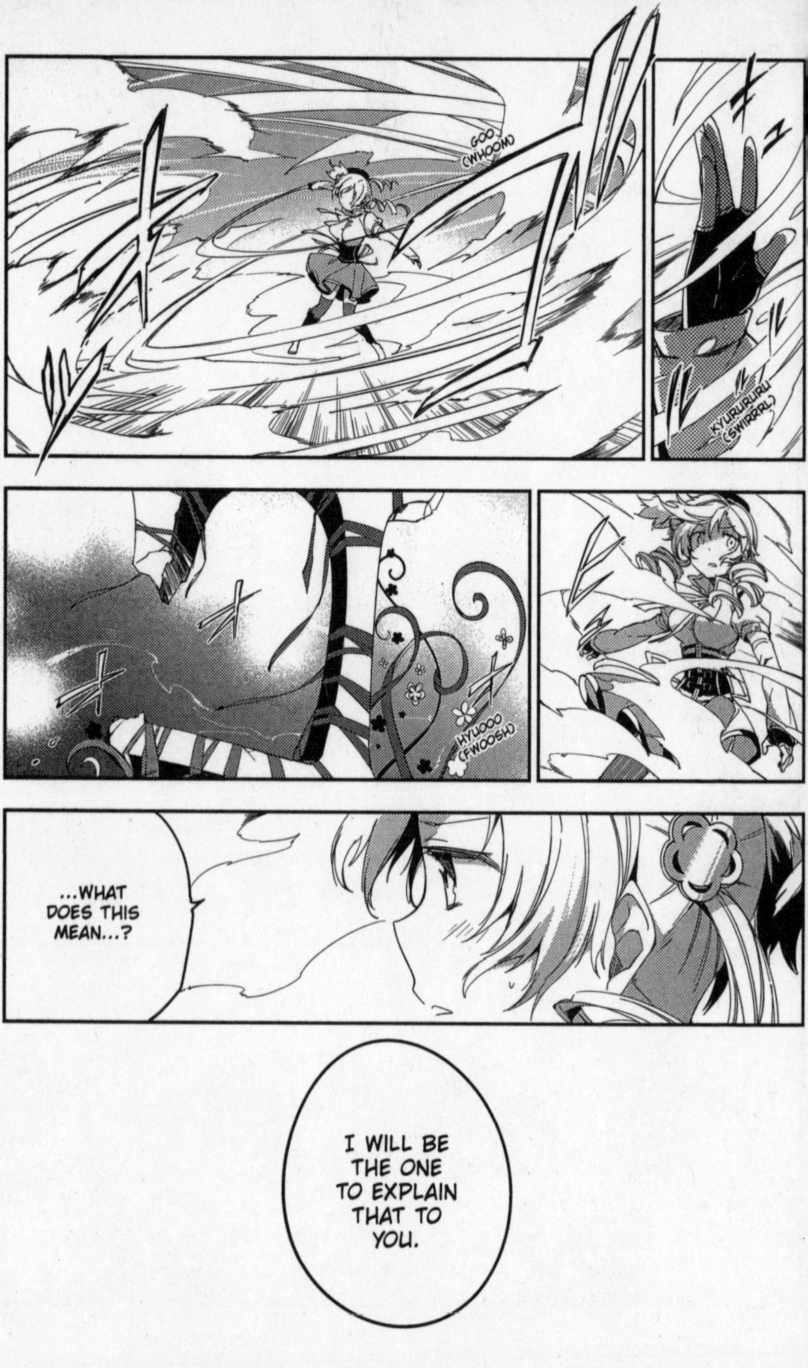
KYURURURU (SWIRRRL)
GOO (WHOOM)
HYUOOO (FWOOSH)
...WHAT DOES THIS MEAN...?
I WILL BE THE ONE TO EXPLAIN THAT TO YOU.

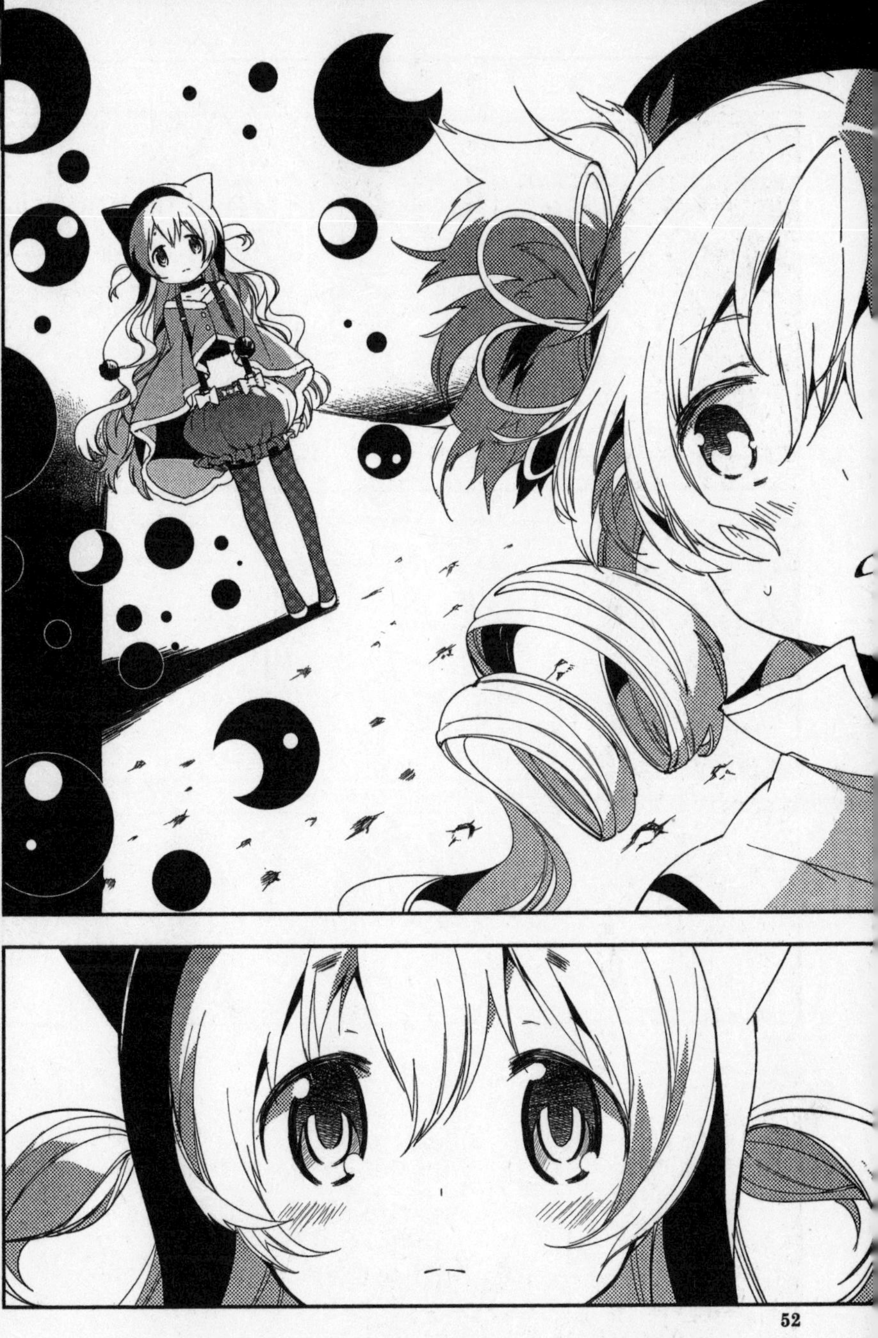

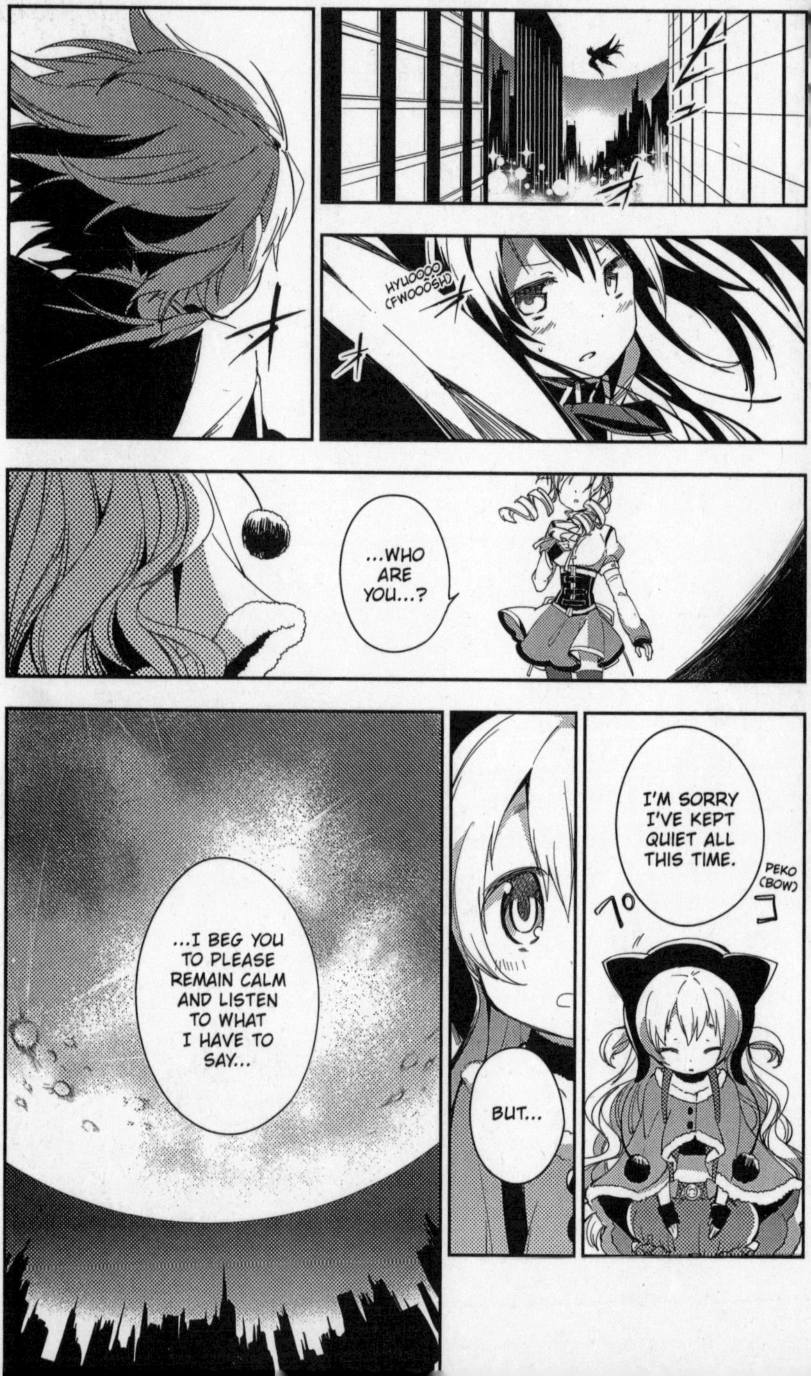
HYUOOOO (FWOOOSH)
...WHO ARE YOU...?
I'M SORRY I'VE KEPT QUIET ALL THIS TIME.
PEKO (BOW)
BUT...
...I BEG YOU TO PLEASE REMAIN CALM AND LISTEN TO WHAT I HAVE TO SAY...

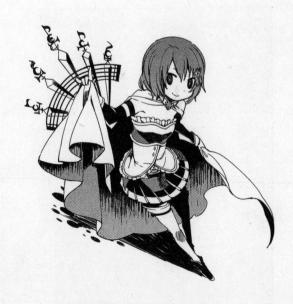

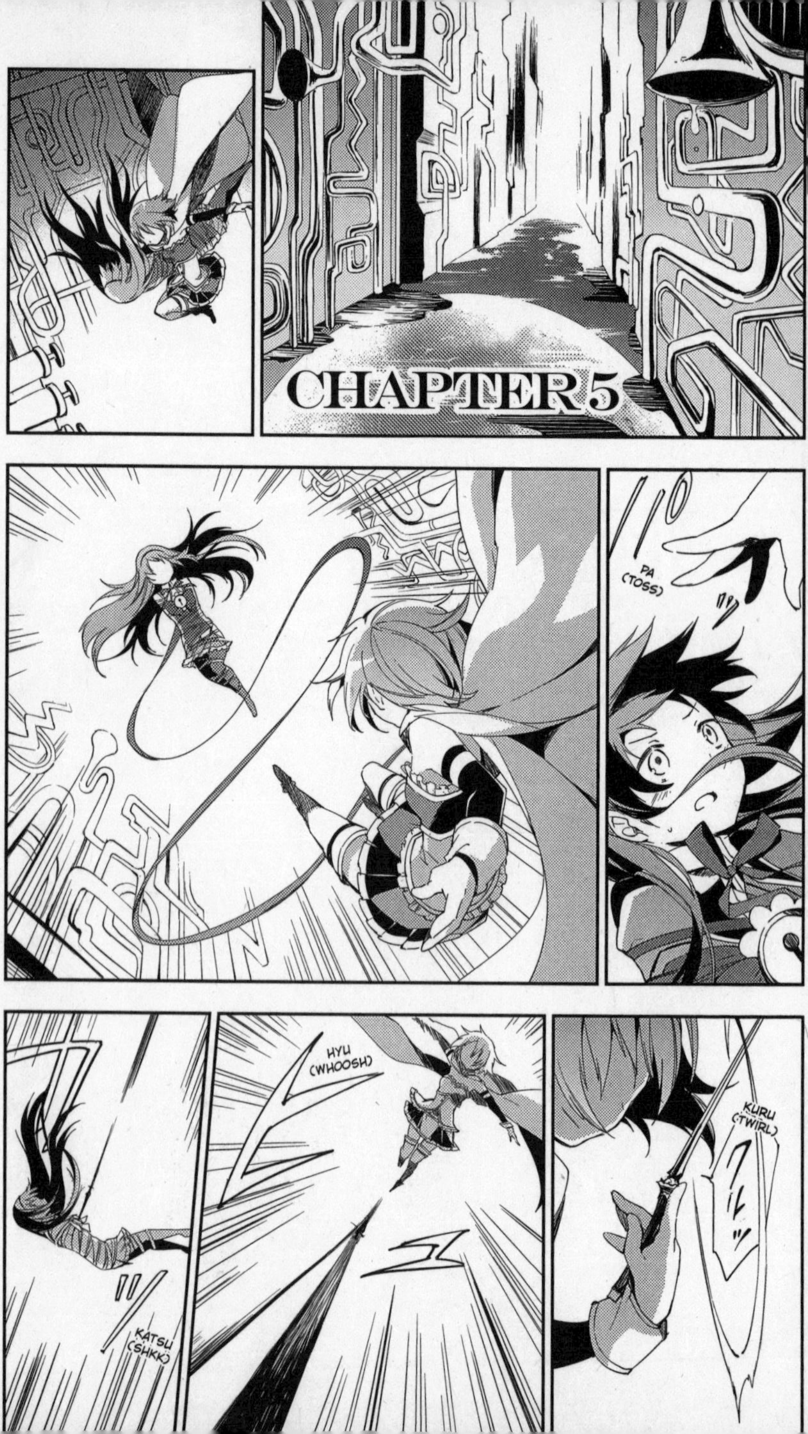
CHAPTER 5
PA (TOSS)
KURU (TWIRL)
HYU (WHOOSH)
KATSU (SHKK)

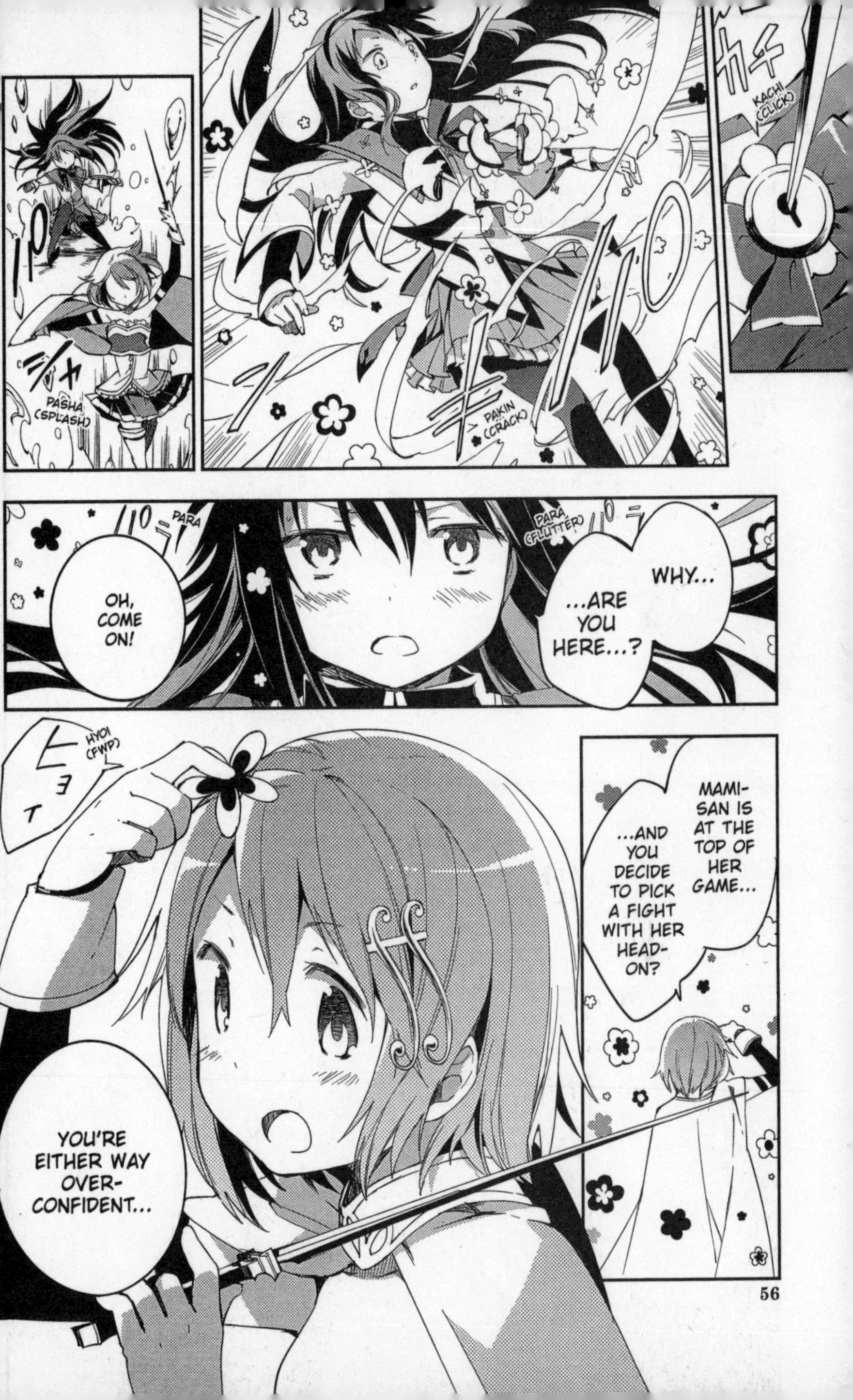
KACHI (CLICK)
PAKIN (CRACK)
PASHA (SPLASH)
PARA (FLUTTER)
WHY...
...ARE YOU HERE...?
PARA
OH, COME ON!
MAMI-SAN IS AT THE TOP OF HER GAME...
...AND YOU DECIDE TO PICK A FIGHT WITH HER HEAD-ON?
HYOI (FWP)
YOU'RE EITHER WAY OVER-CONFIDENT...

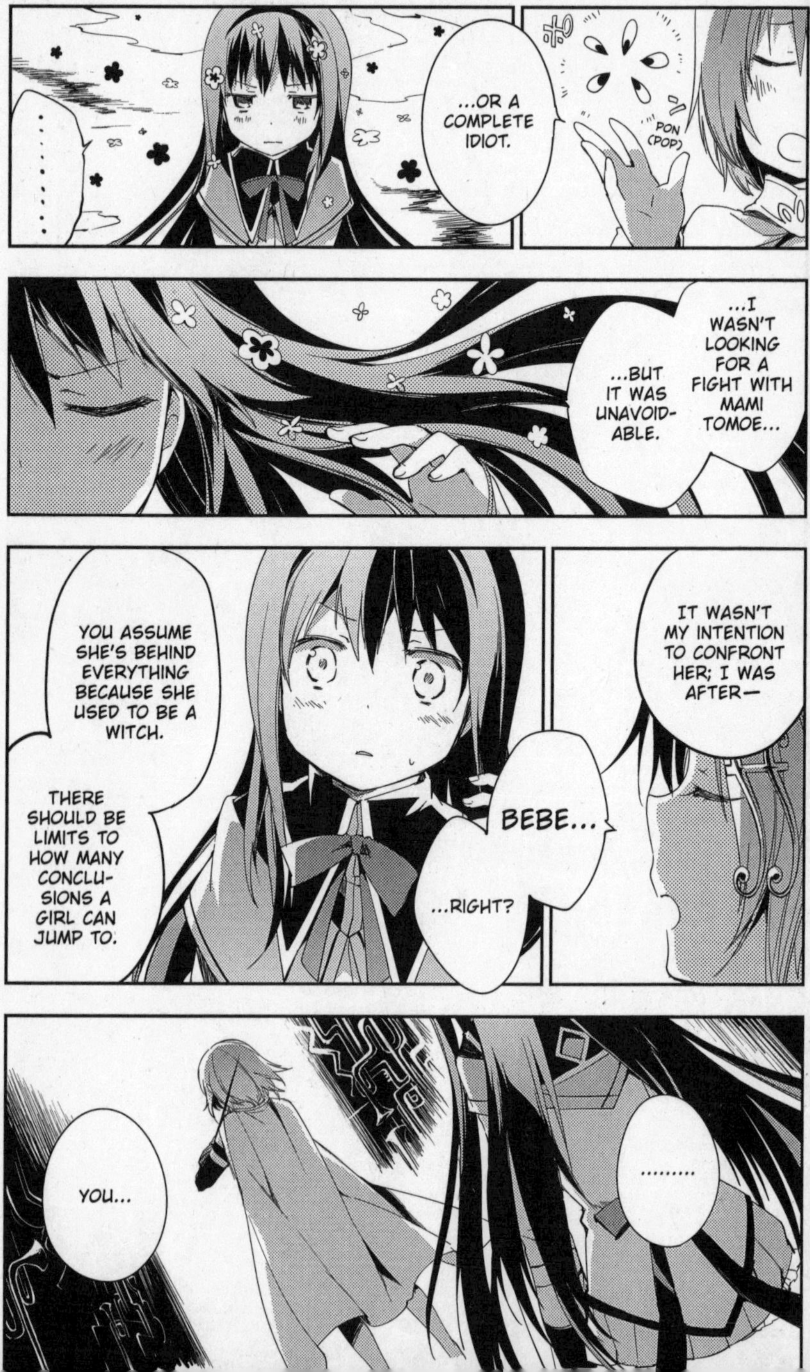
PON (POP)
...OR A COMPLETE IDIOT.
......
...I WASN'T LOOKING FOR A FIGHT WITH MAMI TOMOE...
...BUT IT WAS UNAVOIDABLE.
IT WASN'T MY INTENTION TO CONFRONT HER; I WAS AFTER—
BEBE...
...RIGHT?
YOU ASSUME SHE'S BEHIND EVERYTHING BECAUSE SHE USED TO BE A WITCH.
THERE SHOULD BE LIMITS TO HOW MANY CONCLUSIONS A GIRL CAN JUMP TO.
....
YOU...

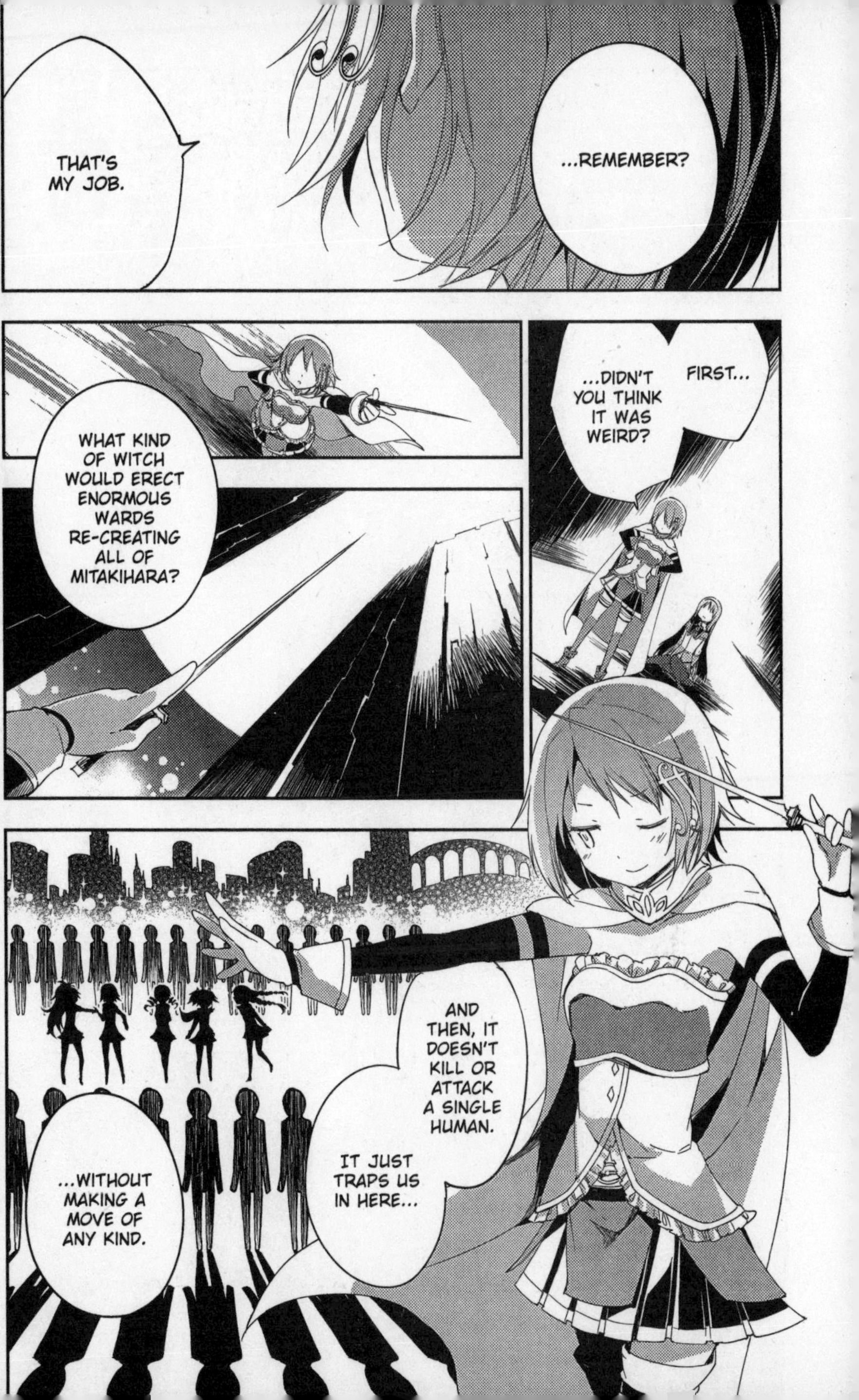
...REMEMBER?
THAT'S MY JOB.
FIRST...
...DIDN'T YOU THINK IT WAS WEIRD?
WHAT KIND OF WITCH WOULD ERECT ENORMOUS WARDS RE-CREATING ALL OF MITAKIHARA?
AND THEN, IT DOESN'T KILL OR ATTACK A SINGLE HUMAN.
IT JUST TRAPS US IN HERE...
...WITHOUT MAKING A MOVE OF ANY KIND.

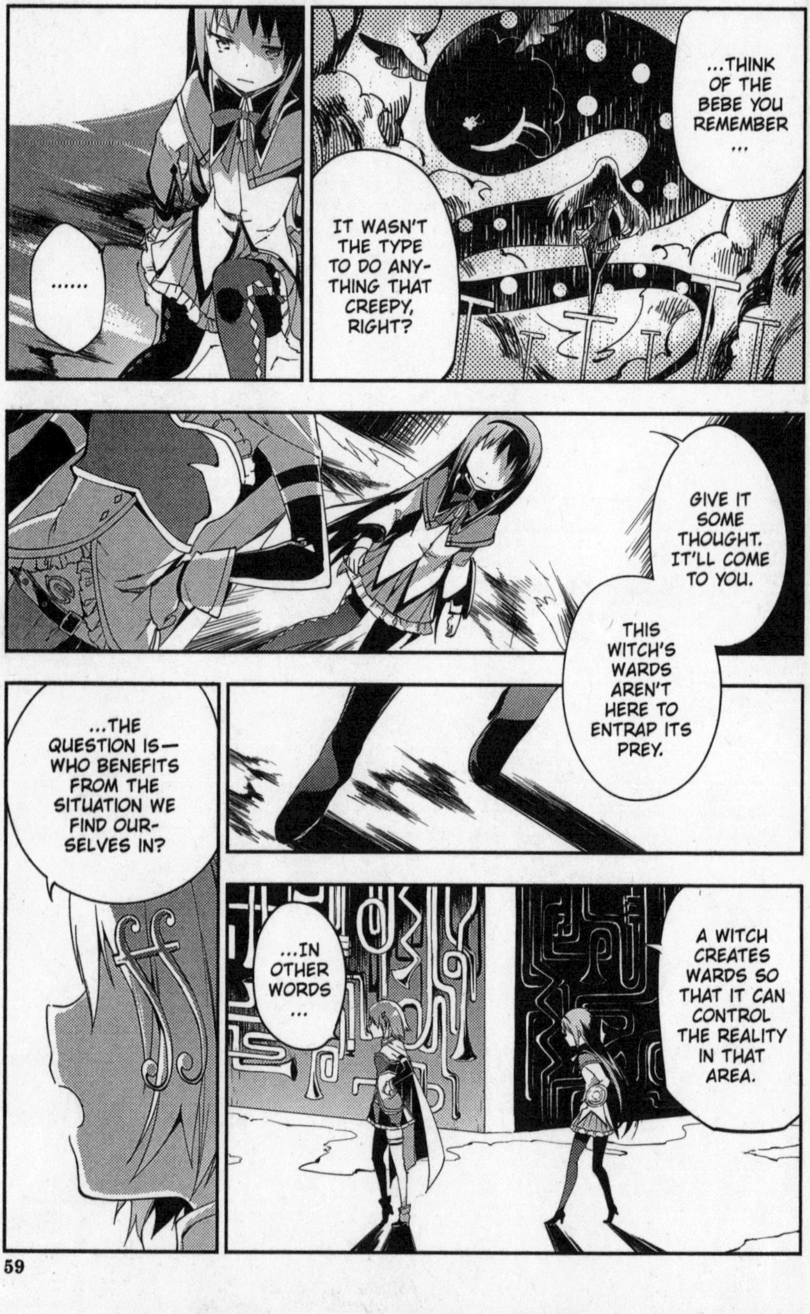
...THINK OF THE BEBE YOU REMEMBER ...
IT WASN'T THE TYPE TO DO ANY-THING THAT CREEPY, RIGHT?
......
GIVE IT SOME THOUGHT. IT'LL COME TO YOU.
THIS WITCH'S WARDS AREN'T HERE TO ENTRAP ITS PREY.
A WITCH CREATES WARDS SO THAT IT CAN CONTROL THE REALITY IN THAT AREA.
...IN OTHER WORDS ...
...THE QUESTION IS—WHO BENEFITS FROM THE SITUATION WE FIND OUR-SELVES IN?

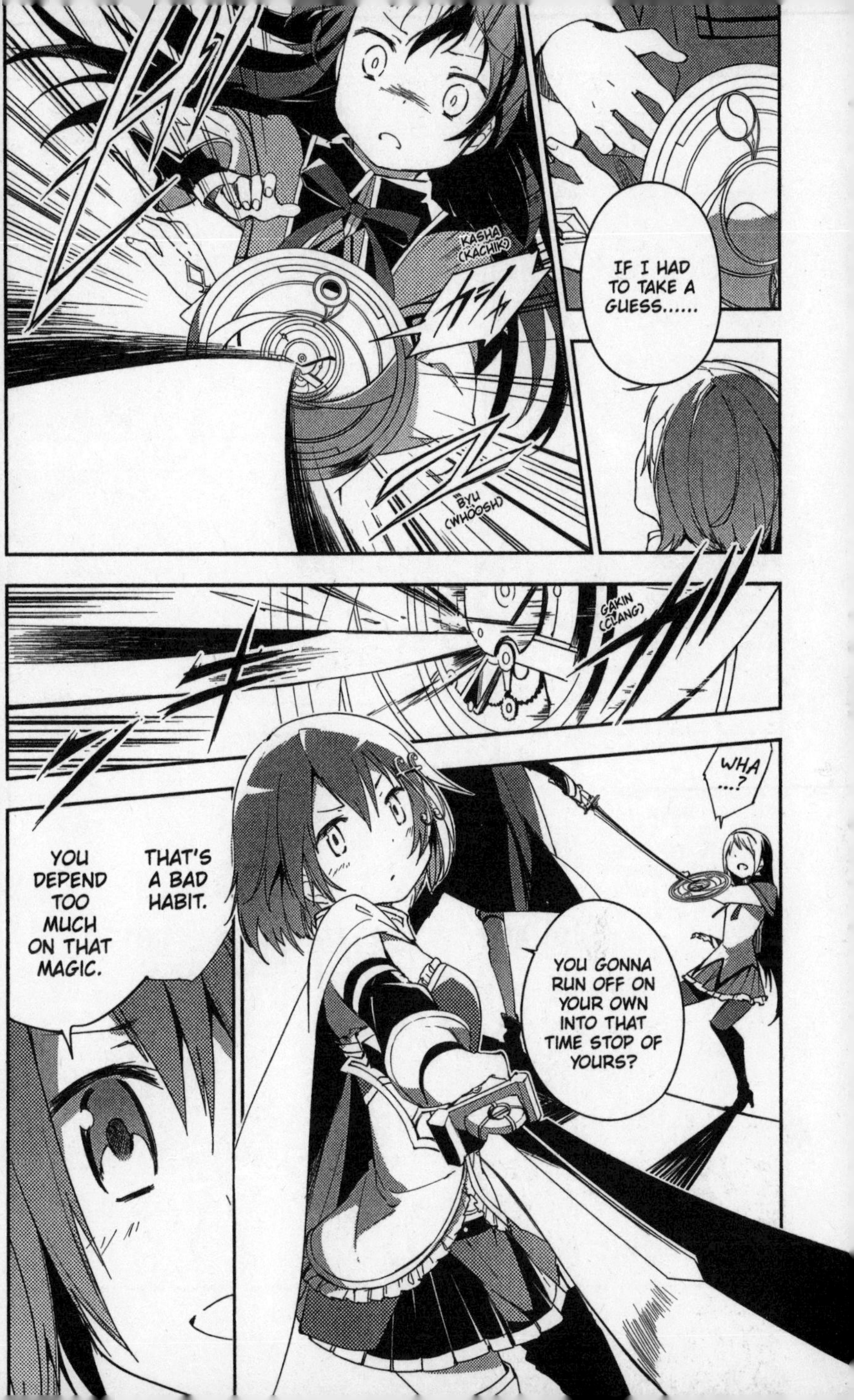
IF I HAD TO TAKE A GUESS......
KASHA (KACHIK)
BYU (WHOOSH)
GAKIN (CLANG)
WHA ...?
YOU GONNA RUN OFF ON YOUR OWN INTO THAT TIME STOP OF YOURS?
THAT'S A BAD HABIT.
YOU DEPEND TOO MUCH ON THAT MAGIC.

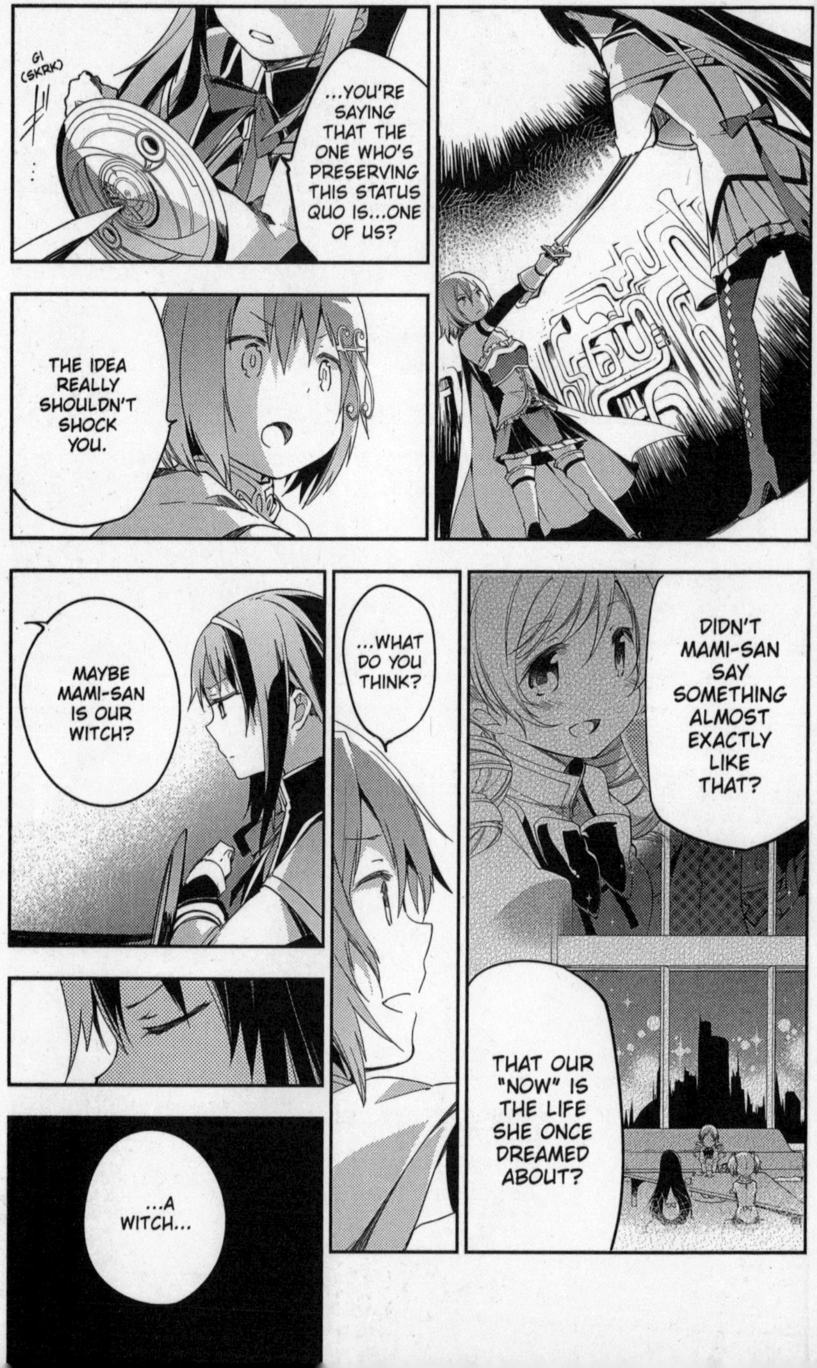
GI (SKRK)
...YOU'RE SAYING THAT THE ONE WHO'S PRESERVING THIS STATUS QUO IS...ONE OF US?
THE IDEA REALLY SHOULDN'T SHOCK YOU.
DIDN'T MAMI-SAN SAY SOMETHING ALMOST EXACTLY LIKE THAT?
THAT OUR "NOW" IS THE LIFE SHE ONCE DREAMED ABOUT?
...WHAT DO YOU THINK?
MAYBE MAMI-SAN IS OUR WITCH?
...A WITCH...

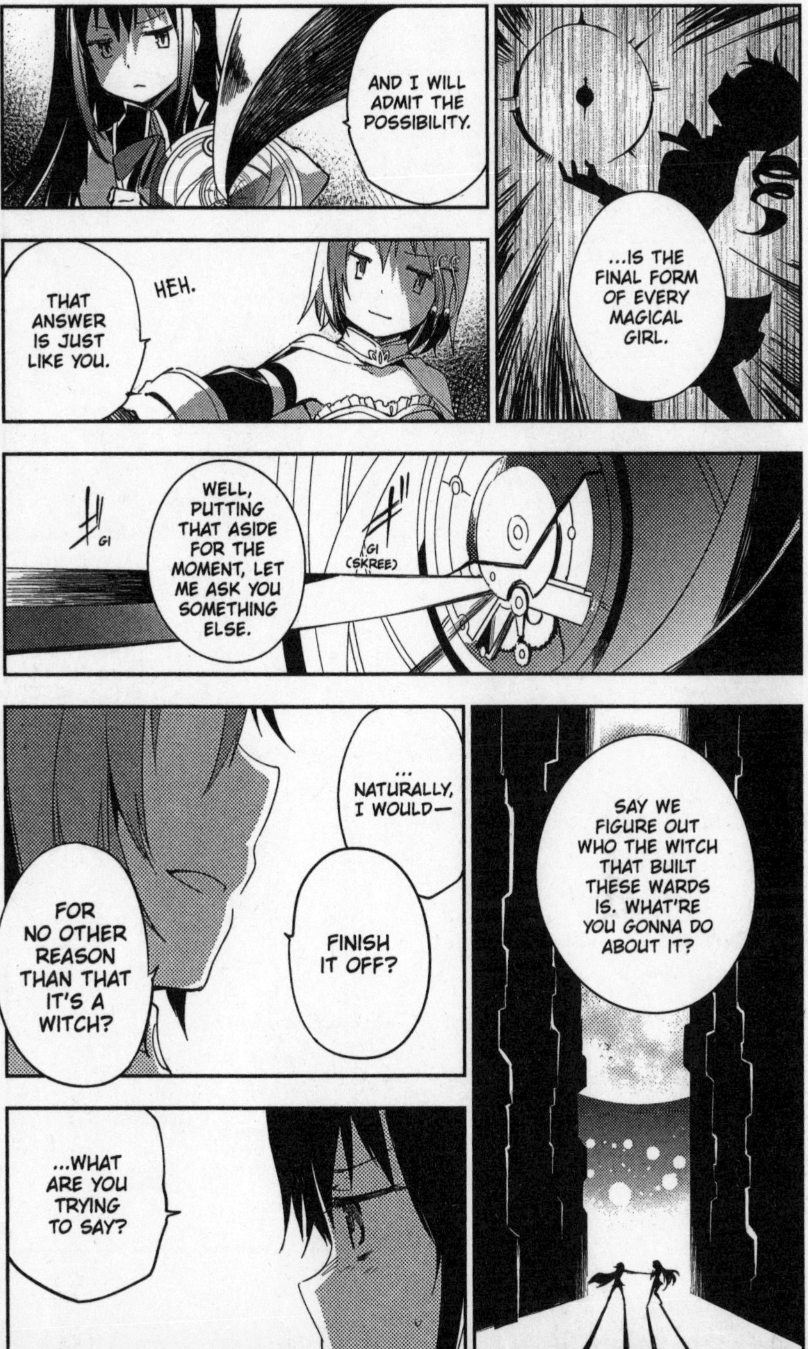
...IS THE FINAL FORM OF EVERY MAGICAL GIRL.
AND I WILL ADMIT THE POSSIBILITY.
HEH.
THAT ANSWER IS JUST LIKE YOU.
GI (SKREE)
WELL, PUTTING THAT ASIDE FOR THE MOMENT, LET ME ASK YOU SOMETHING ELSE.
GI
SAY WE FIGURE OUT WHO THE WITCH THAT BUILT THESE WARDS IS. WHAT'RE YOU GONNA DO ABOUT IT?
... NATURALLY, I WOULD—
FINISH IT OFF?
FOR NO OTHER REASON THAN THAT IT'S A WITCH?
...WHAT ARE YOU TRYING TO SAY?

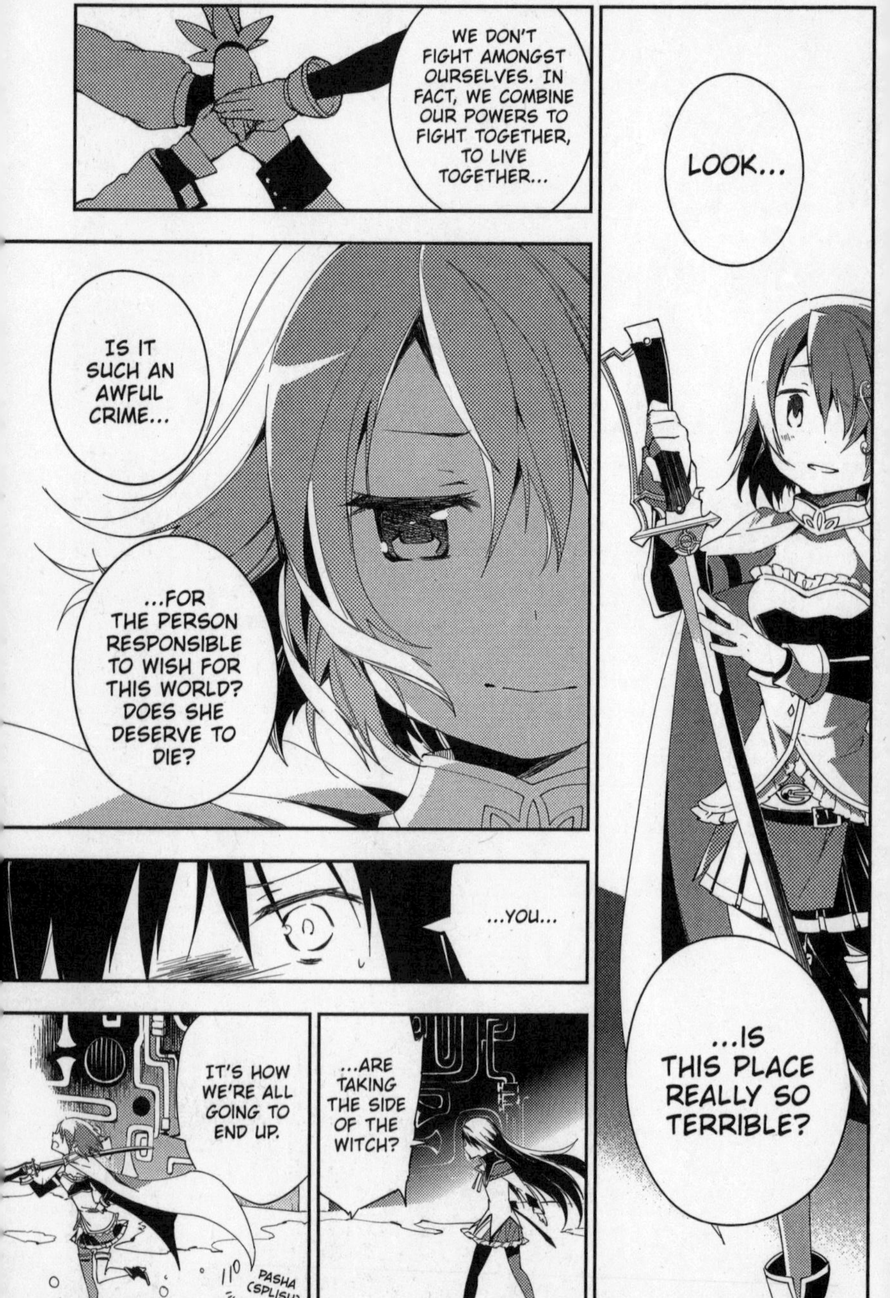
LOOK...
...IS THIS PLACE REALLY SO TERRIBLE?
WE DON'T FIGHT AMONGST OURSELVES. IN FACT, WE COMBINE OUR POWERS TO FIGHT TOGETHER, TO LIVE TOGETHER...
IS IT SUCH AN AWFUL CRIME...
...FOR THE PERSON RESPONSIBLE TO WISH FOR THIS WORLD? DOES SHE DESERVE TO DIE?
...YOU...
...ARE TAKING THE SIDE OF THE WITCH?
IT'S HOW WE'RE ALL GOING TO END UP.
PASHA (SPLISH)

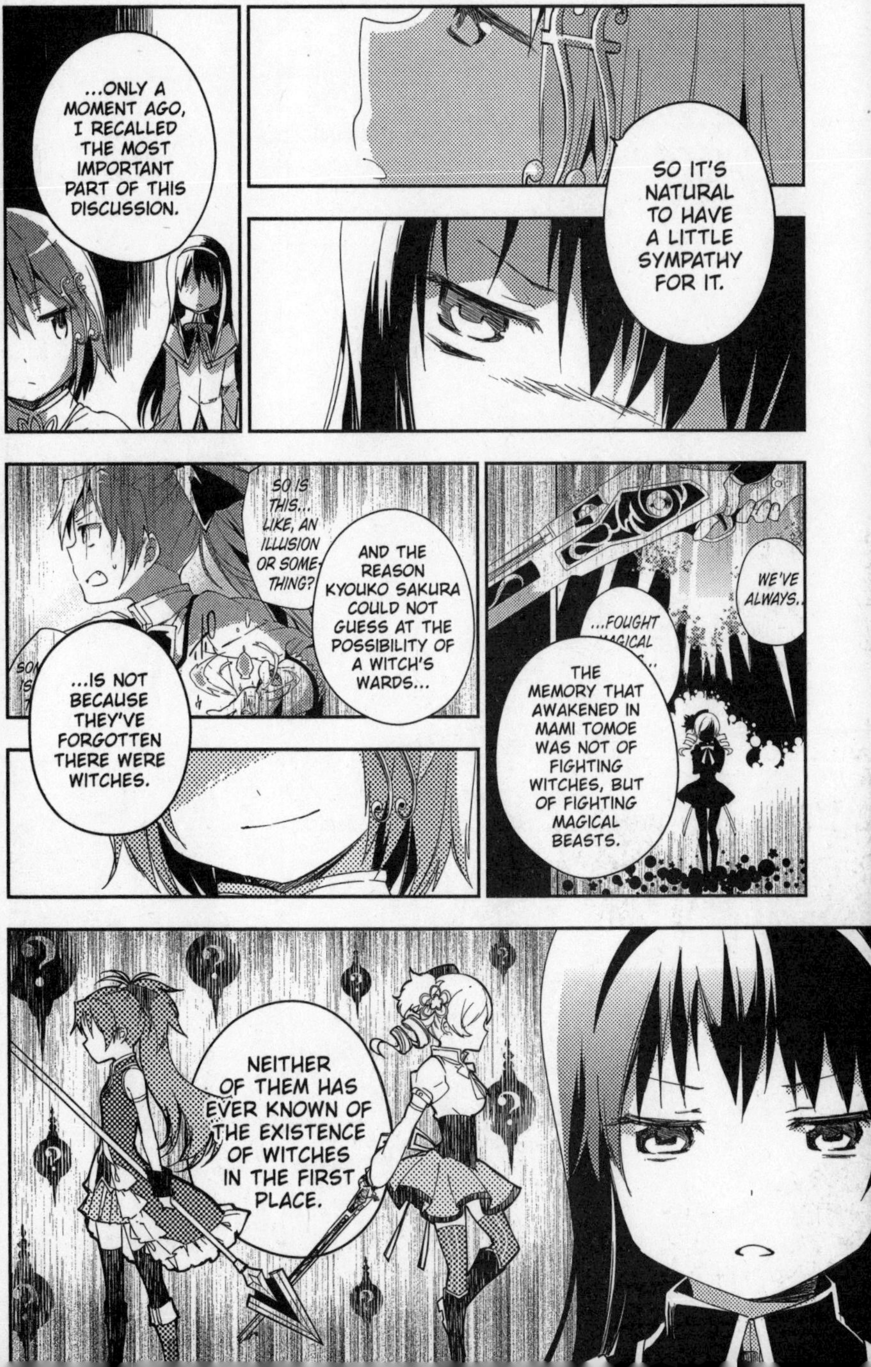
SO IT'S NATURAL TO HAVE A LITTLE SYMPATHY FOR IT.
...ONLY A MOMENT AGO, I RECALLED THE MOST IMPORTANT PART OF THIS DISCUSSION.
WE'VE ALWAYS...
...FOUGHT
THE MEMORY THAT AWAKENED IN MAMI TOMOE WAS NOT OF FIGHTING WITCHES, BUT OF FIGHTING MAGICAL BEASTS.
SO IS THIS... LIKE, AN ILLUSION OR SOMETHING?
AND THE REASON KYOUKO SAKURA COULD NOT GUESS AT THE POSSIBILITY OF A WITCH'S WARDS...
...IS NOT BECAUSE THEY'VE FORGOTTEN THERE WERE WITCHES.
NEITHER OF THEM HAS EVER KNOWN OF THE EXISTENCE OF WITCHES IN THE FIRST PLACE.

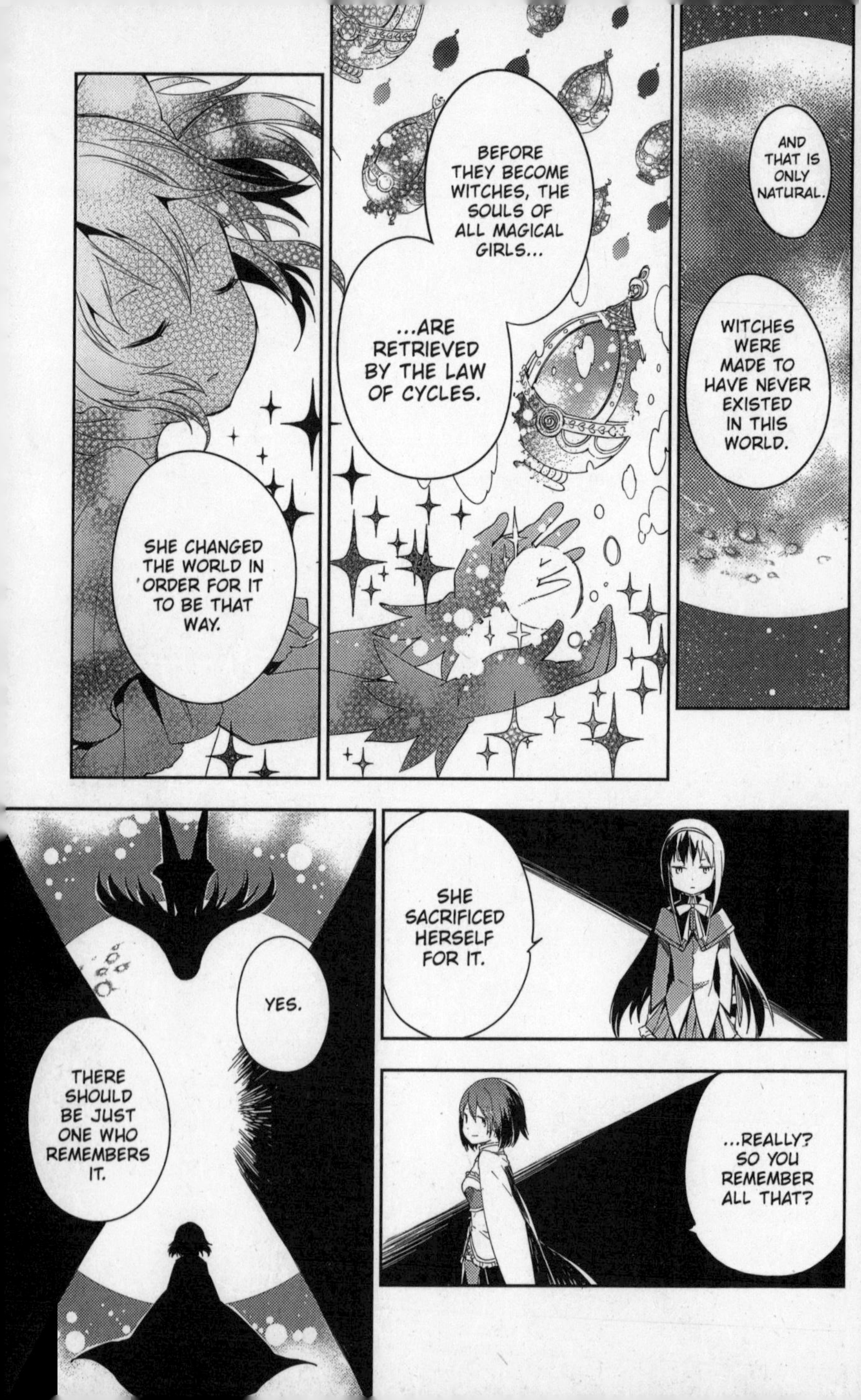
AND THAT IS ONLY NATURAL.
WITCHES WERE MADE TO HAVE NEVER EXISTED IN THIS WORLD.
BEFORE THEY BECOME WITCHES, THE SOULS OF ALL MAGICAL GIRLS...
...ARE RETRIEVED BY THE LAW OF CYCLES.
SHE CHANGED THE WORLD IN ORDER FOR IT TO BE THAT WAY.
SHE SACRIFICED HERSELF FOR IT.
...REALLY? SO YOU REMEMBER ALL THAT?
YES.
THERE SHOULD BE JUST ONE WHO REMEMBERS IT.

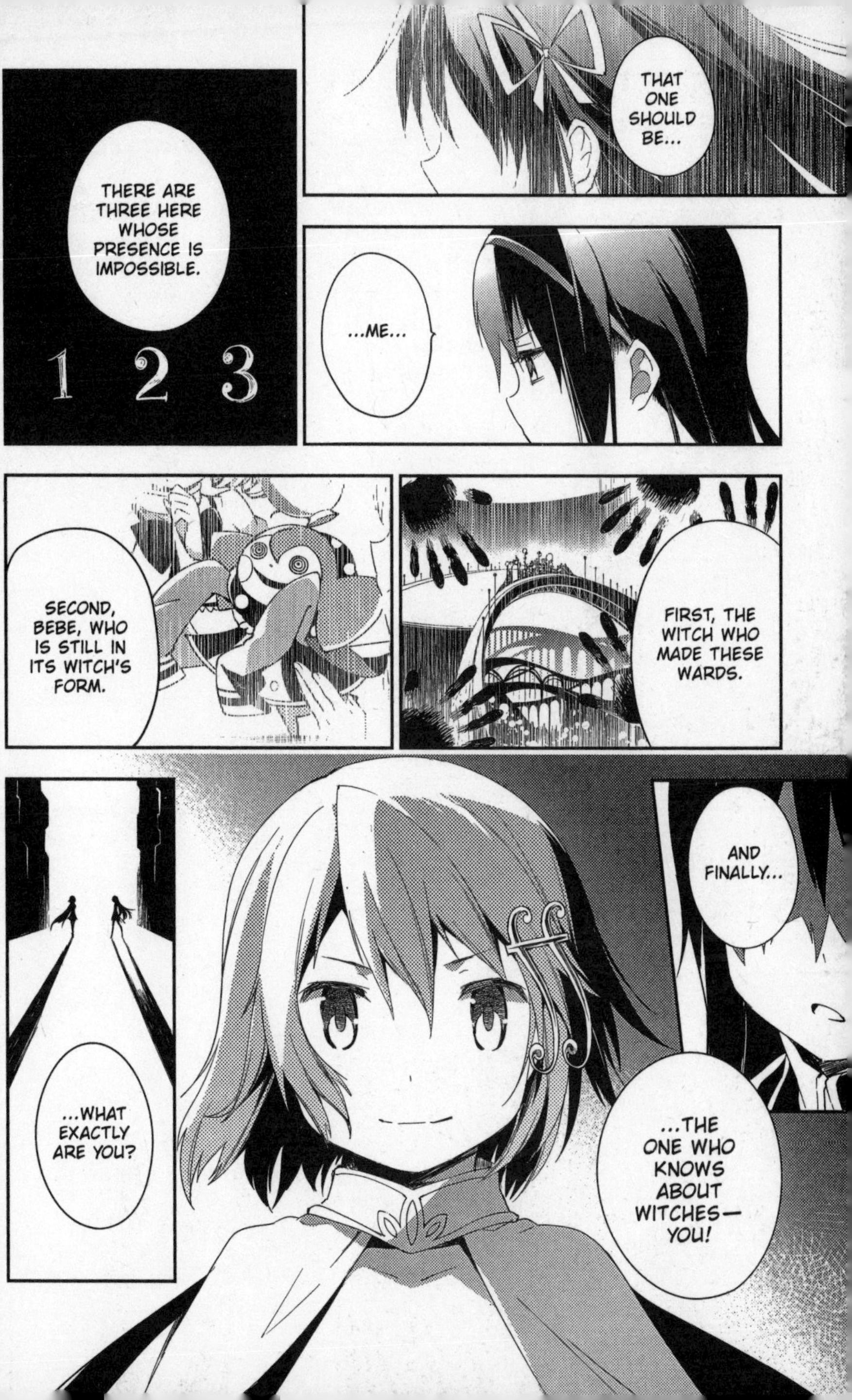
THAT ONE SHOULD BE...
...ME...
THERE ARE THREE HERE WHOSE PRESENCE IS IMPOSSIBLE.
1 2 3
FIRST, THE WITCH WHO MADE THESE WARDS.
SECOND, BEBE, WHO IS STILL IN ITS WITCH'S FORM.
AND FINALLY...
...THE ONE WHO KNOWS ABOUT WITCHES—YOU!
...WHAT EXACTLY ARE YOU?

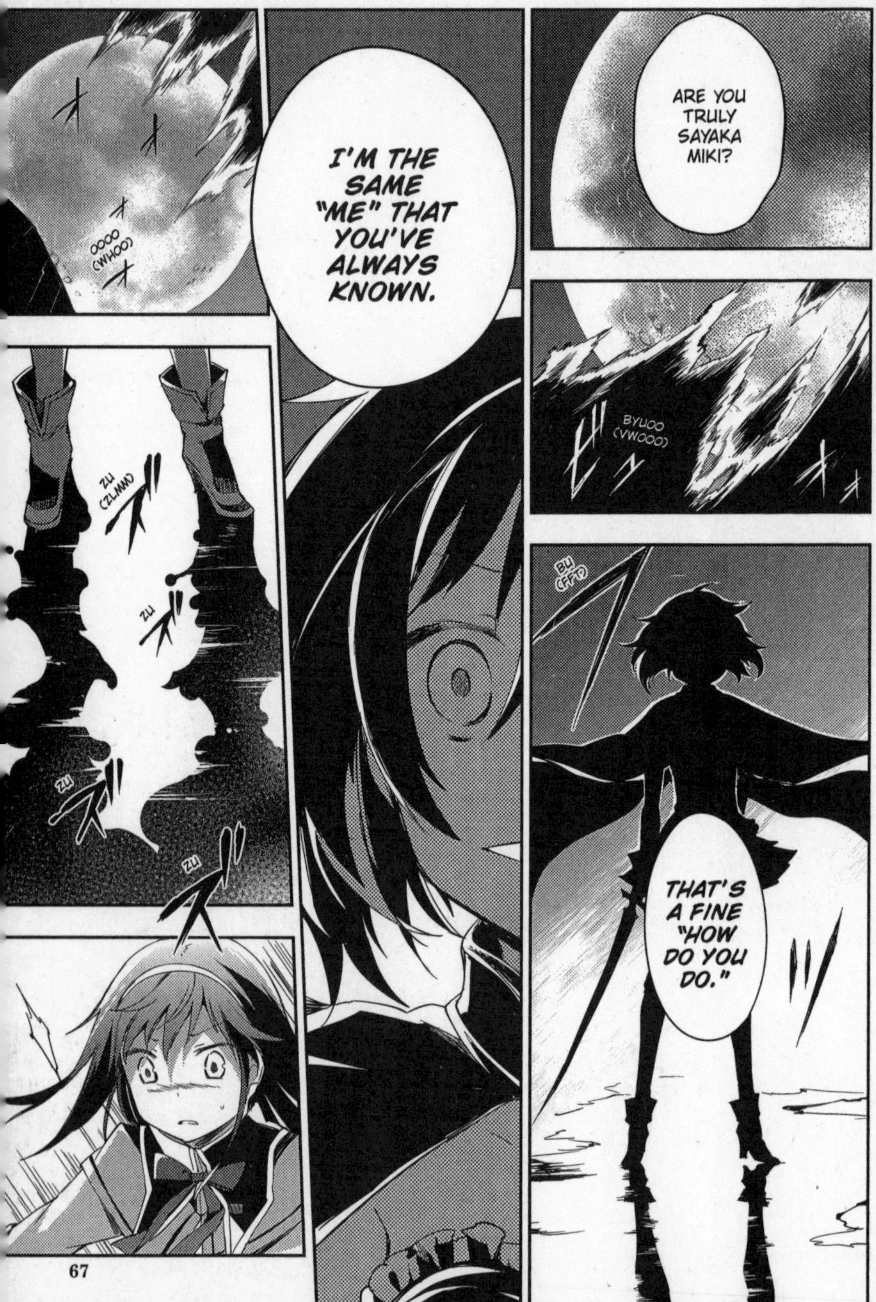
ARE YOU TRULY SAYAKA MIKI?
BYUOO (VWOOO)
BU (FFT)
THAT'S A FINE "HOW DO YOU DO."
I'M THE SAME "ME" THAT YOU'VE ALWAYS KNOWN.
OOOO (WHOO)
ZU (ZLMM)
ZU
ZU
ZU

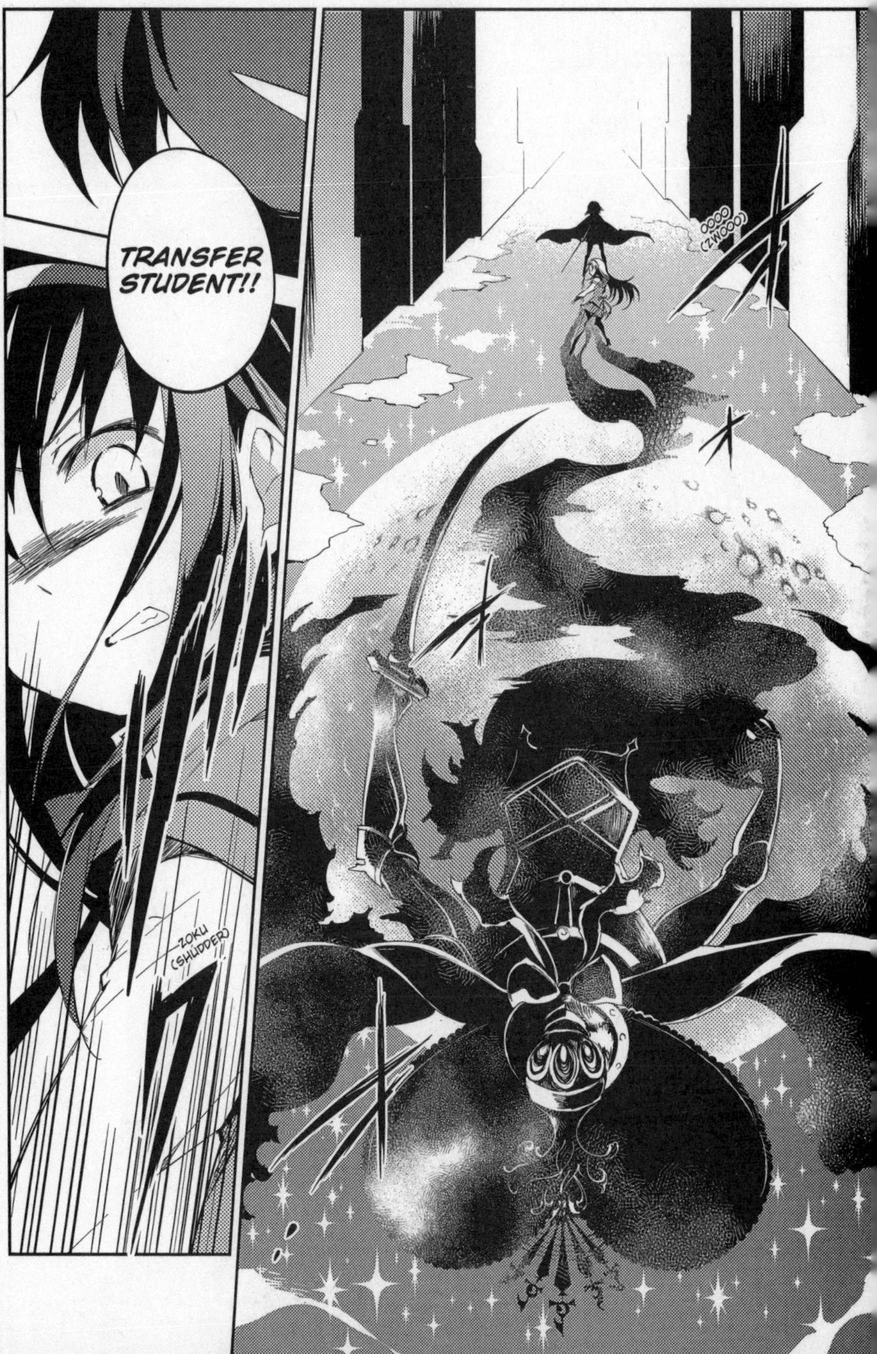
OOOO
(ZWOOO)
TRANSFER STUDENT!!
ZOKU
(SHUDDER)

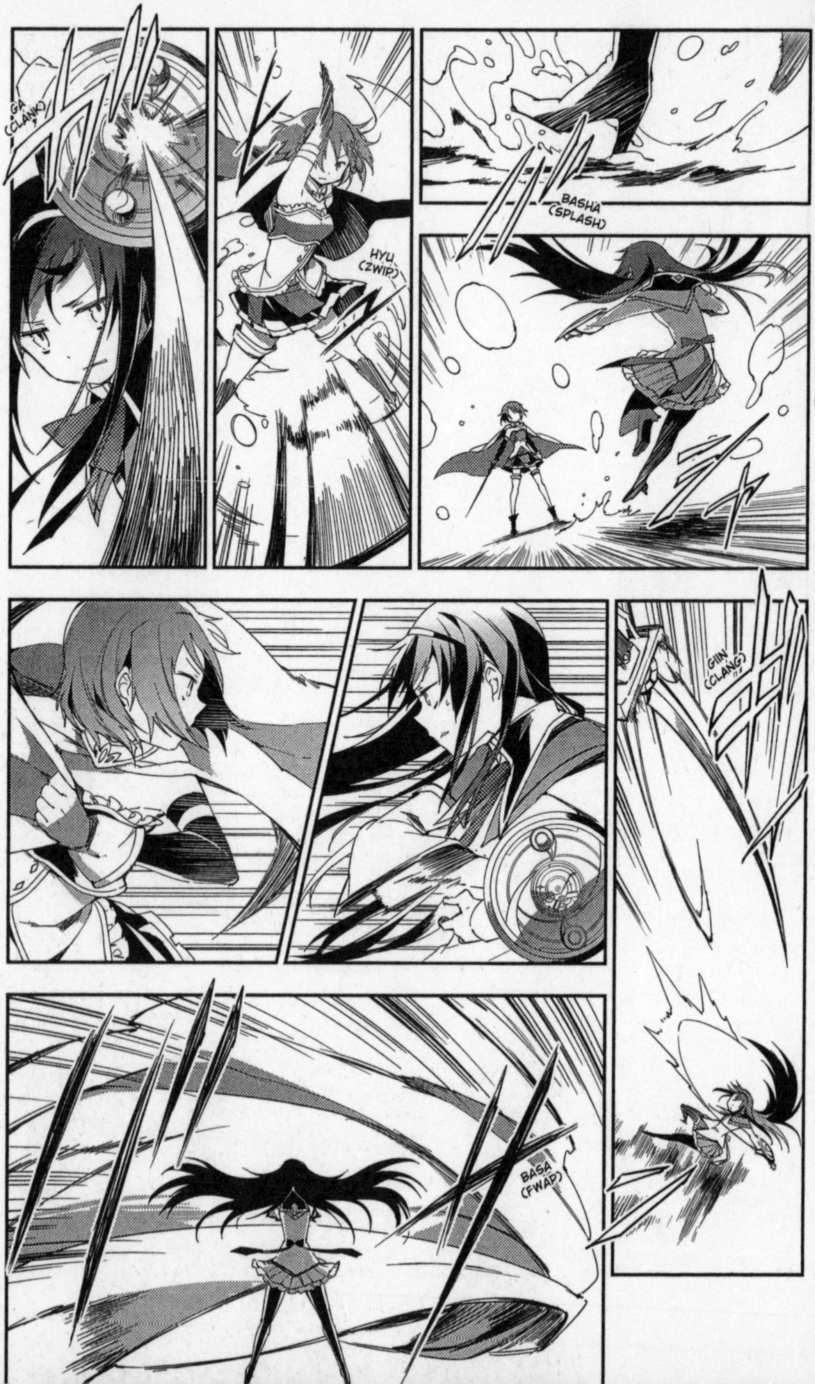
BASHA (SPLASH)
HYU (ZWIP)
GA (CLANK)
GIIN (CLANG)
BASA (FWAP)

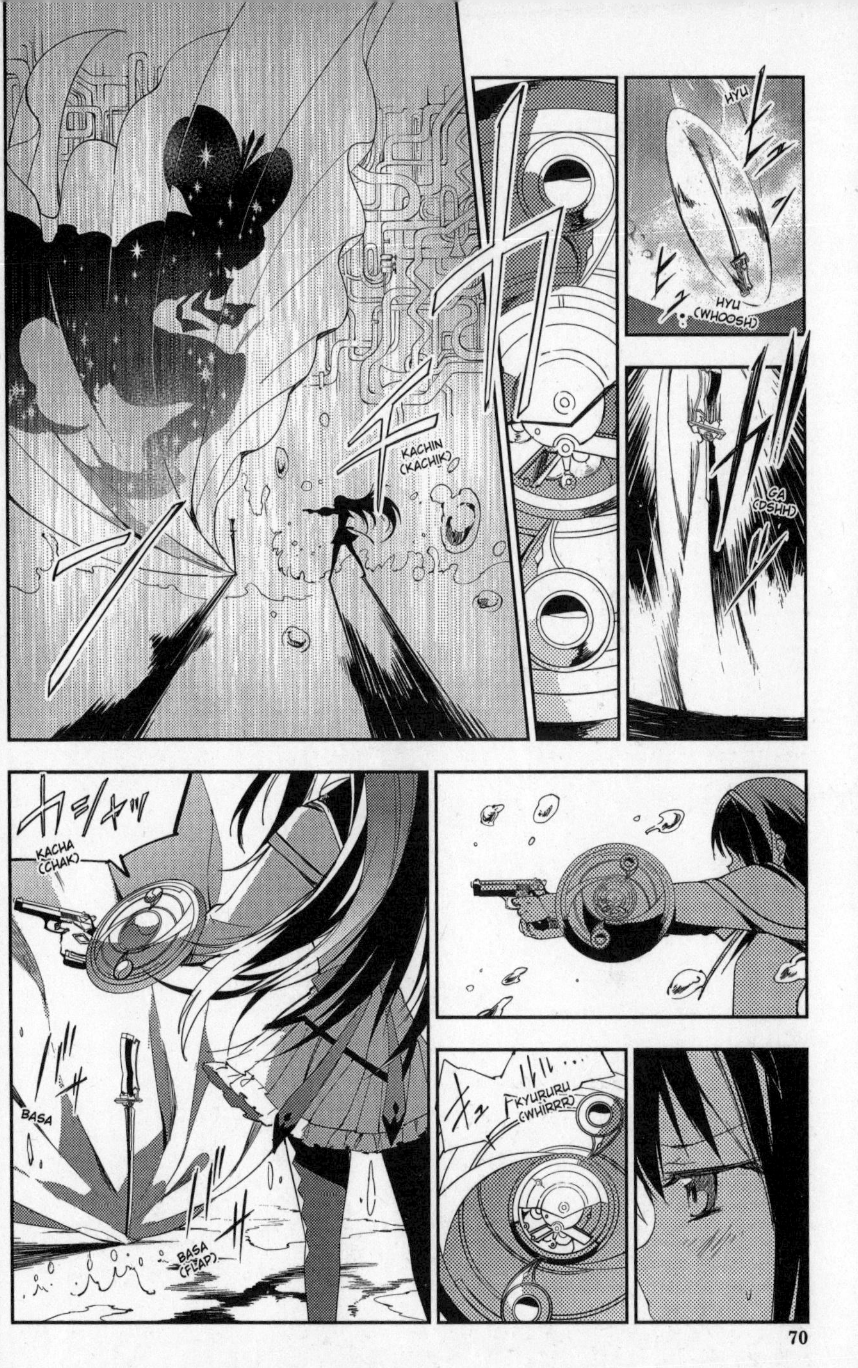
HYU
HYU (WHOOSH)
GA (DSHH)
KACHIN (KACHIK)
KYURURU (WHIRRR)
KACHA (CHAK)
BASA
BASA (FLAP)

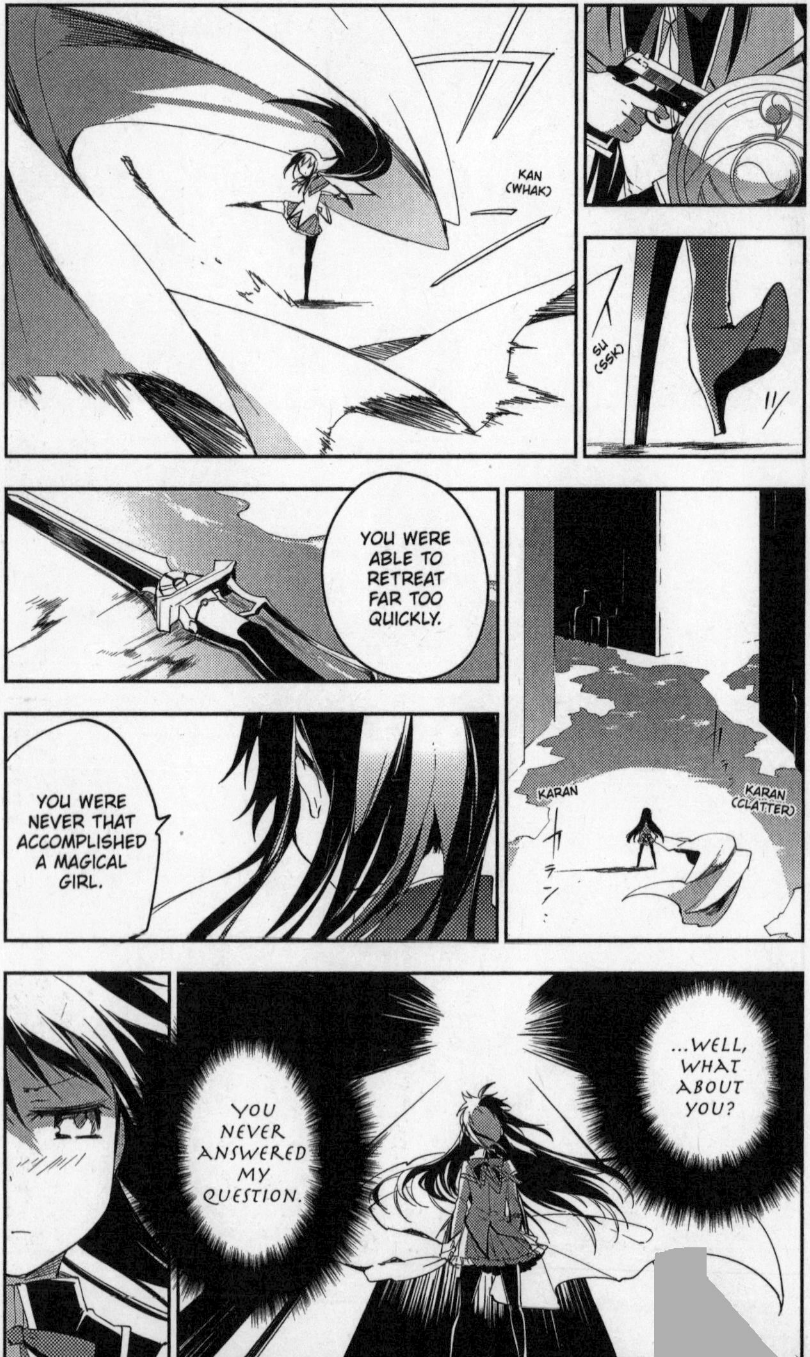
SU (SSK)
KAN (WHAK)
KARAN (CLATTER)
KARAN
YOU WERE ABLE TO RETREAT FAR TOO QUICKLY.
YOU WERE NEVER THAT ACCOMPLISHED A MAGICAL GIRL.
...WELL, WHAT ABOUT YOU?
YOU NEVER ANSWERED MY QUESTION.

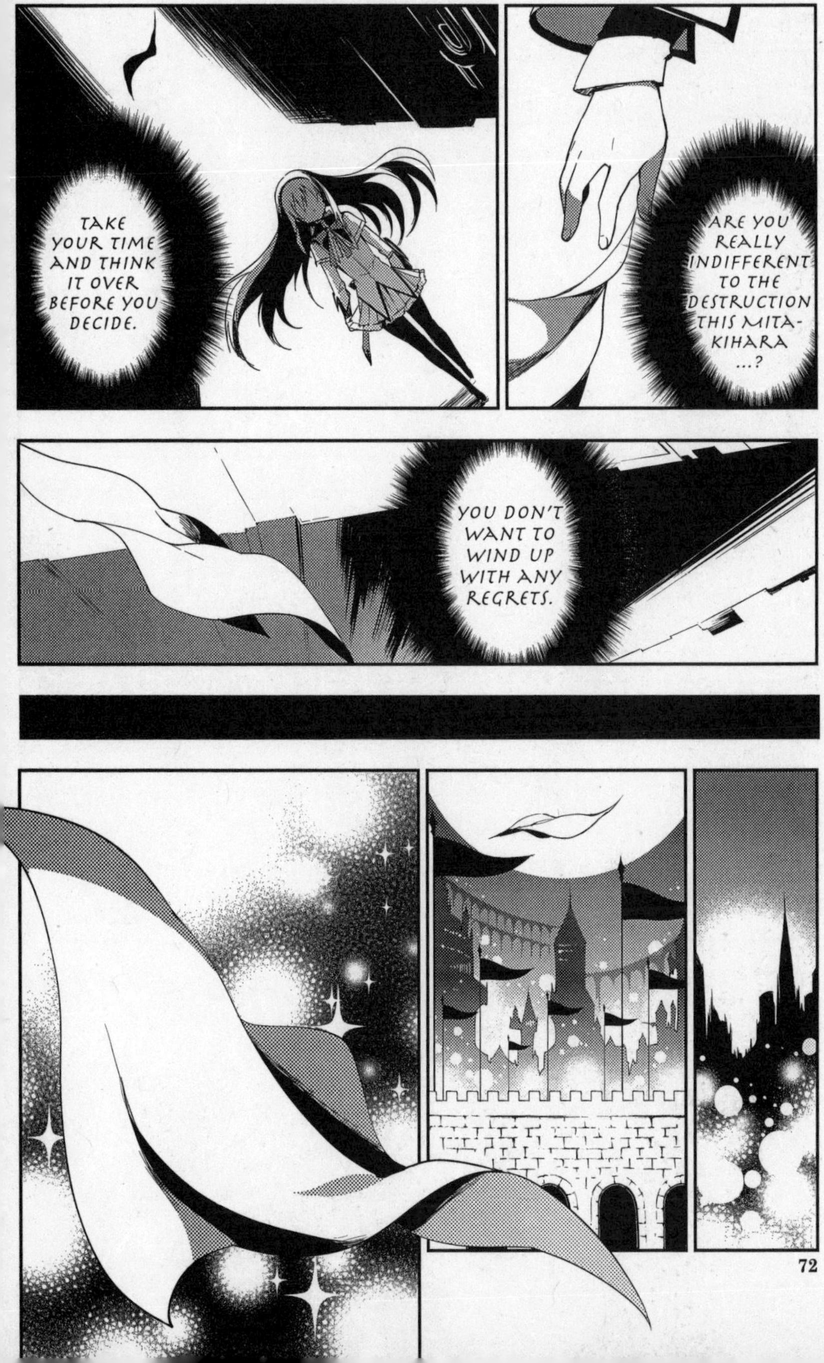
ARE YOU REALLY INDIFFERENT TO THE DESTRUCTION THIS MITA-KIHARA ...?
TAKE YOUR TIME AND THINK IT OVER BEFORE YOU DECIDE.
YOU DON'T WANT TO WIND UP WITH ANY REGRETS.

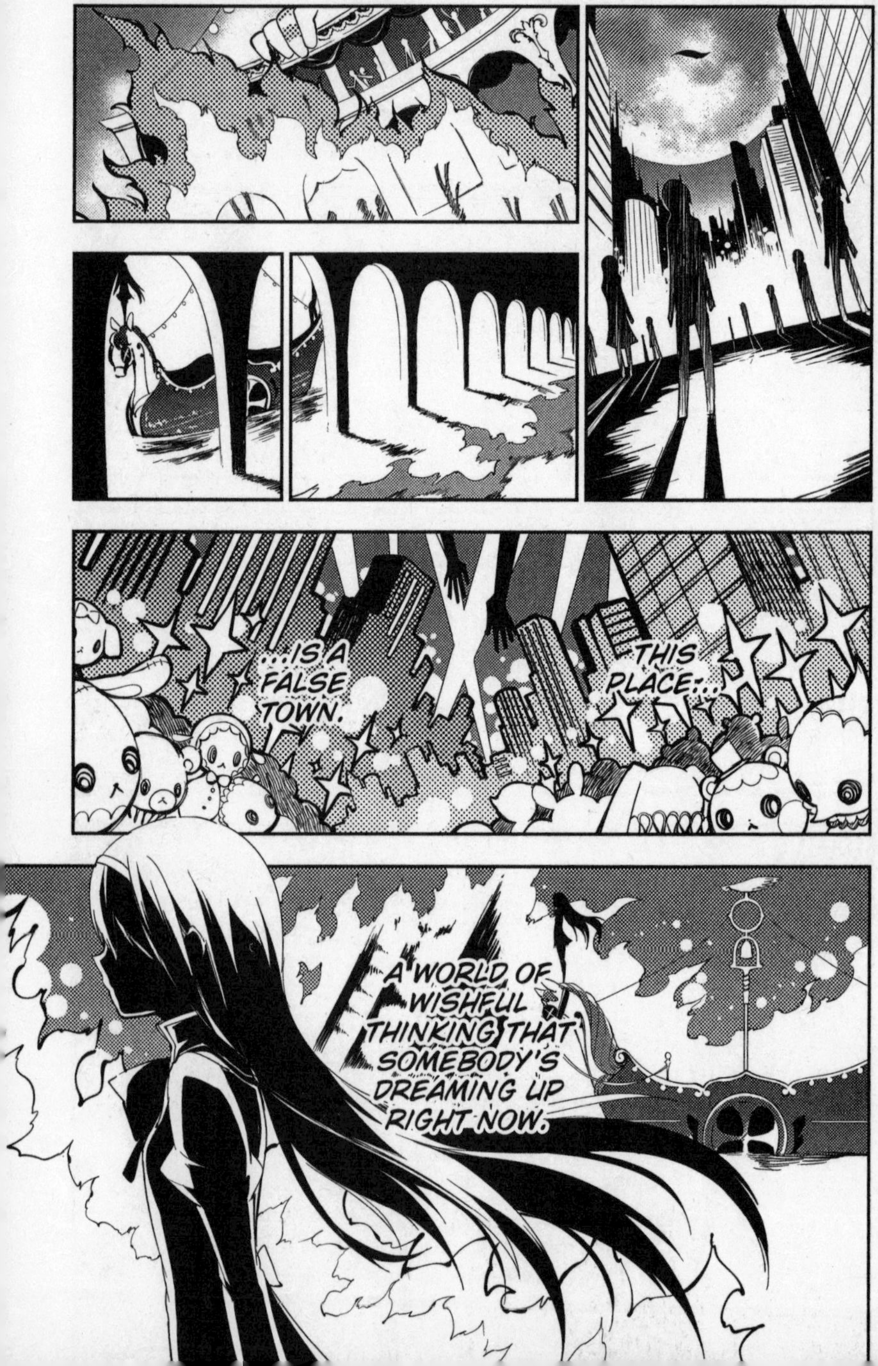
THIS PLACE...
...IS A FALSE TOWN.
A WORLD OF WISHFUL THINKING THAT SOMEBODY'S DREAMING UP RIGHT NOW.

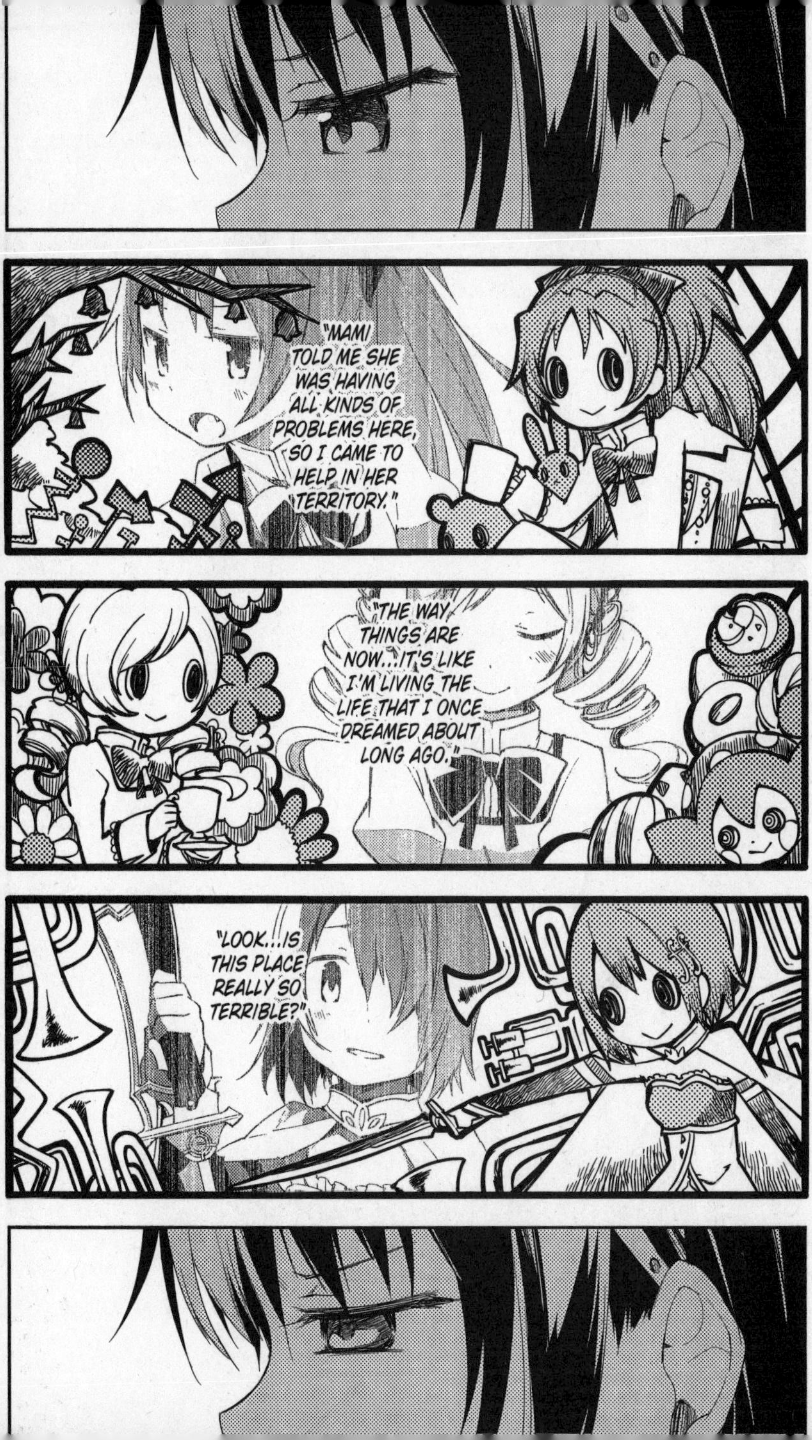
"MAMI TOLD ME SHE WAS HAVING ALL KINDS OF PROBLEMS HERE, SO I CAME TO HELP IN HER TERRITORY."
"THE WAY THINGS ARE NOW...IT'S LIKE I'M LIVING THE LIFE THAT I ONCE DREAMED ABOUT LONG AGO."
"LOOK...IS THIS PLACE REALLY SO TERRIBLE?"

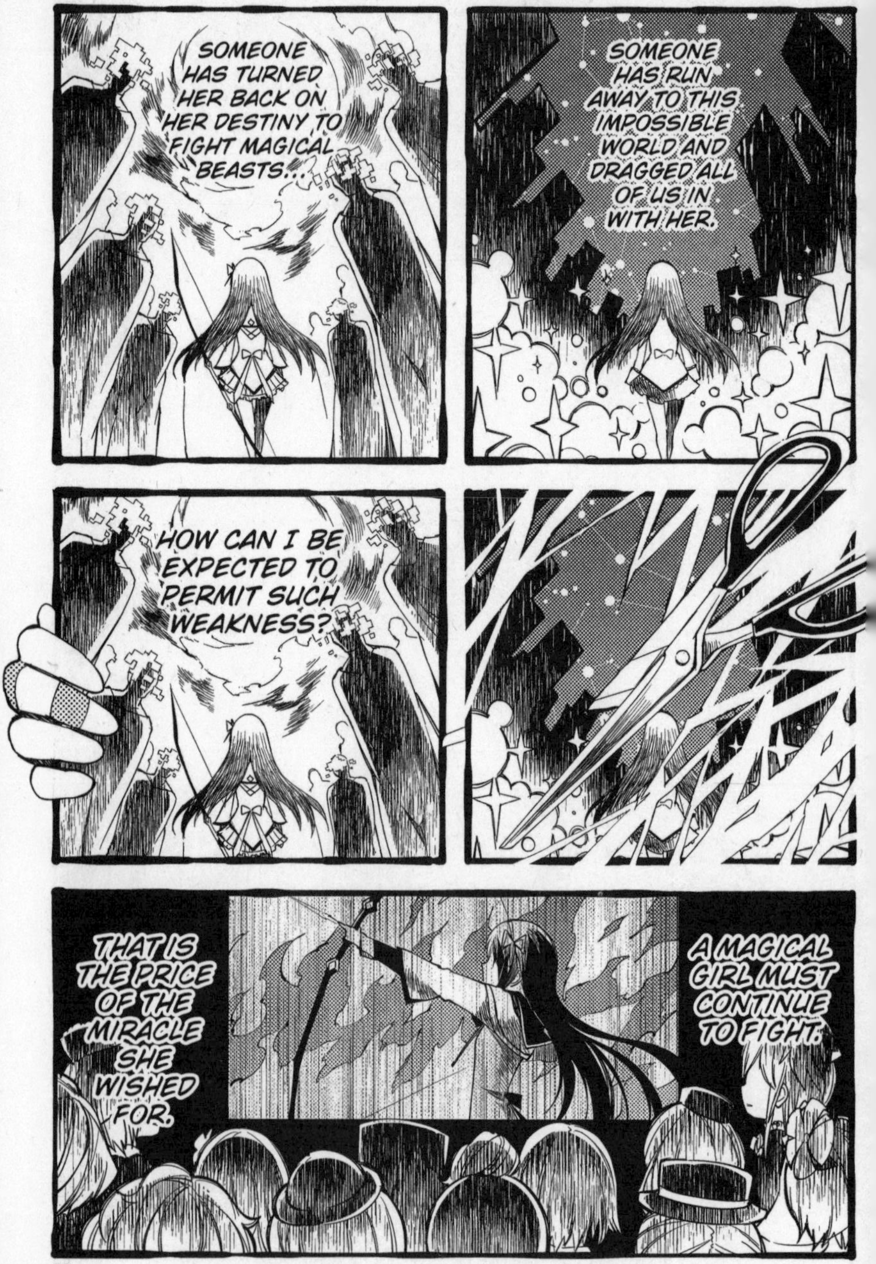
SOMEONE HAS RUN AWAY TO THIS IMPOSSIBLE WORLD AND DRAGGED ALL OF US IN WITH HER.
SOMEONE HAS TURNED HER BACK ON HER DESTINY TO FIGHT MAGICAL BEASTS...
HOW CAN I BE EXPECTED TO PERMIT SUCH WEAKNESS?
A MAGICAL GIRL MUST CONTINUE TO FIGHT.
THAT IS THE PRICE OF THE MIRACLE SHE WISHED FOR.

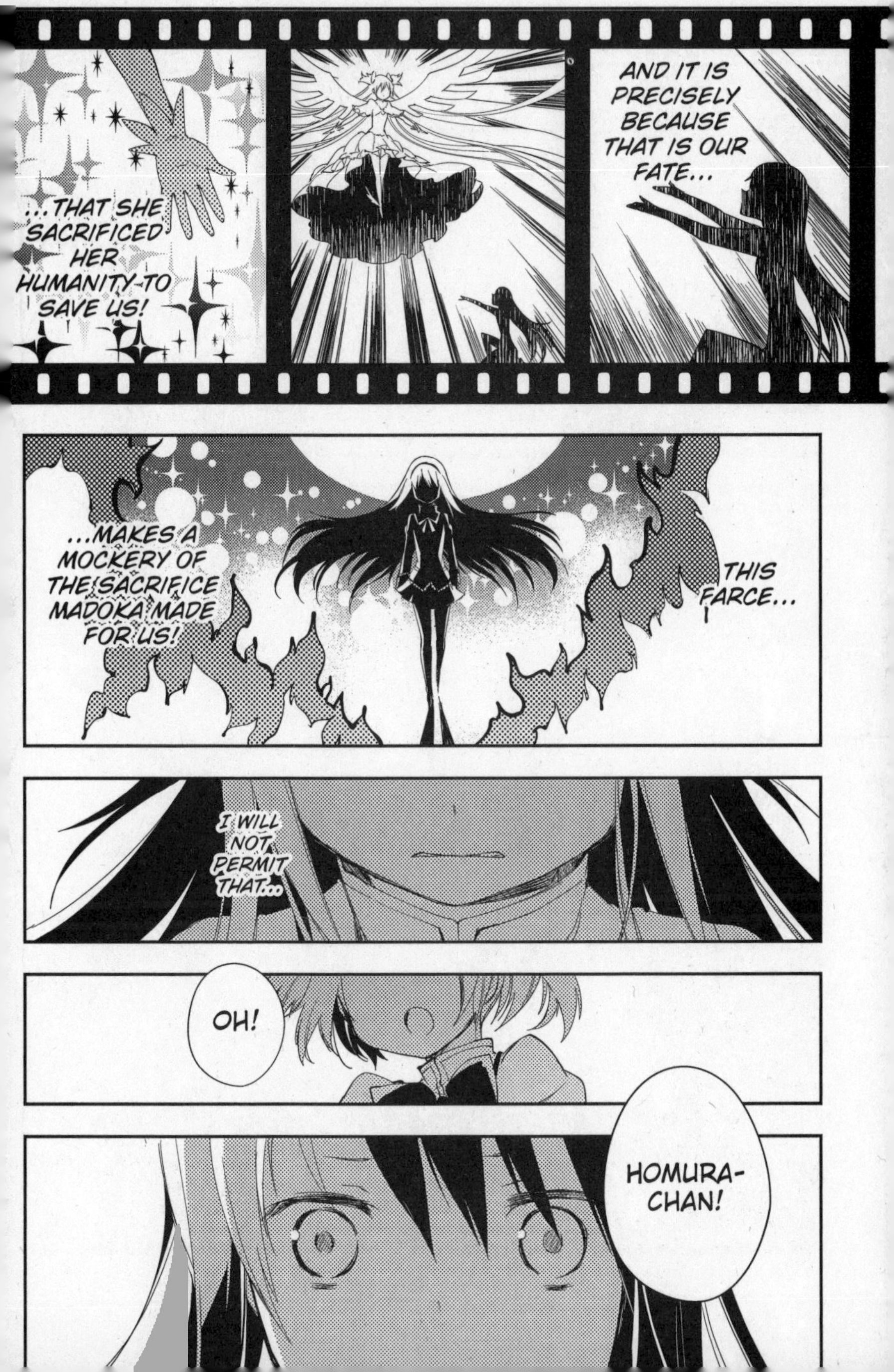
AND IT IS PRECISELY BECAUSE THAT IS OUR FATE...
...THAT SHE SACRIFICED HER HUMANITY TO SAVE US!
THIS FARCE...
...MAKES A MOCKERY OF THE SACRIFICE MADOKA MADE FOR US!
I WILL NOT PERMIT THAT...
OH!
HOMURA-CHAN!

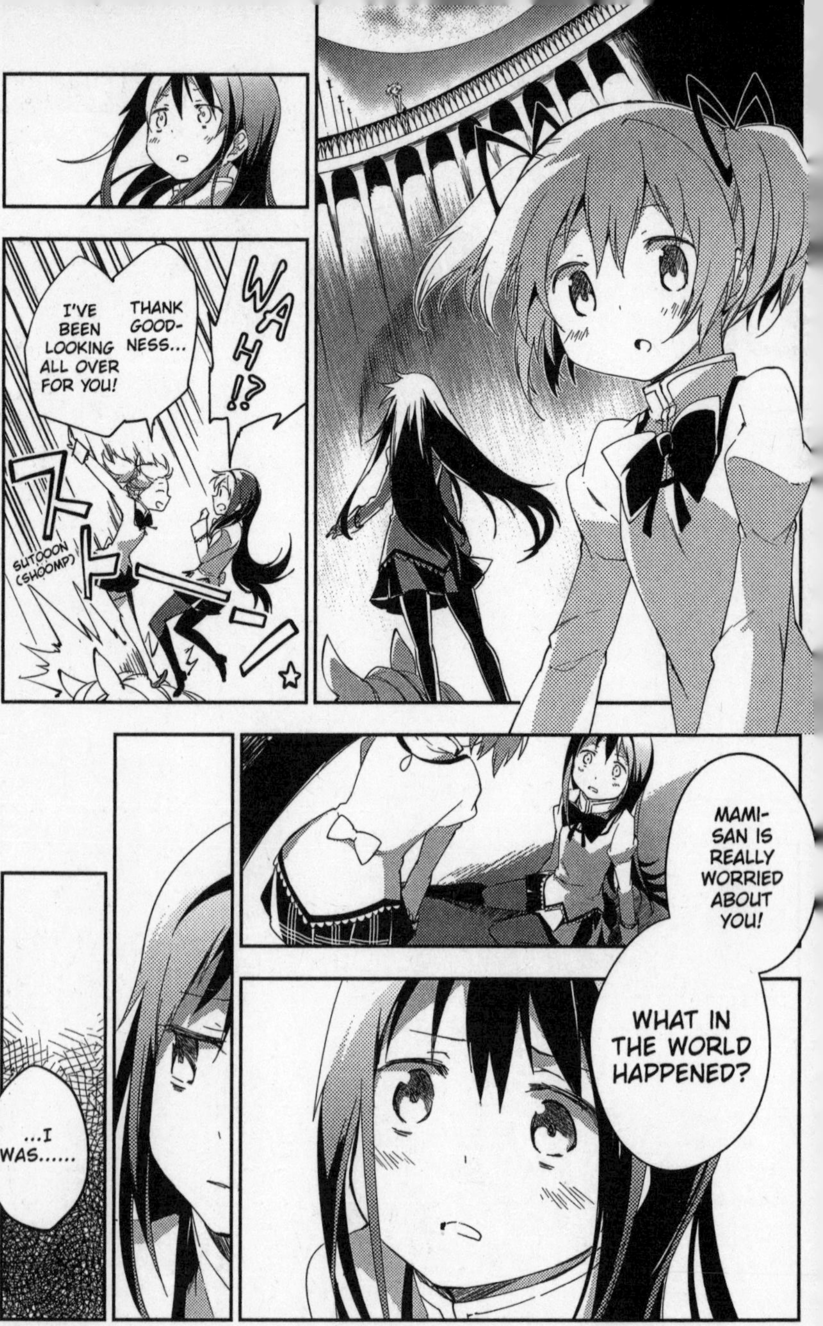
WAH!?
THANK GOODNESS... I'VE BEEN LOOKING ALL OVER FOR YOU!
SUTOOON (SHOOMP)
MAMI-SAN IS REALLY WORRIED ABOUT YOU!
WHAT IN THE WORLD HAPPENED?
...I WAS......

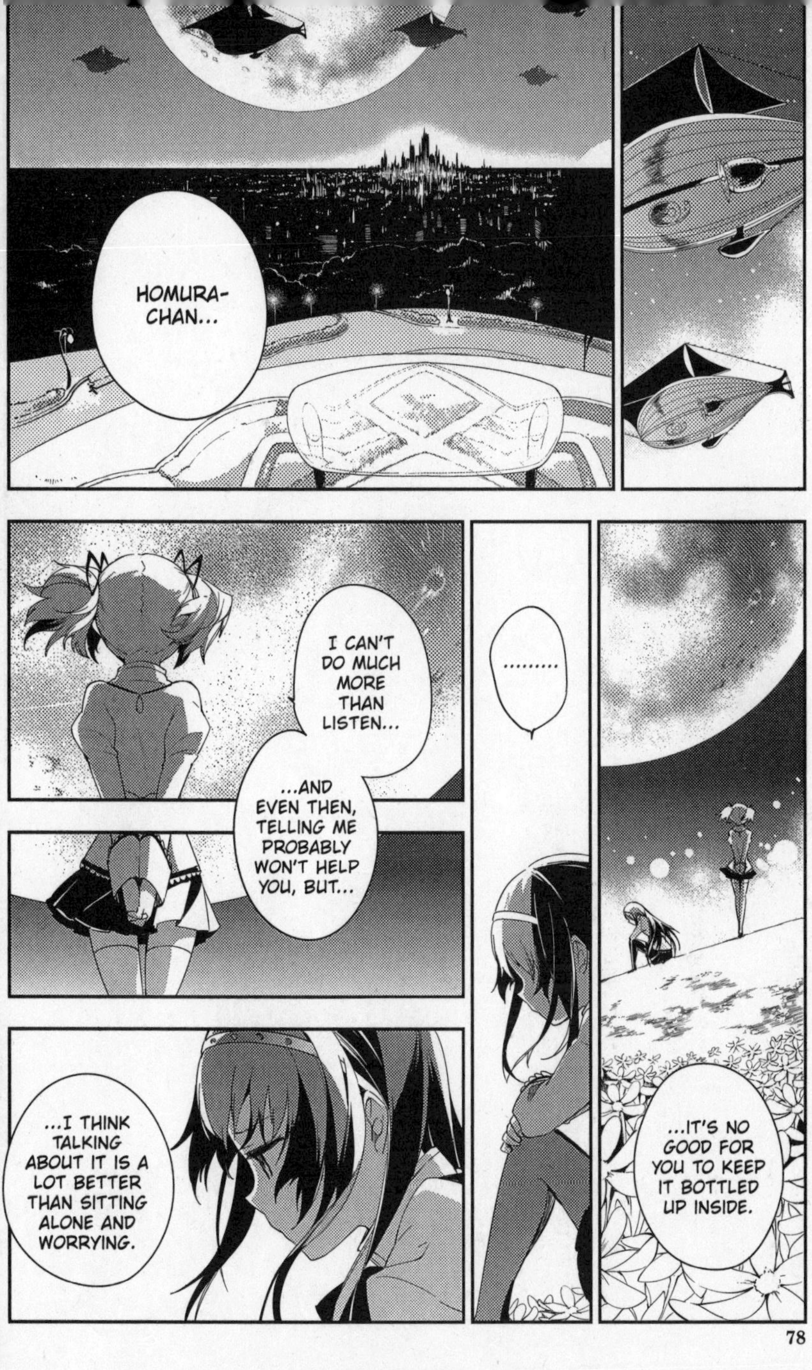
HOMURA-CHAN...
...IT'S NO GOOD FOR YOU TO KEEP IT BOTTLED UP INSIDE.
....
I CAN'T DO MUCH MORE THAN LISTEN...
...AND EVEN THEN, TELLING ME PROBABLY WON'T HELP YOU, BUT...
...I THINK TALKING ABOUT IT IS A LOT BETTER THAN SITTING ALONE AND WORRYING.

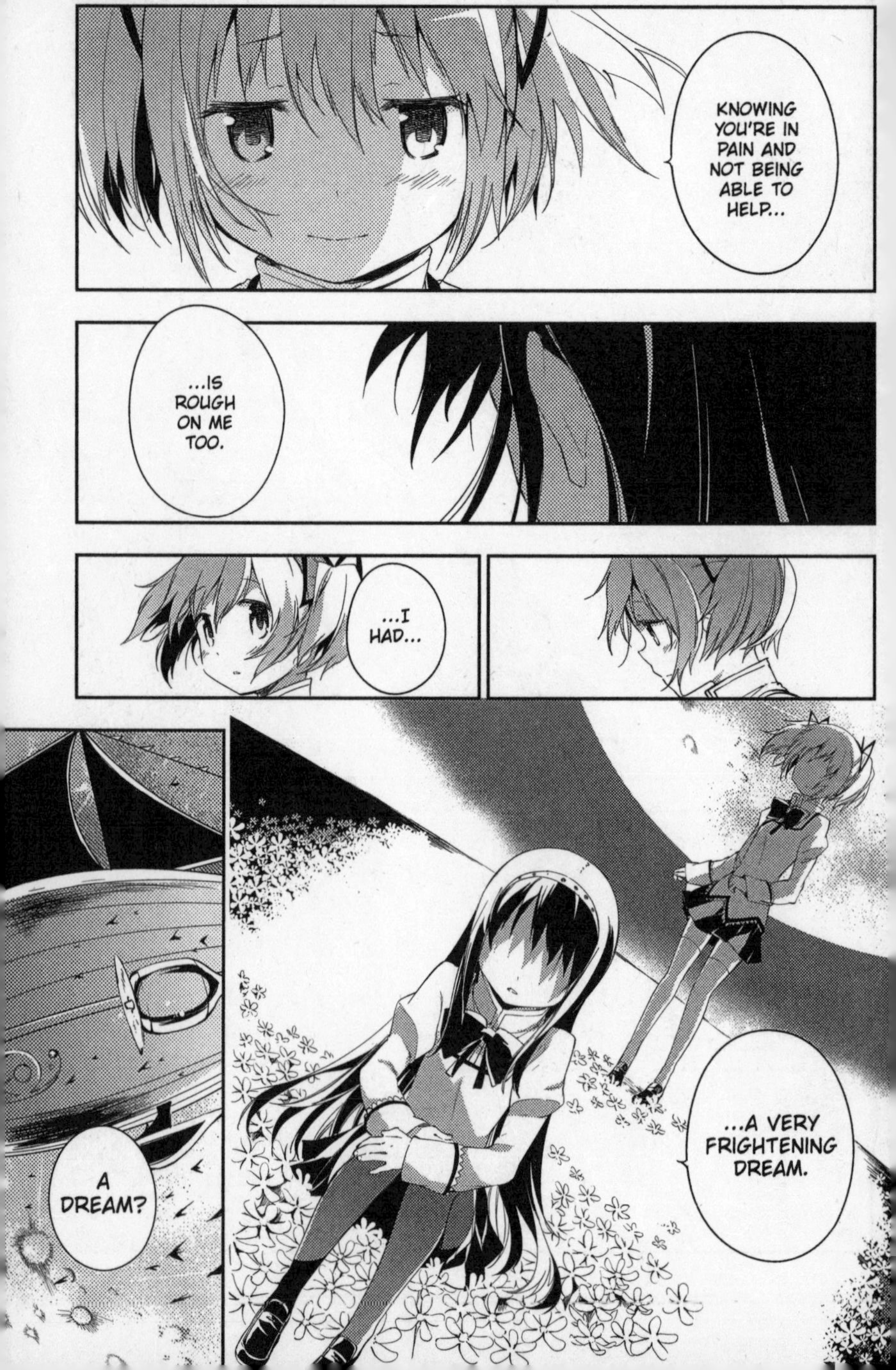
KNOWING YOU'RE IN PAIN AND NOT BEING ABLE TO HELP...
...IS ROUGH ON ME TOO.
...I HAD...
...A VERY FRIGHTENING DREAM.
A DREAM?

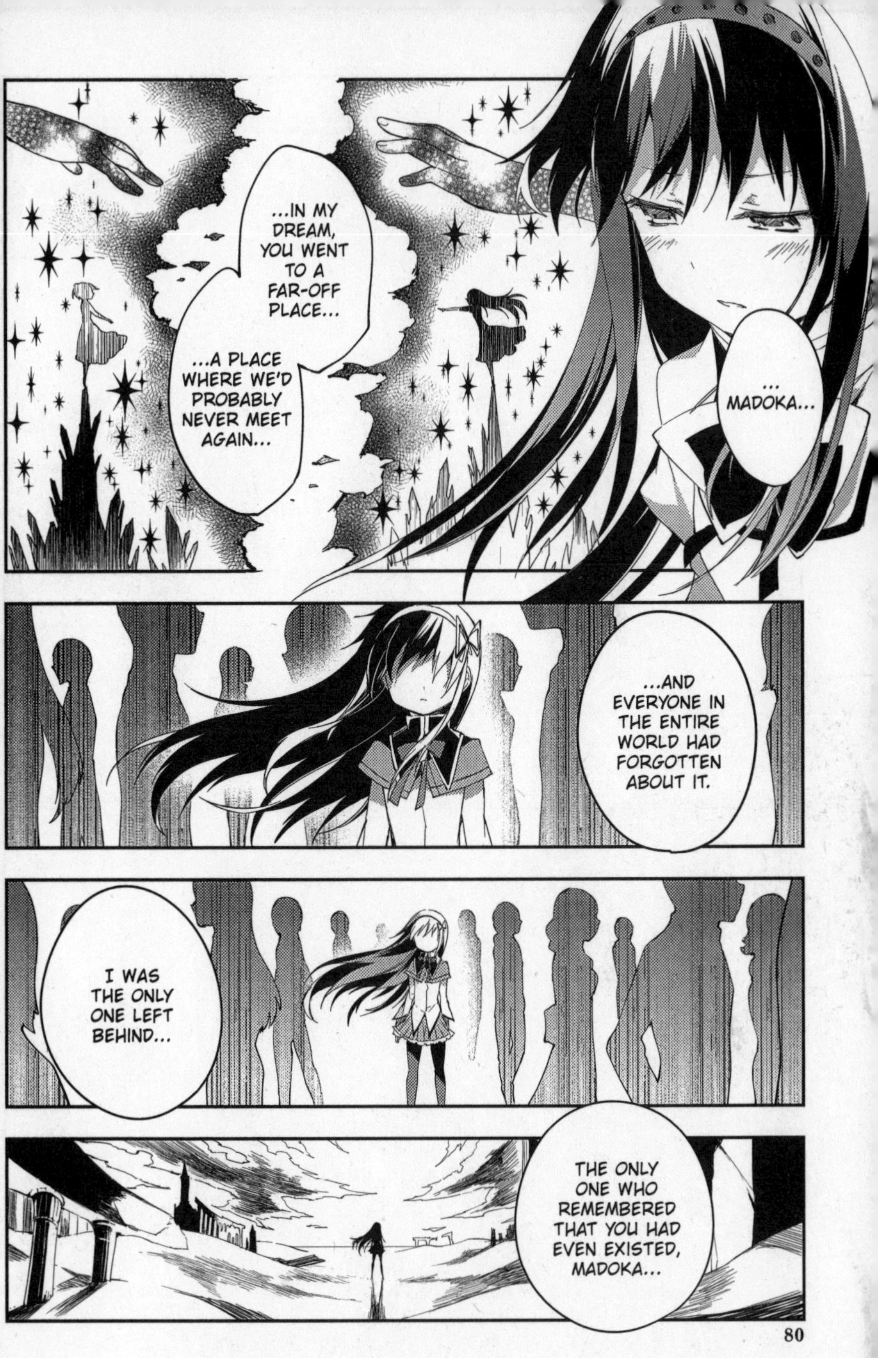
... MADOKA...
...IN MY DREAM, YOU WENT TO A FAR-OFF PLACE...
...A PLACE WHERE WE'D PROBABLY NEVER MEET AGAIN...
...AND EVERYONE IN THE ENTIRE WORLD HAD FORGOTTEN ABOUT IT.
I WAS THE ONLY ONE LEFT BEHIND...
THE ONLY ONE WHO REMEMBERED THAT YOU HAD EVEN EXISTED, MADOKA...

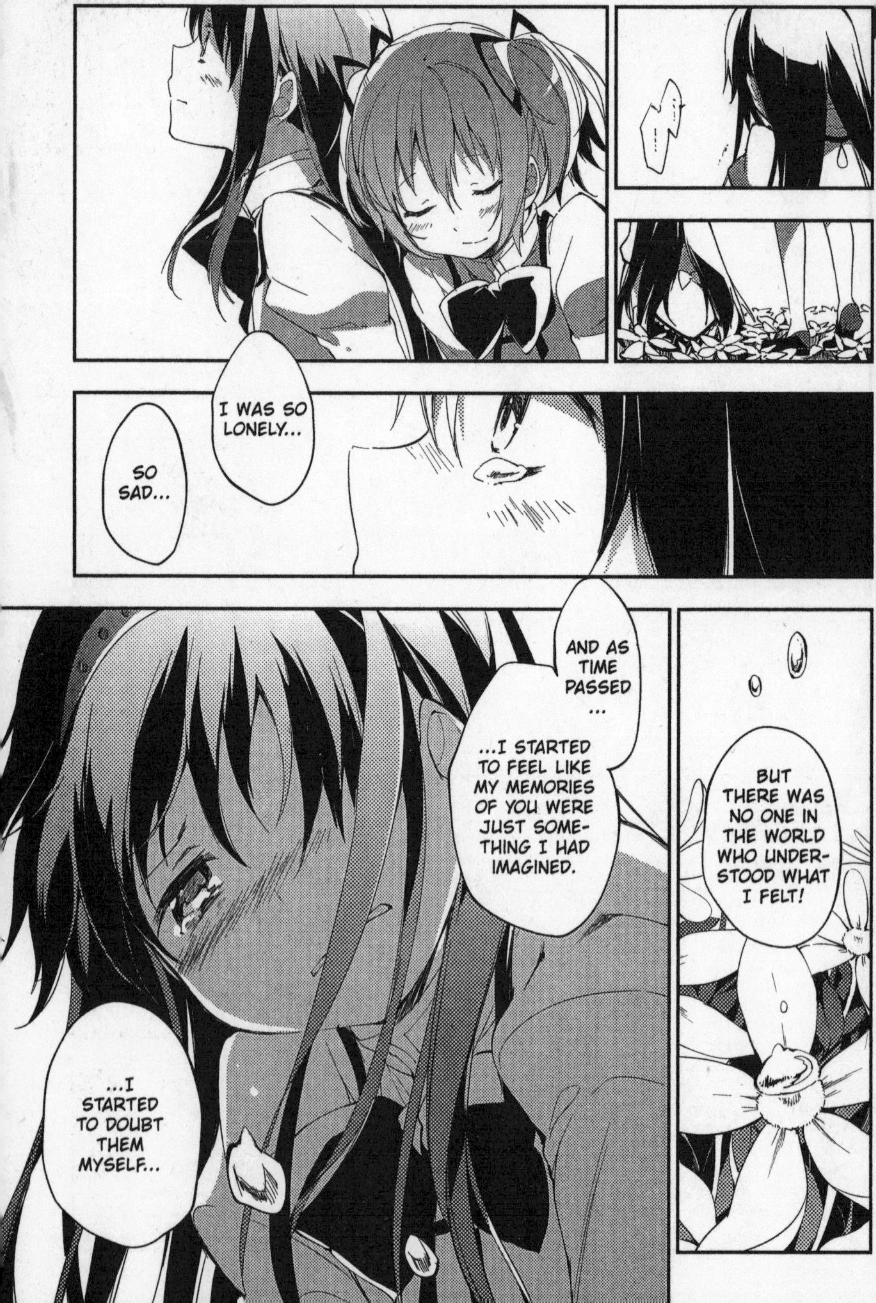
...
I WAS SO LONELY...
SO SAD...
BUT THERE WAS NO ONE IN THE WORLD WHO UNDER-STOOD WHAT I FELT!
AND AS TIME PASSED ...
...I STARTED TO FEEL LIKE MY MEMORIES OF YOU WERE JUST SOME-THING I HAD IMAGINED.
...I STARTED TO DOUBT THEM MYSELF...

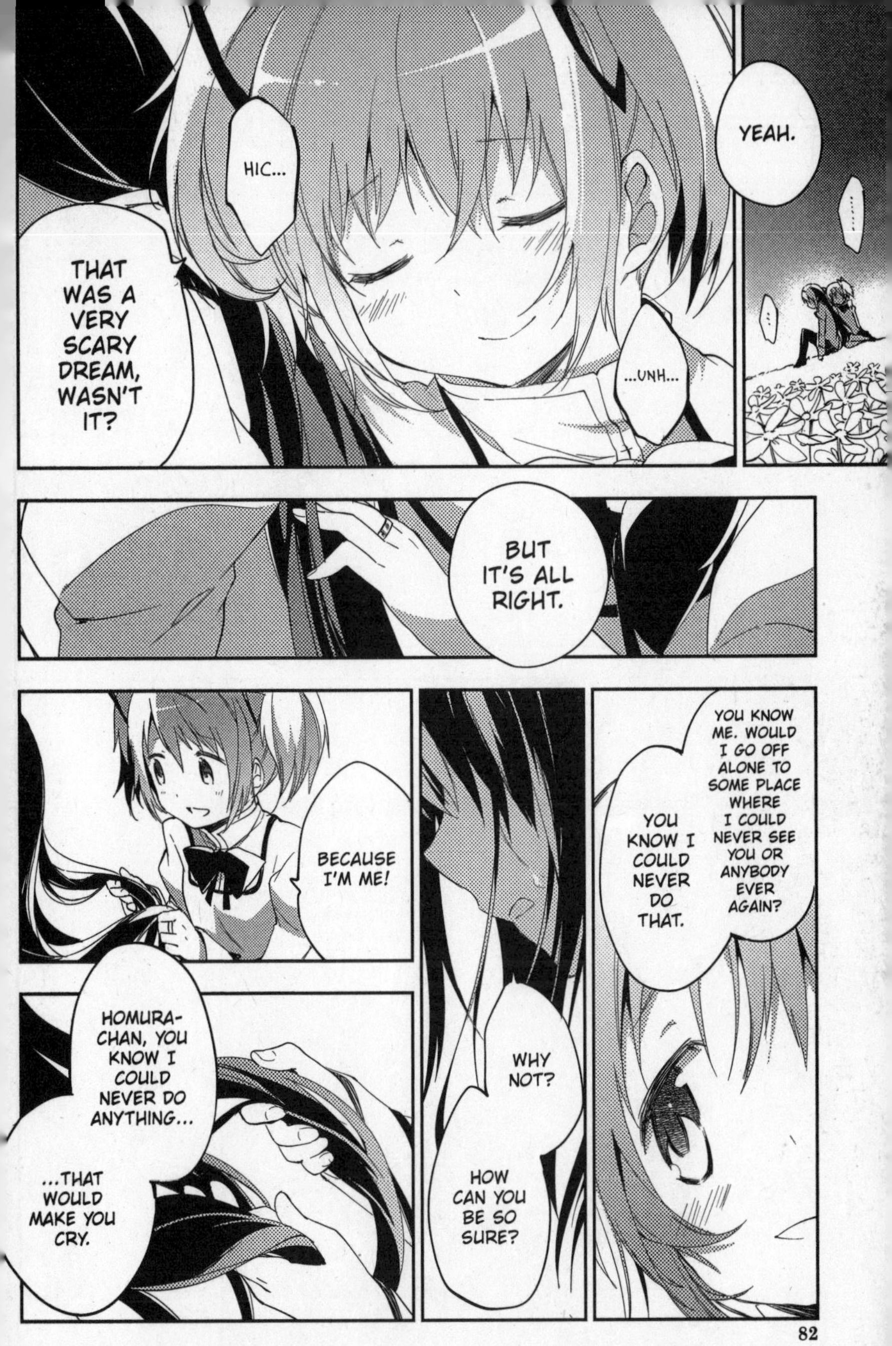
YEAH.
......
...
HIC...
THAT WAS A VERY SCARY DREAM, WASN'T IT?
...UNH...
BUT IT'S ALL RIGHT.
YOU KNOW ME. WOULD I GO OFF ALONE TO SOME PLACE WHERE I COULD NEVER SEE YOU OR ANYBODY EVER AGAIN?
YOU KNOW I COULD NEVER DO THAT.
WHY NOT?
HOW CAN YOU BE SO SURE?
BECAUSE I'M ME!
HOMURA-CHAN, YOU KNOW I COULD NEVER DO ANYTHING...
...THAT WOULD MAKE YOU CRY.

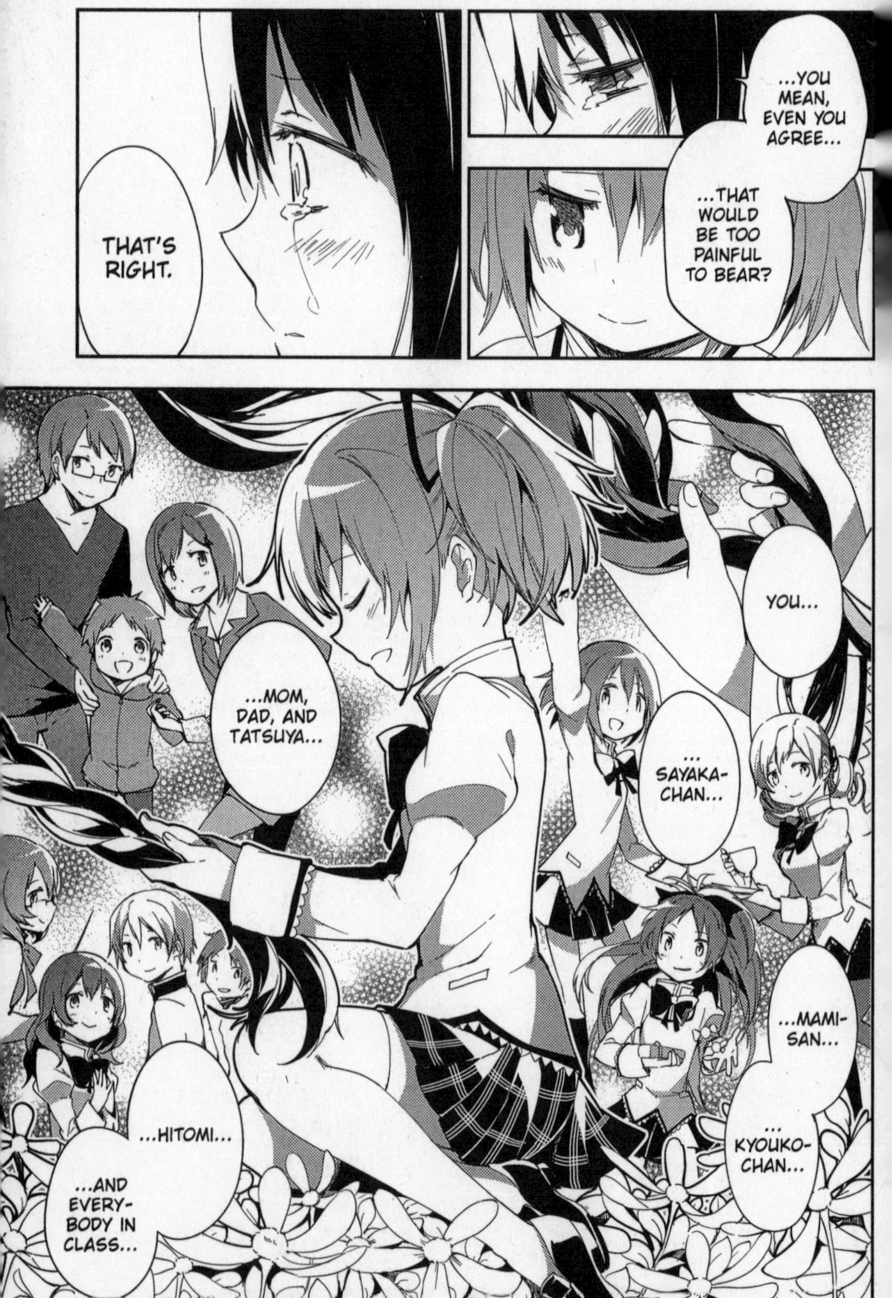
...YOU MEAN, EVEN YOU AGREE...
...THAT WOULD BE TOO PAINFUL TO BEAR?
THAT'S RIGHT.
YOU...
...MOM, DAD, AND TATSUYA...
...SAYAKA-CHAN...
...MAMI-SAN...
...KYOUKO-CHAN...
...HITOMI...
...AND EVERYBODY IN CLASS...

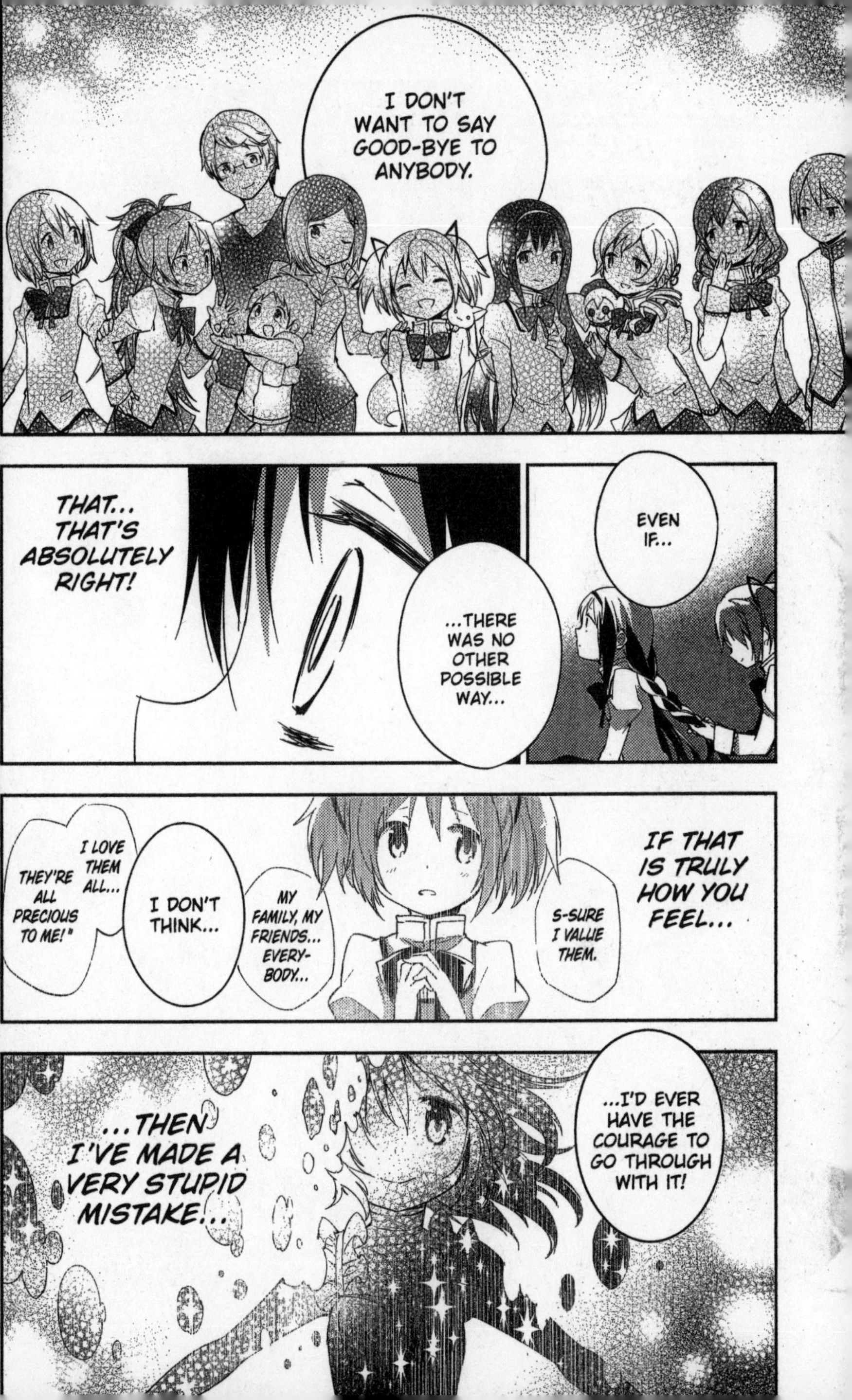
I DON'T WANT TO SAY GOOD-BYE TO ANYBODY.
EVEN IF...
...THERE WAS NO OTHER POSSIBLE WAY...
THAT... THAT'S ABSOLUTELY RIGHT!
IF THAT IS TRULY HOW YOU FEEL...
S-SURE I VALUE THEM.
MY FAMILY, MY FRIENDS... EVERYBODY...
I DON'T THINK...
I LOVE THEM ALL...
THEY'RE ALL PRECIOUS TO ME!"
...I'D EVER HAVE THE COURAGE TO GO THROUGH WITH IT!
...THEN I'VE MADE A VERY STUPID MISTAKE...

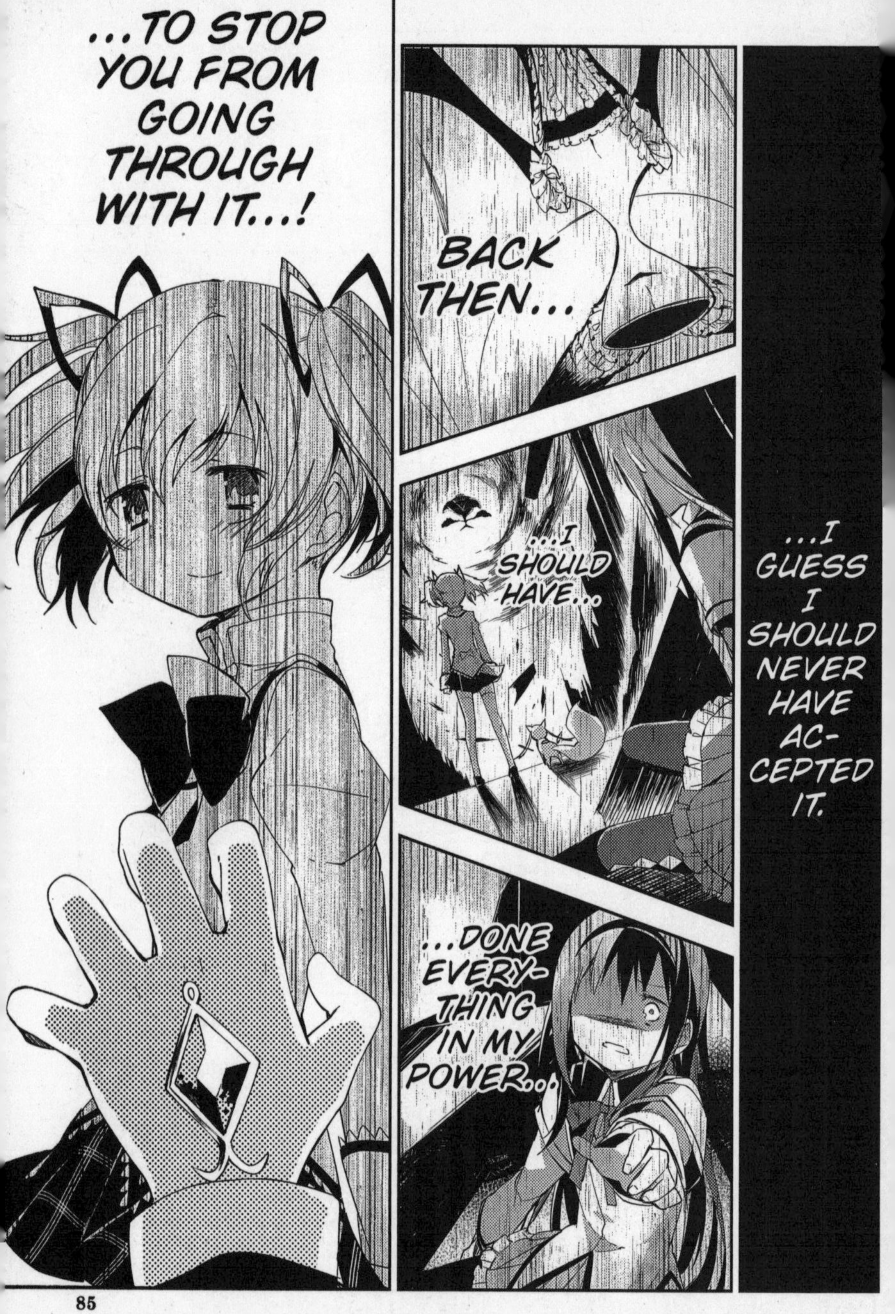

...I GUESS I SHOULD NEVER HAVE AC-CEPTED IT.
BACK THEN...
...I SHOULD HAVE...
...DONE EVERY-THING IN MY POWER...
...TO STOP YOU FROM GOING THROUGH WITH IT...!

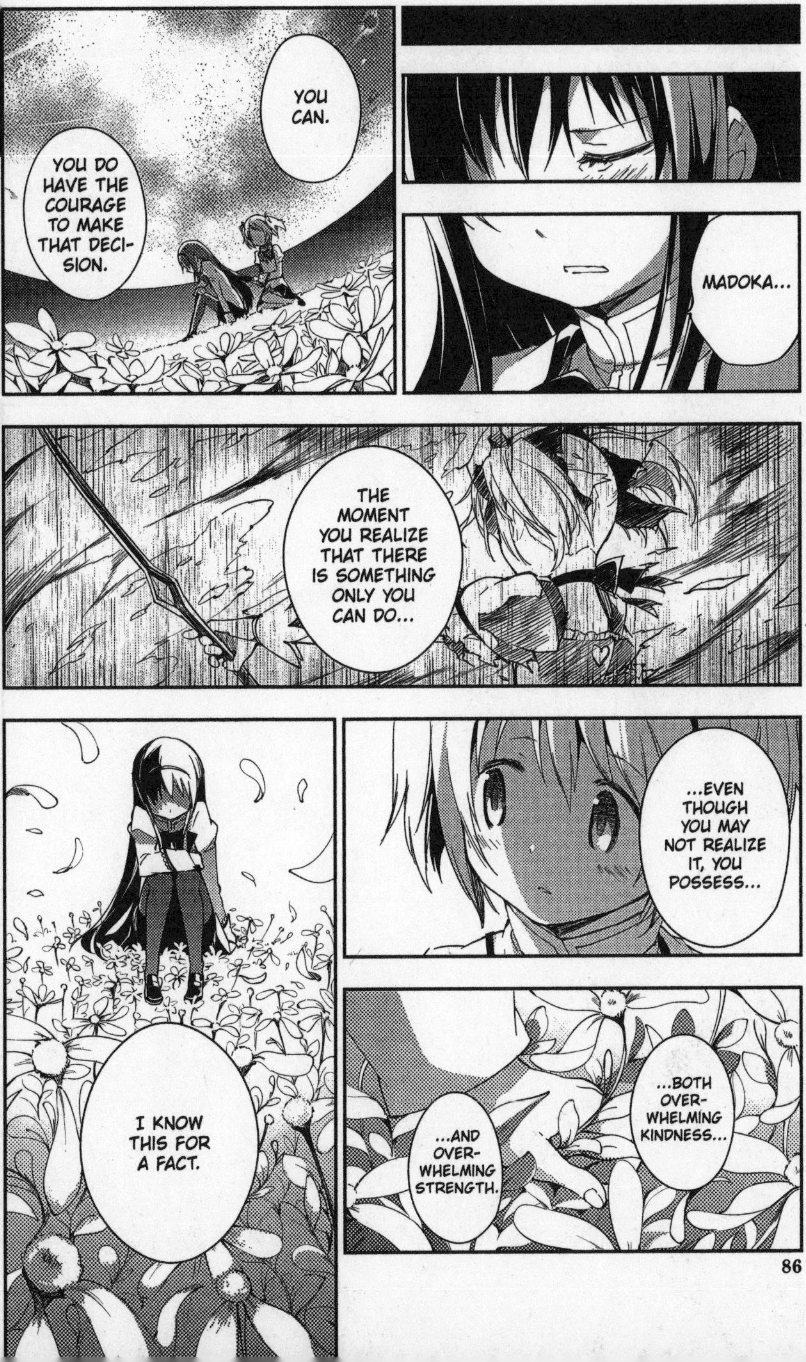
MADOKA...
YOU CAN.
YOU DO HAVE THE COURAGE TO MAKE THAT DECISION.
THE MOMENT YOU REALIZE THAT THERE IS SOMETHING ONLY YOU CAN DO...
...EVEN THOUGH YOU MAY NOT REALIZE IT, YOU POSSESS...
...BOTH OVERWHELMING KINDNESS...
...AND OVERWHELMING STRENGTH.
I KNOW THIS FOR A FACT.

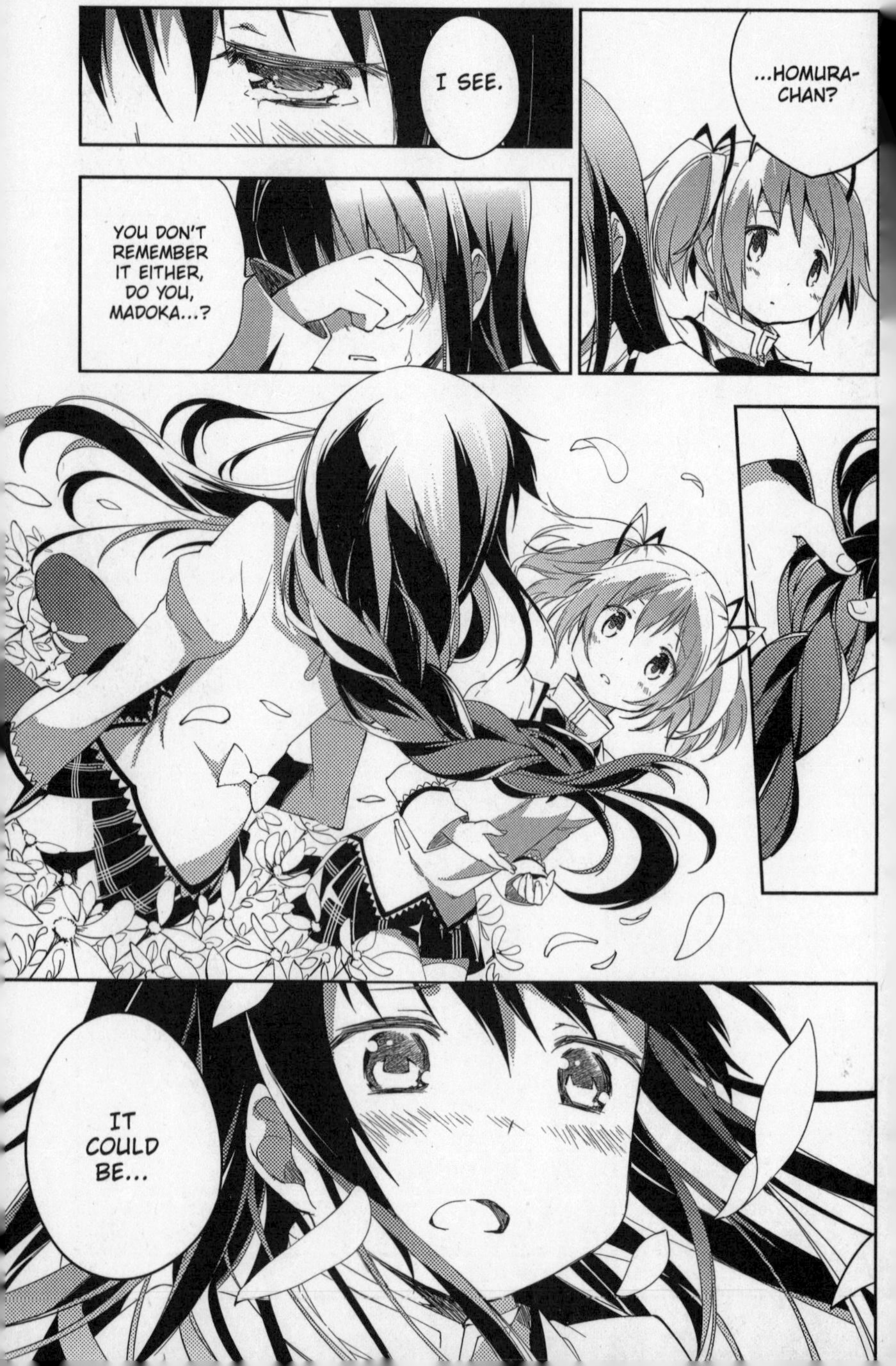
...HOMURA-CHAN?
I SEE.
YOU DON'T REMEMBER IT EITHER, DO YOU, MADOKA...?
IT COULD BE...

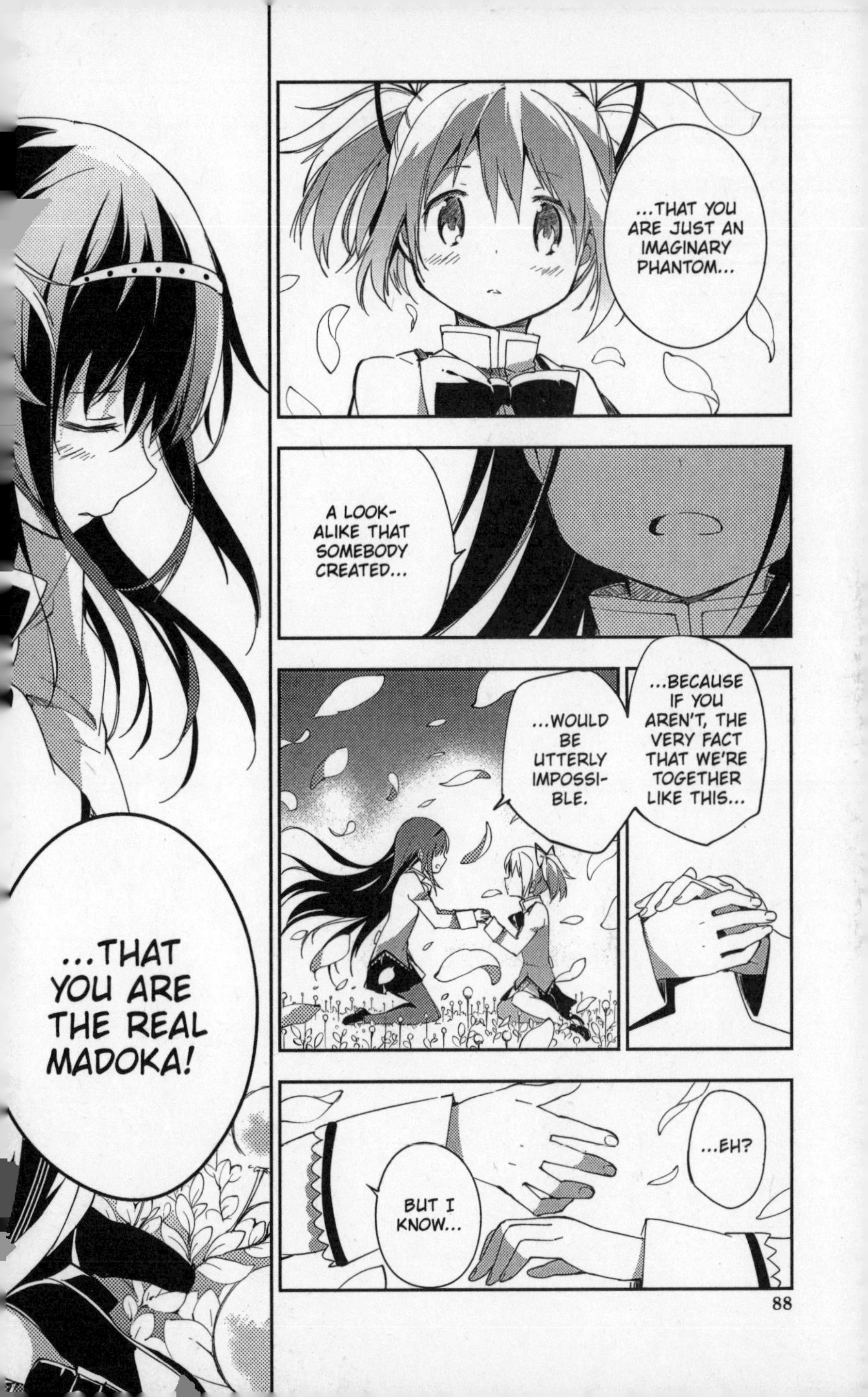
...THAT YOU ARE JUST AN IMAGINARY PHANTOM...
A LOOK-ALIKE THAT SOMEBODY CREATED...
...BECAUSE IF YOU AREN'T, THE VERY FACT THAT WE'RE TOGETHER LIKE THIS...
...WOULD BE UTTERLY IMPOSSI-BLE.
...EH?
BUT I KNOW...
...THAT YOU ARE THE REAL MADOKA!

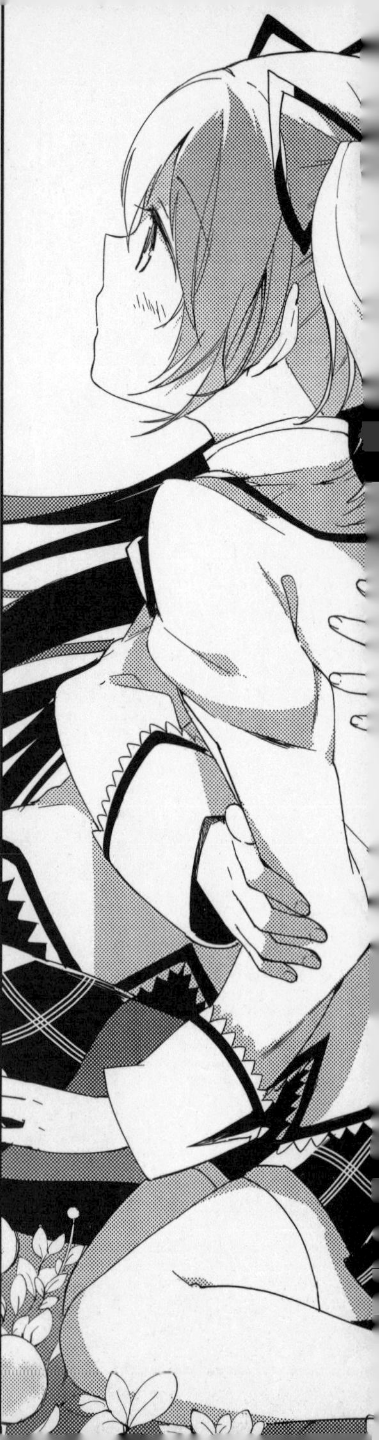

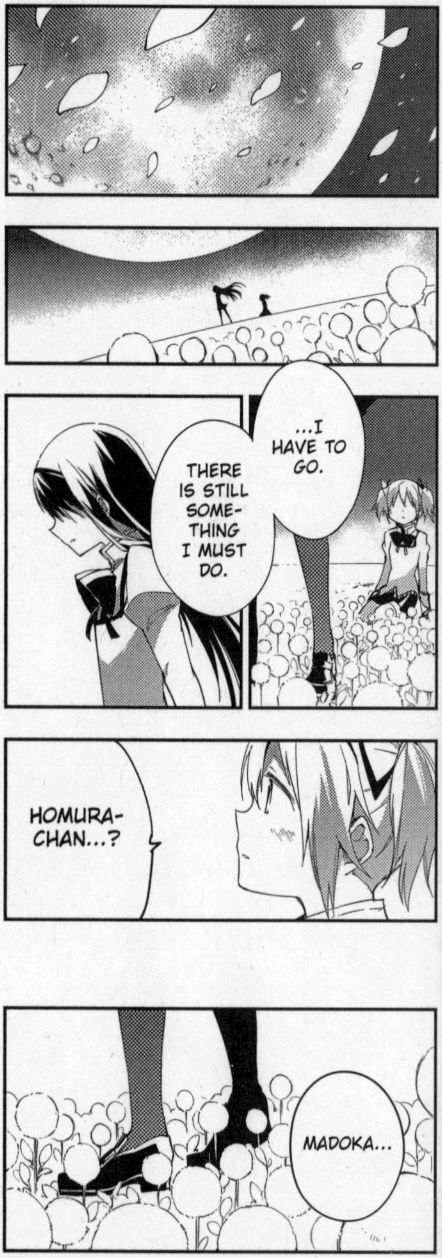

...I HAVE TO GO.
THERE IS STILL SOMETHING I MUST DO.
HOMURA-CHAN...?
MADOKA...

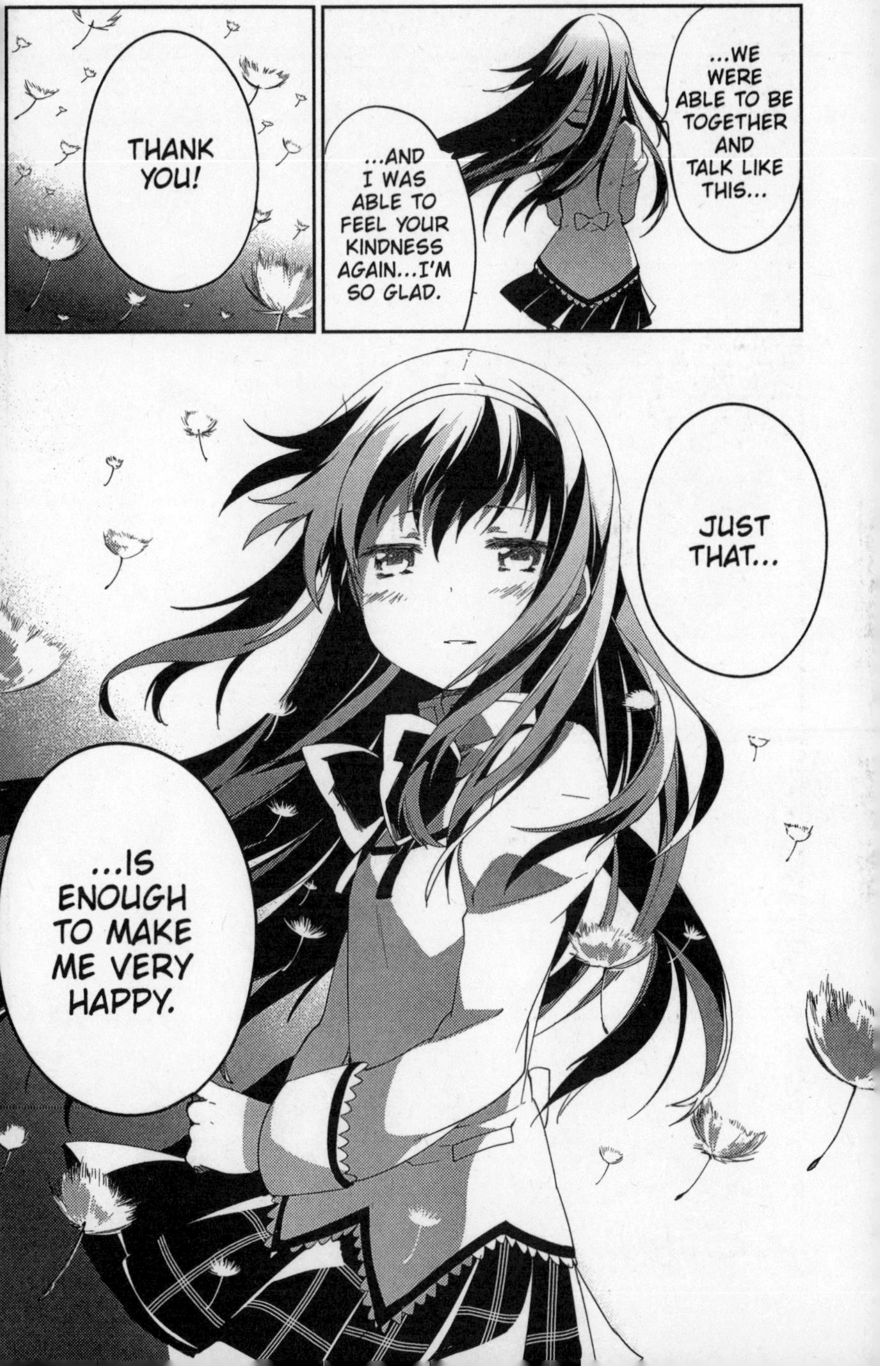
...WE WERE ABLE TO BE TOGETHER AND TALK LIKE THIS...
...AND I WAS ABLE TO FEEL YOUR KINDNESS AGAIN...I'M SO GLAD.
THANK YOU!
JUST THAT...
...IS ENOUGH TO MAKE ME VERY HAPPY.

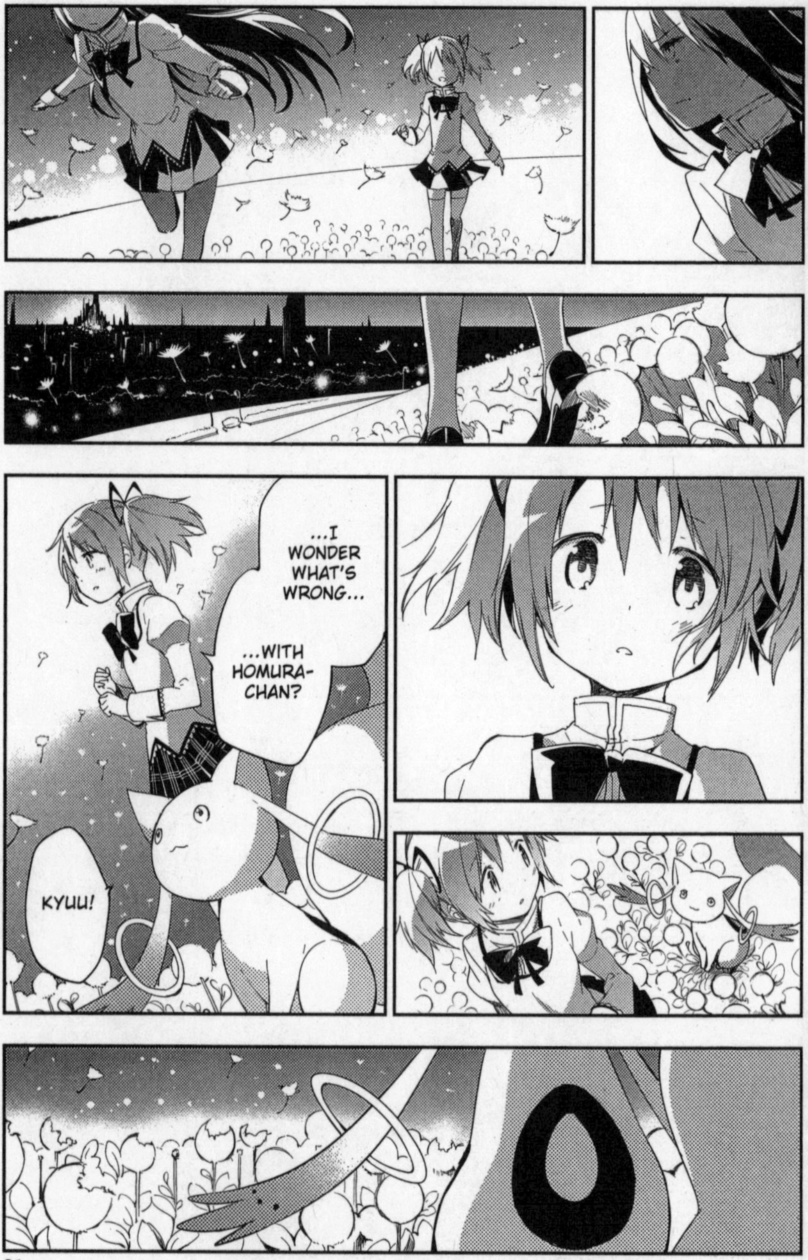
...I WONDER WHAT'S WRONG...
...WITH HOMURA-CHAN?
KYUU!

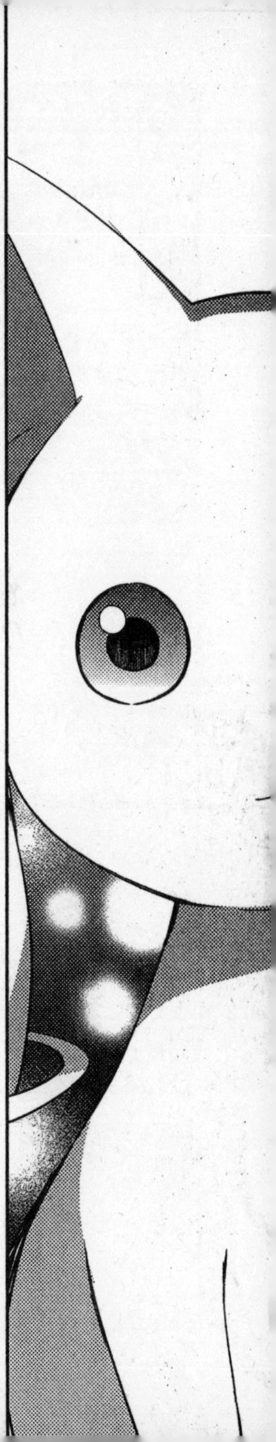

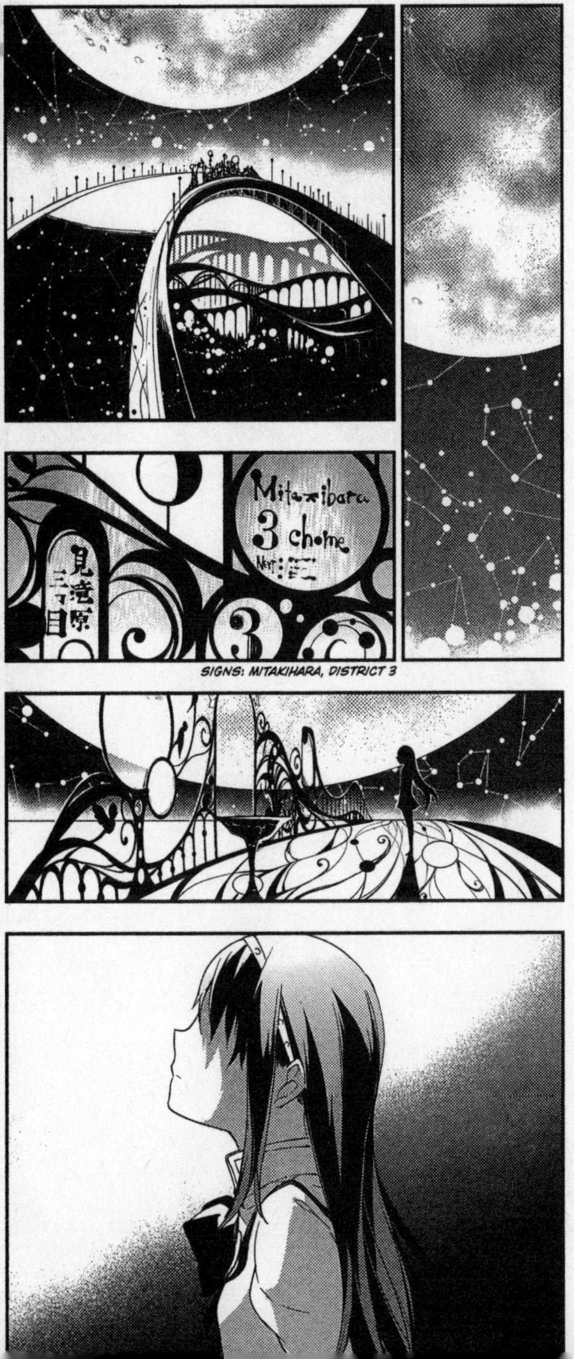

Mitakibara
3 chome
見滝原三丁目

SIGNS: MITAKIHARA, DISTRICT 3

SCREEN: KYOUKO SAKURA

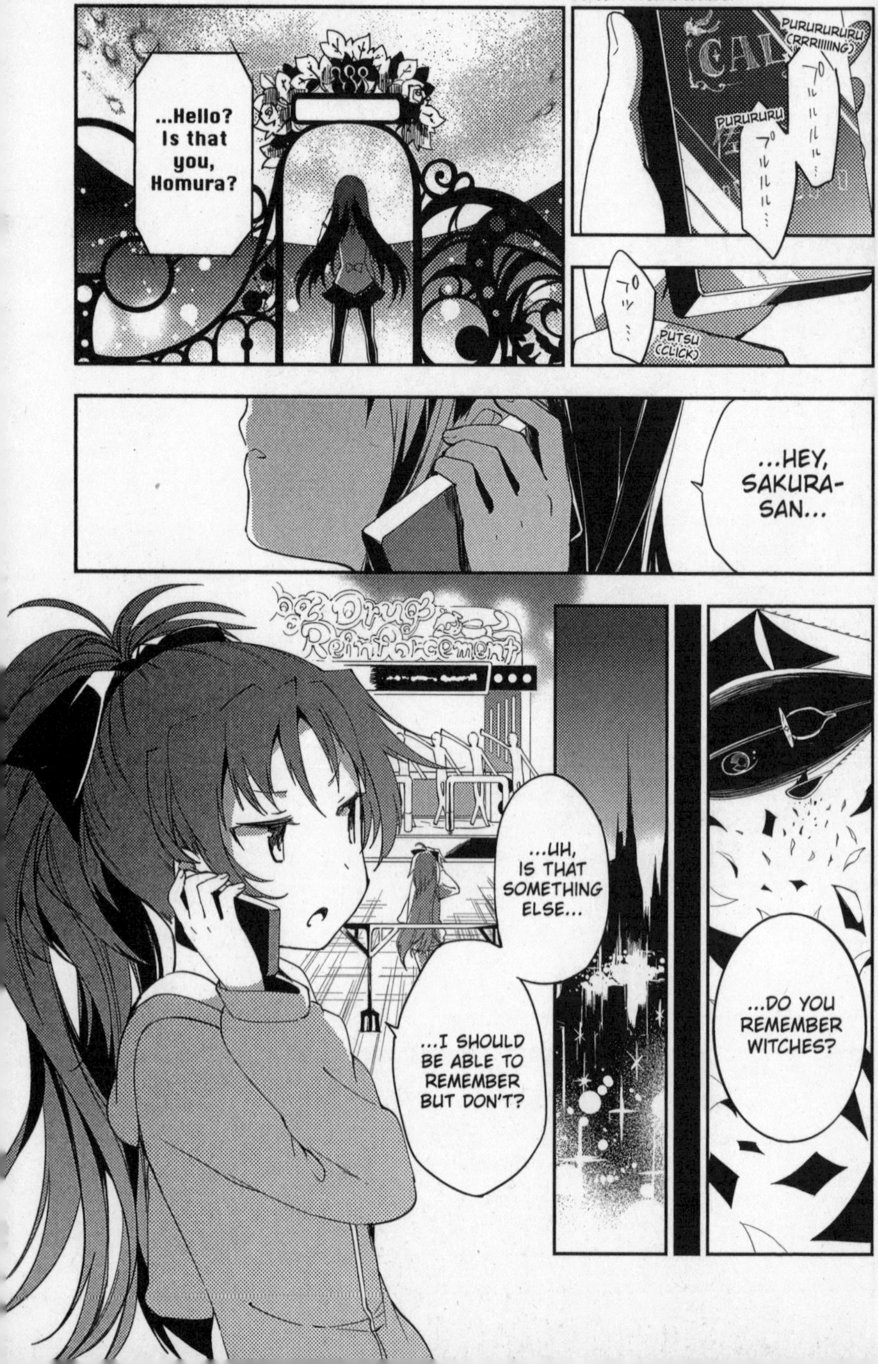
PURURURURU (RRRIIIIING)
プルルル…
PURURURU
プルルル…
プツ…
PUTSU (CLICK)
...Hello? Is that you, Homura?
...HEY, SAKURA-SAN...
...DO YOU REMEMBER WITCHES?
...UH, IS THAT SOMETHING ELSE...
...I SHOULD BE ABLE TO REMEMBER BUT DON'T?

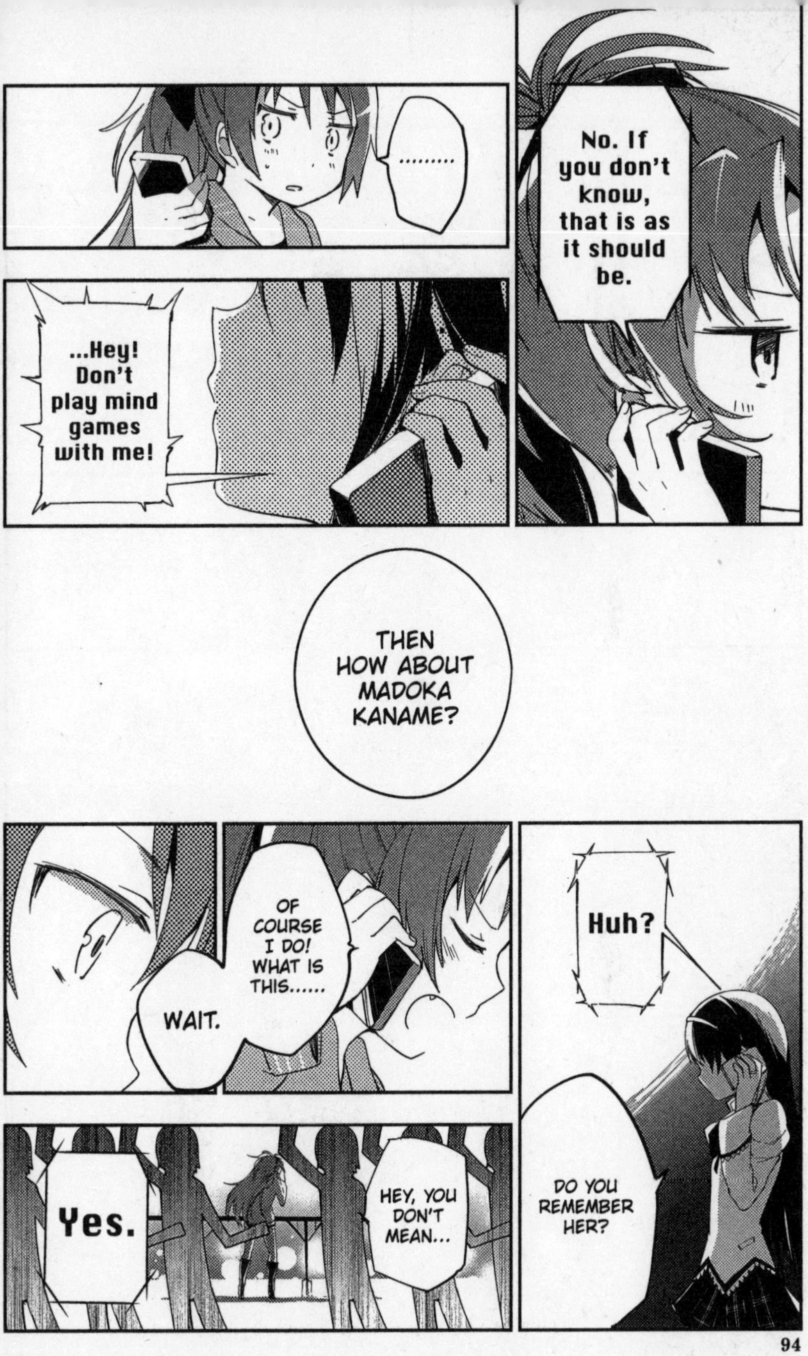
No. If you don't know, that is as it should be.
....
...Hey! Don't play mind games with me!
THEN HOW ABOUT MADOKA KANAME?
Huh?
DO YOU REMEMBER HER?
OF COURSE I DO! WHAT IS THIS......
WAIT.
HEY, YOU DON'T MEAN...
Yes.

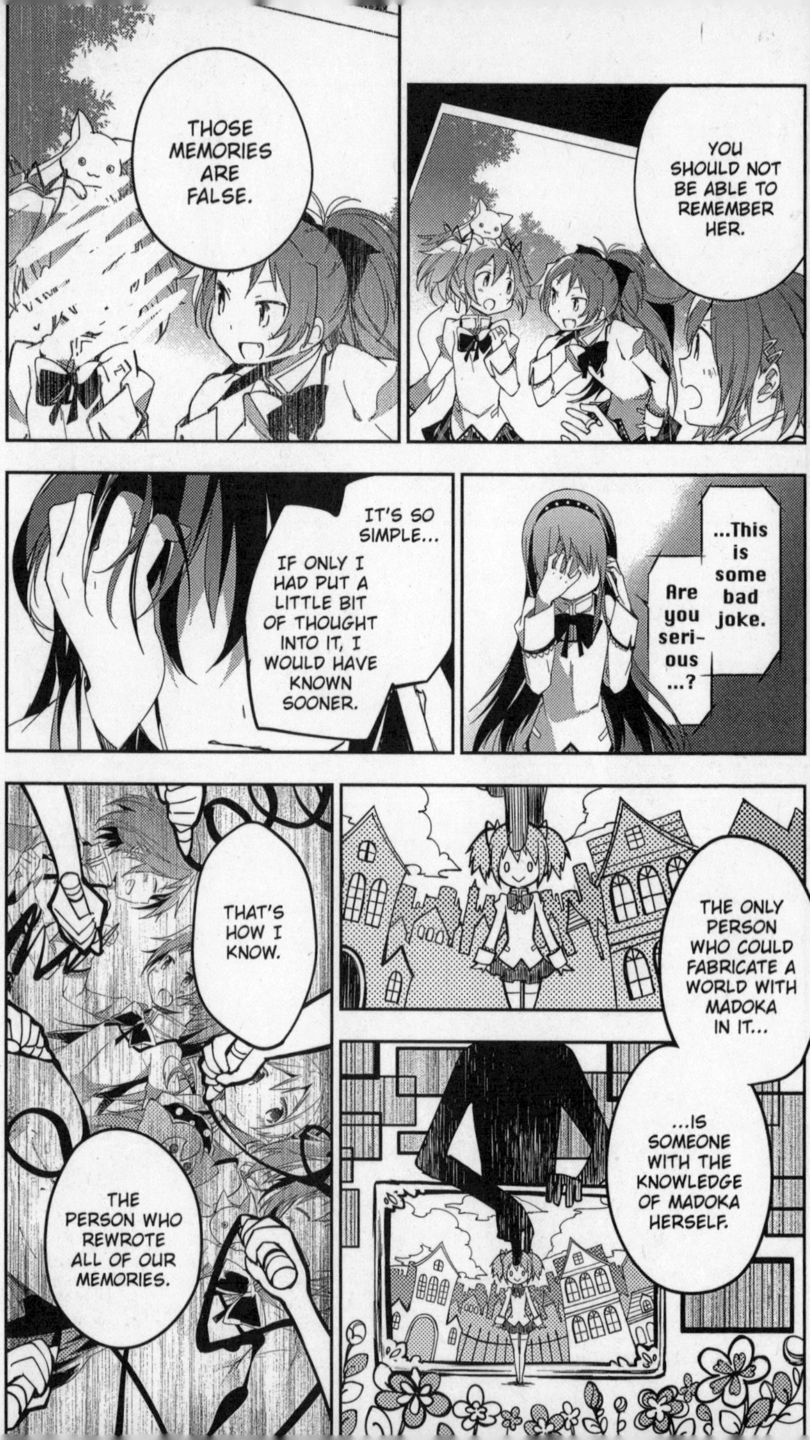
YOU SHOULD NOT BE ABLE TO REMEMBER HER.
THOSE MEMORIES ARE FALSE.
...This is some bad joke.
Are you seri-ous...?
IT'S SO SIMPLE...
IF ONLY I HAD PUT A LITTLE BIT OF THOUGHT INTO IT, I WOULD HAVE KNOWN SOONER.
THE ONLY PERSON WHO COULD FABRICATE A WORLD WITH MADOKA IN IT...
...IS SOMEONE WITH THE KNOWLEDGE OF MADOKA HERSELF.
THAT'S HOW I KNOW.
THE PERSON WHO REWROTE ALL OF OUR MEMORIES.

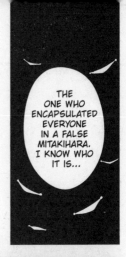

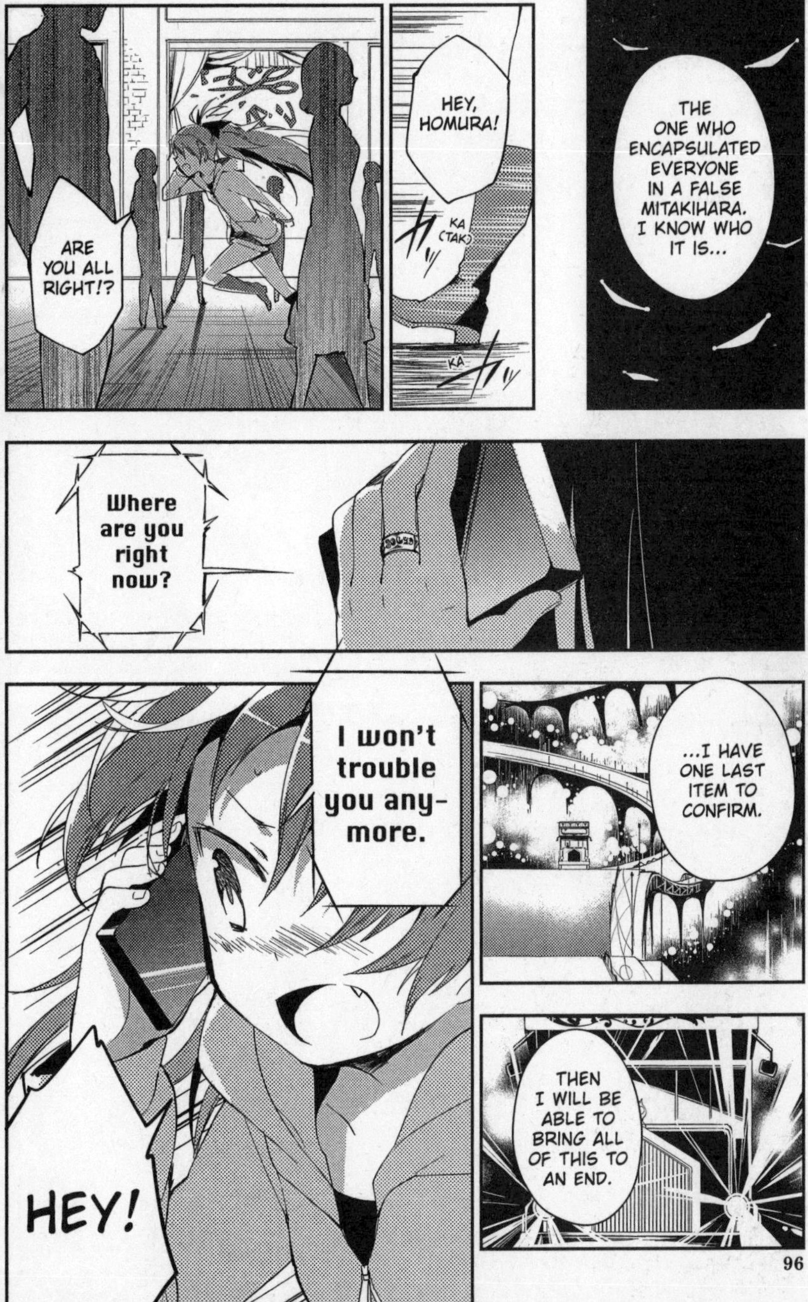
THE ONE WHO ENCAPSULATED EVERYONE IN A FALSE MITAKIHARA. I KNOW WHO IT IS...
HEY, HOMURA!
KA (TAK)
KA
ARE YOU ALL RIGHT!?
Where are you right now?
...I HAVE ONE LAST ITEM TO CONFIRM.
THEN I WILL BE ABLE TO BRING ALL OF THIS TO AN END.
I won't trouble you any-more.
HEY!

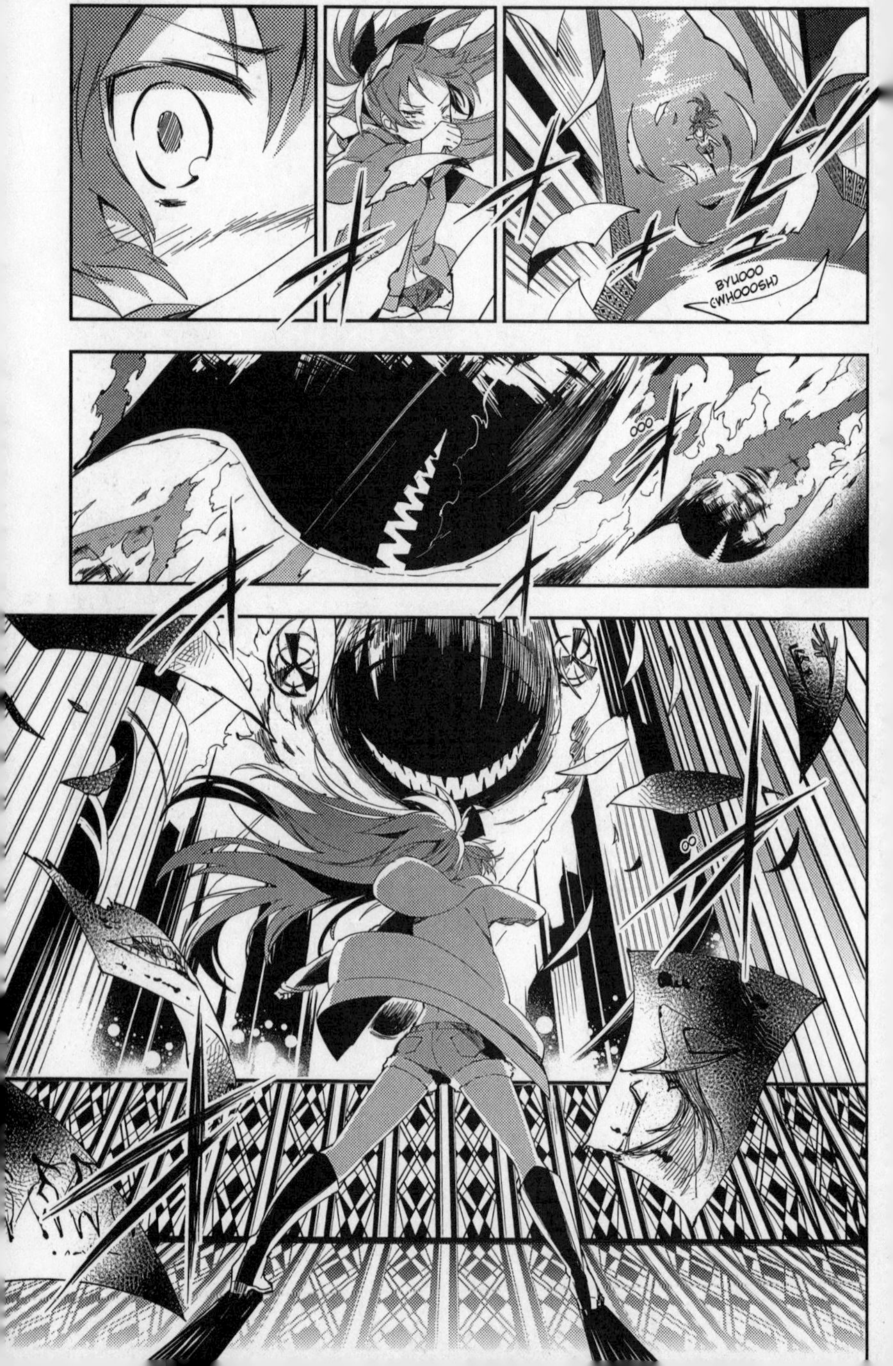
BYUOOO
(WHOOOSH)

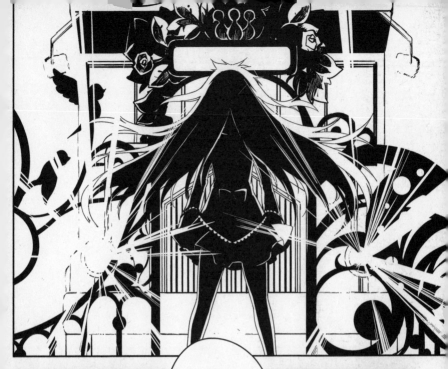

I APOLOGIZE FOR INVOLVING YOU IN THIS.

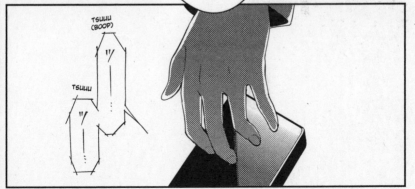

TSUUU (BOOP)

TSUUU

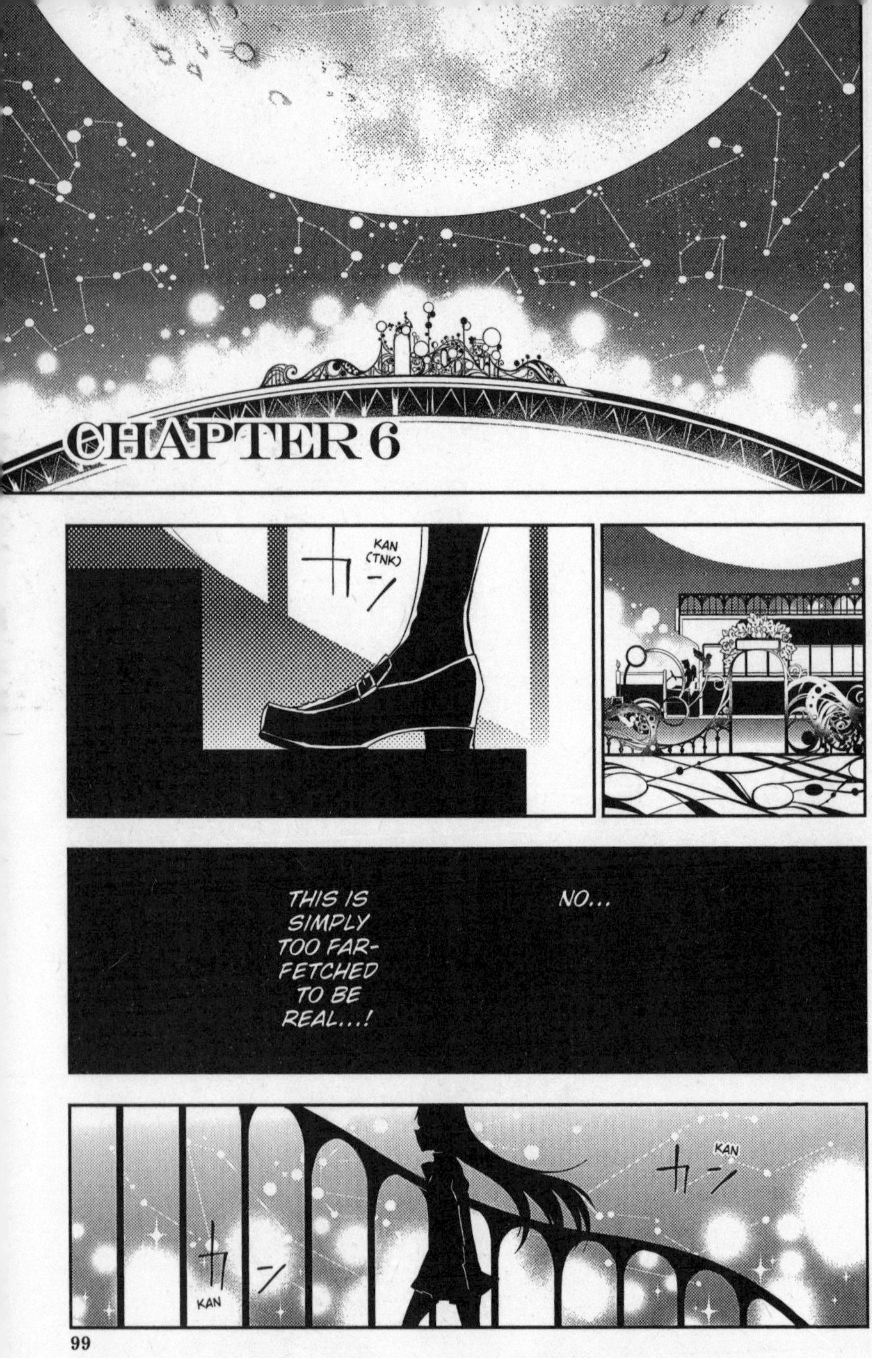
CHAPTER 6
KAN (TNK)
カーン
NO...
THIS IS SIMPLY TOO FAR-FETCHED TO BE REAL...!
KAN
カーン
KAN
カーン

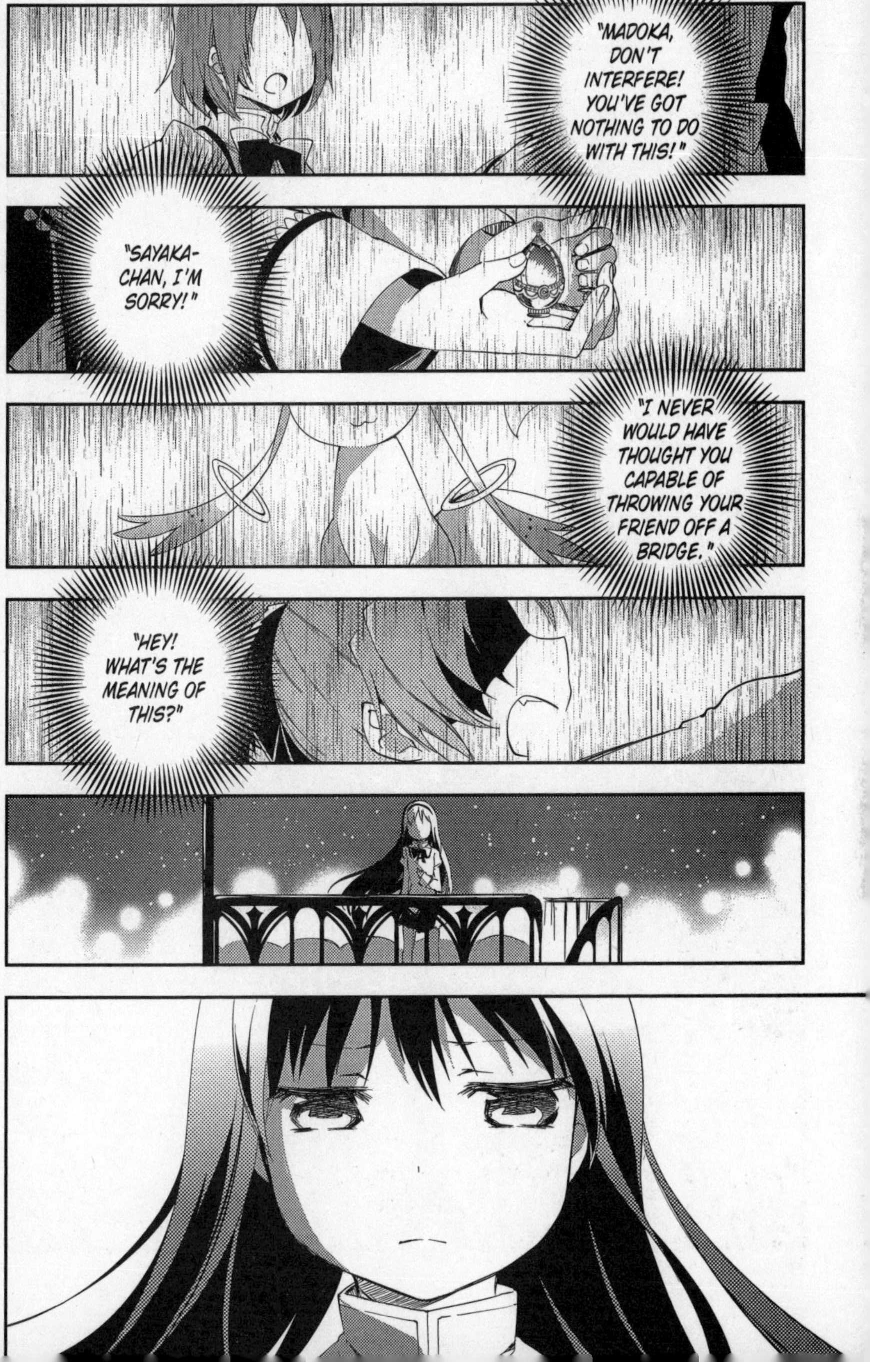
"MADOKA, DON'T INTERFERE! YOU'VE GOT NOTHING TO DO WITH THIS!"
"SAYAKA-CHAN, I'M SORRY!"
"I NEVER WOULD HAVE THOUGHT YOU CAPABLE OF THROWING YOUR FRIEND OFF A BRIDGE."
"HEY! WHAT'S THE MEANING OF THIS?"

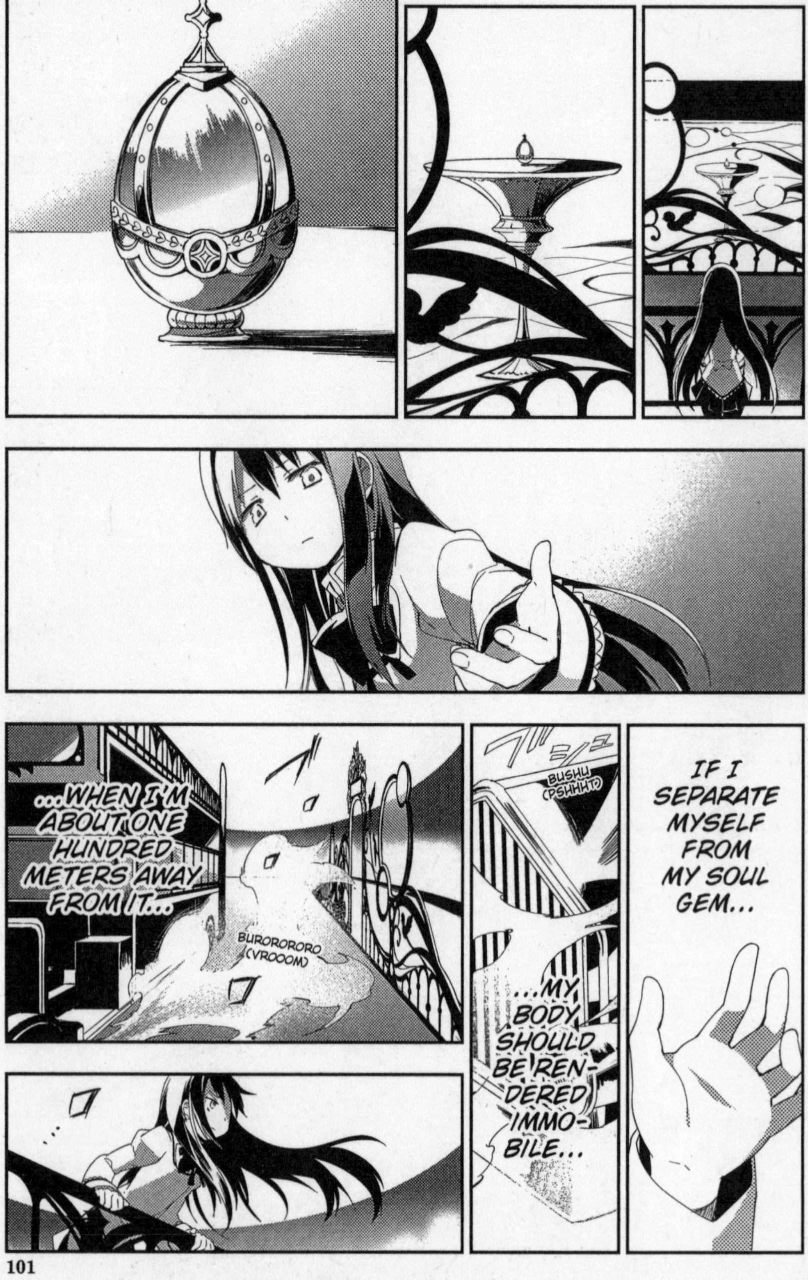
IF I SEPARATE MYSELF FROM MY SOUL GEM...
BUSHU (PSHHHT)
...MY BODY SHOULD BE REN-DERED IMMO-BILE...
...WHEN I'M ABOUT ONE HUNDRED METERS AWAY FROM IT...
BURORORORO (VROOOM)
...

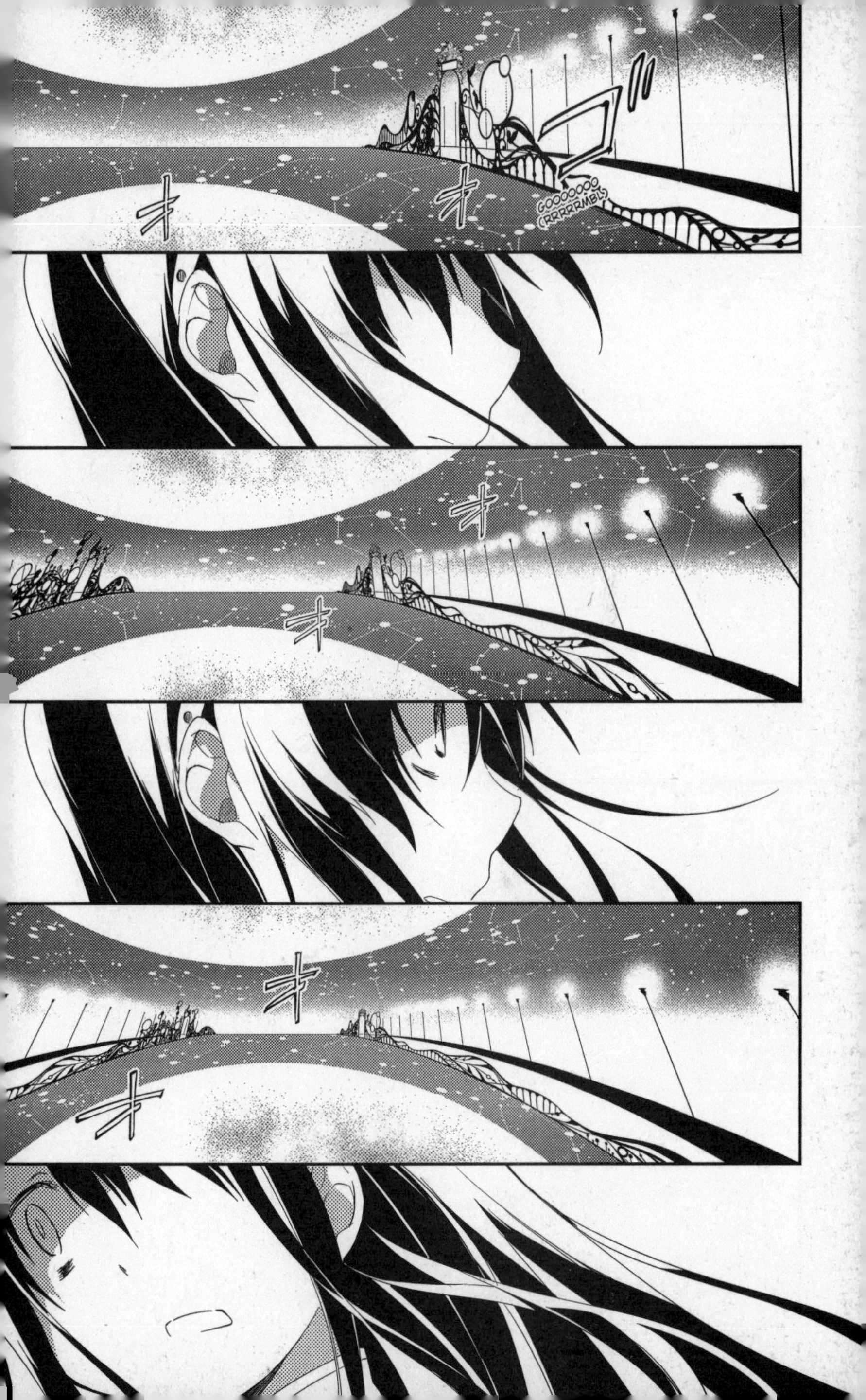
GOOOOOOO
(RRRRRRMBL)

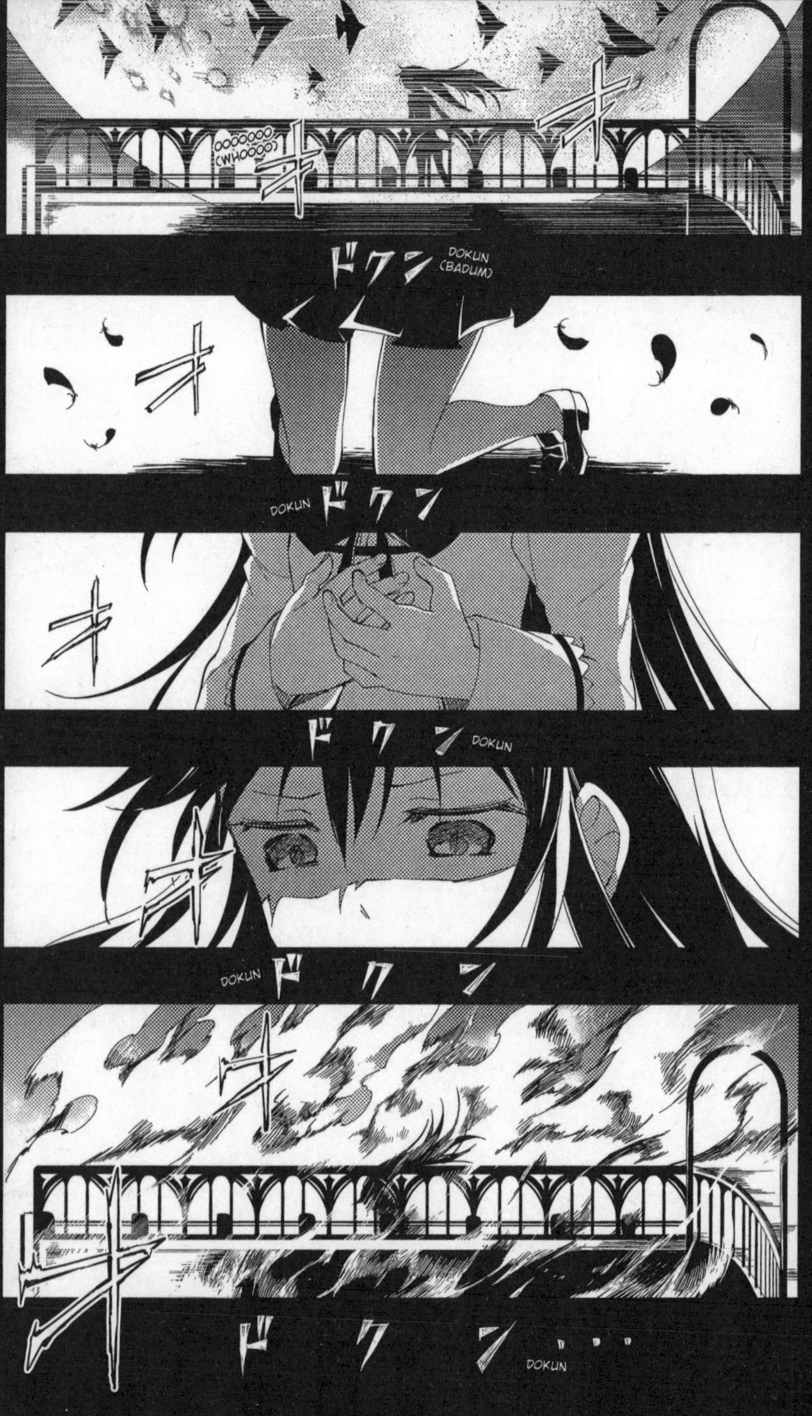

オオ
OOOOOOO (WHOOOOO)
ドクン
DOKUN (BADUM)
オ
ドクン
DOKUN
オ
ドクン
DOKUN
オ
ドクン
DOKUN
オオ
ドクン…
DOKUN

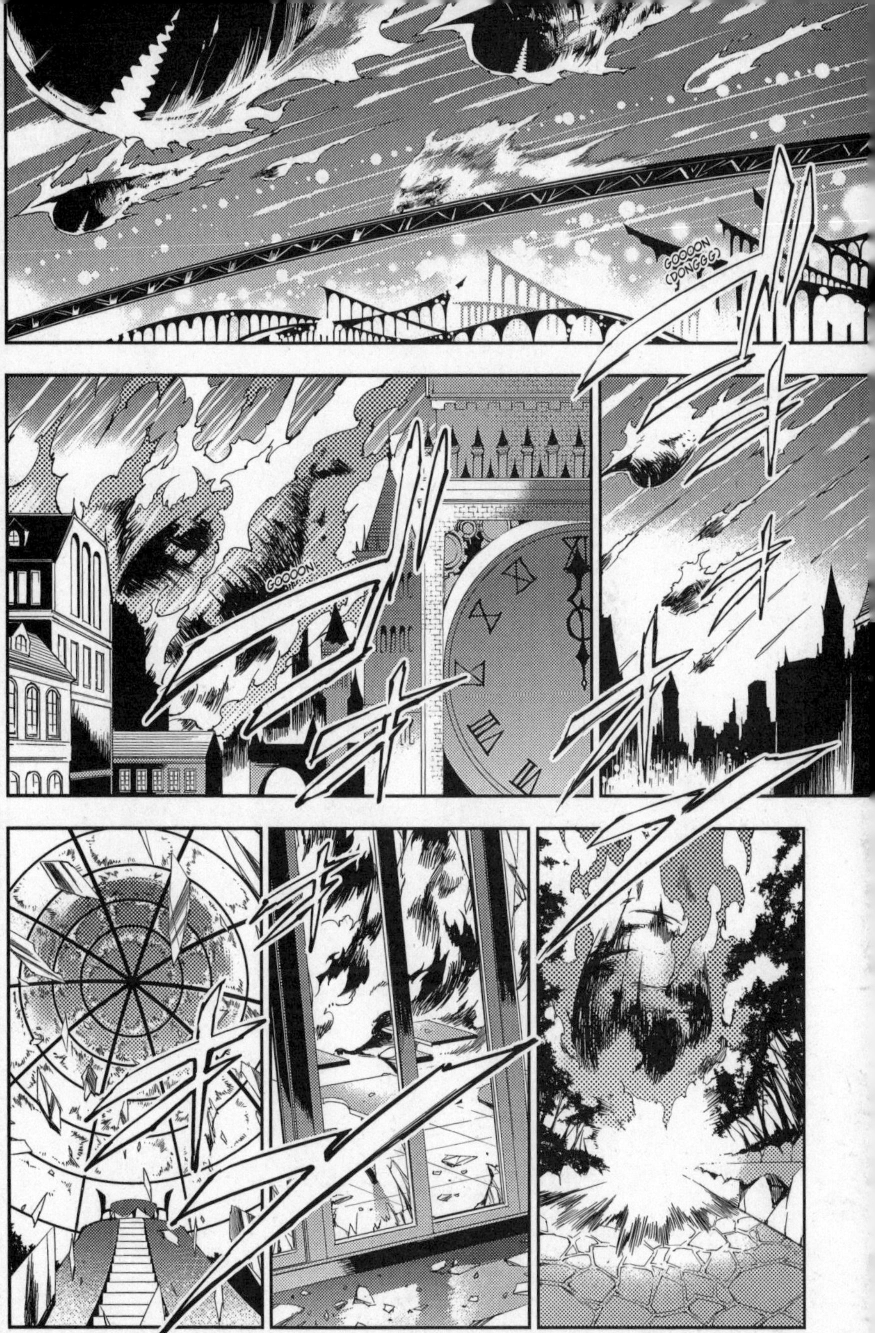
GOOOON
(DONGGG)
GOOOON!

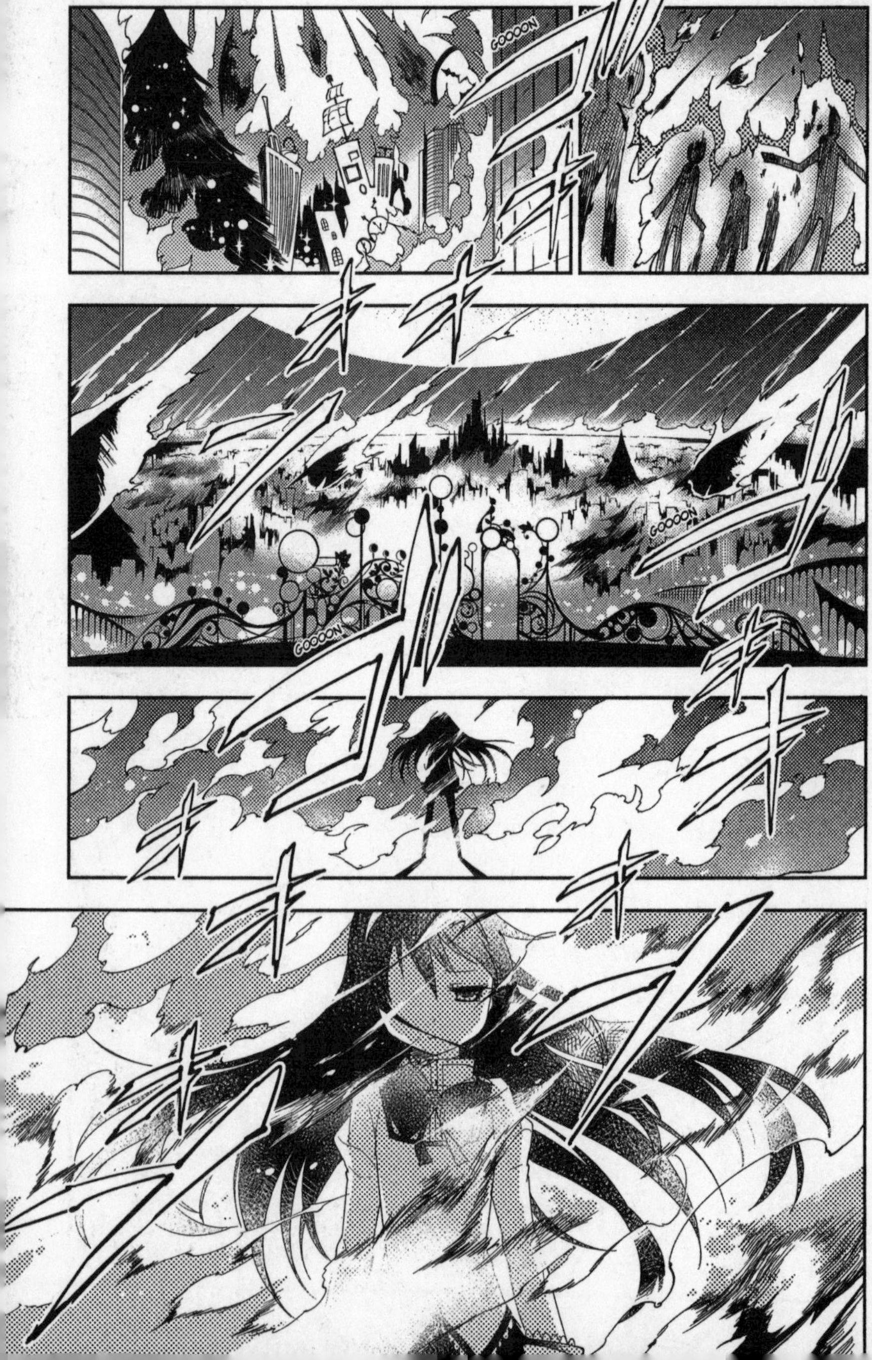
GOOOON
GOOOON
GOOOON

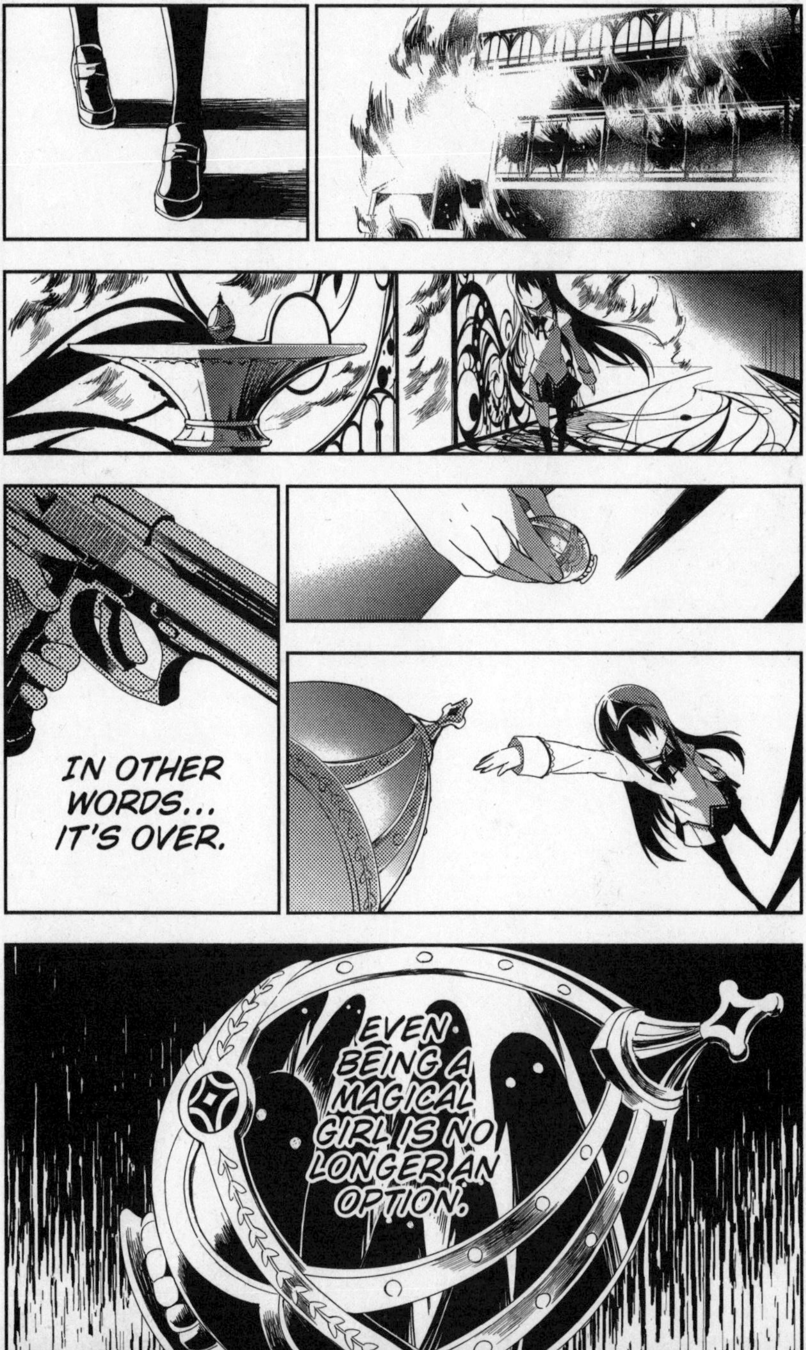
IN OTHER WORDS... IT'S OVER.
EVEN BEING A MAGICAL GIRL IS NO LONGER AN OPTION.

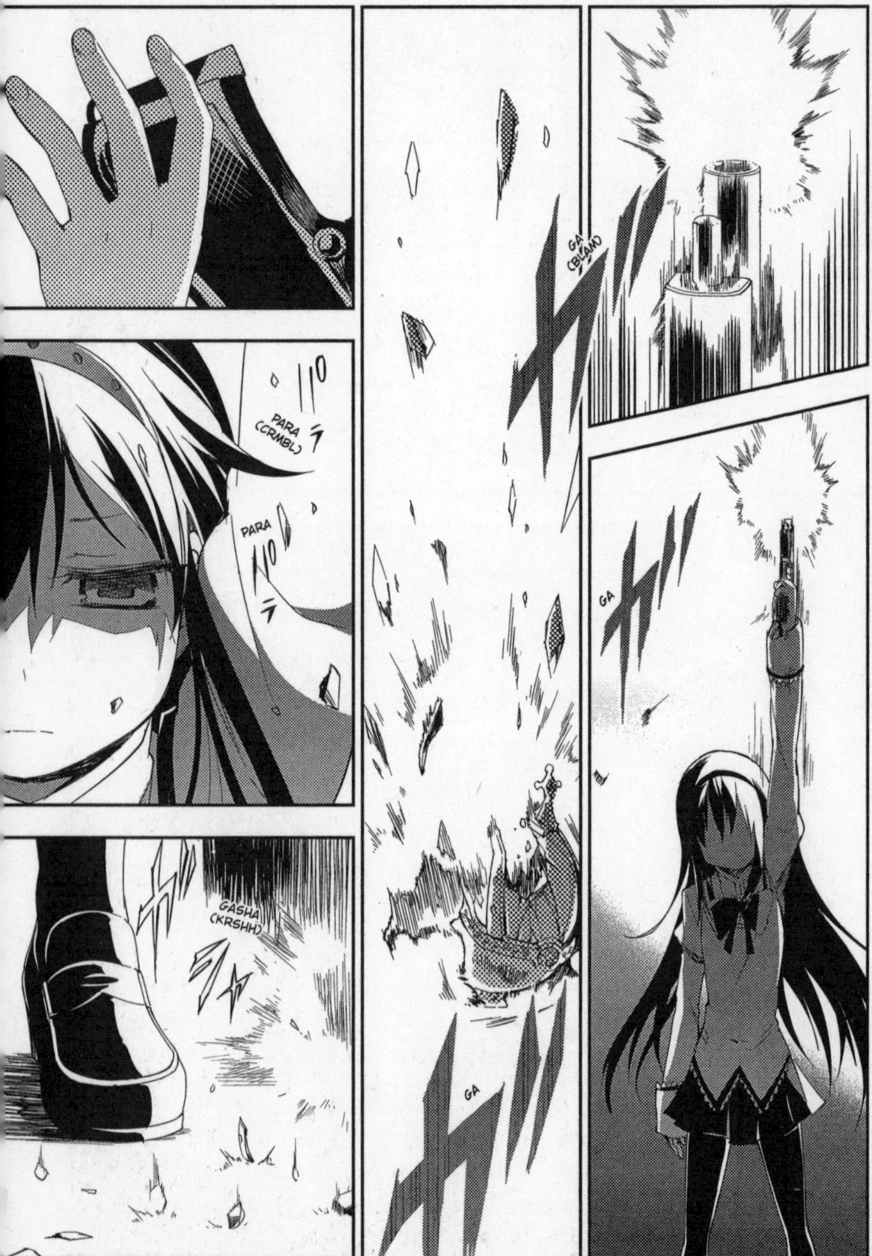
GA
GA (BLAM)
GA
PARA (CRMBL)
PARA
GASHA (KRSHH)

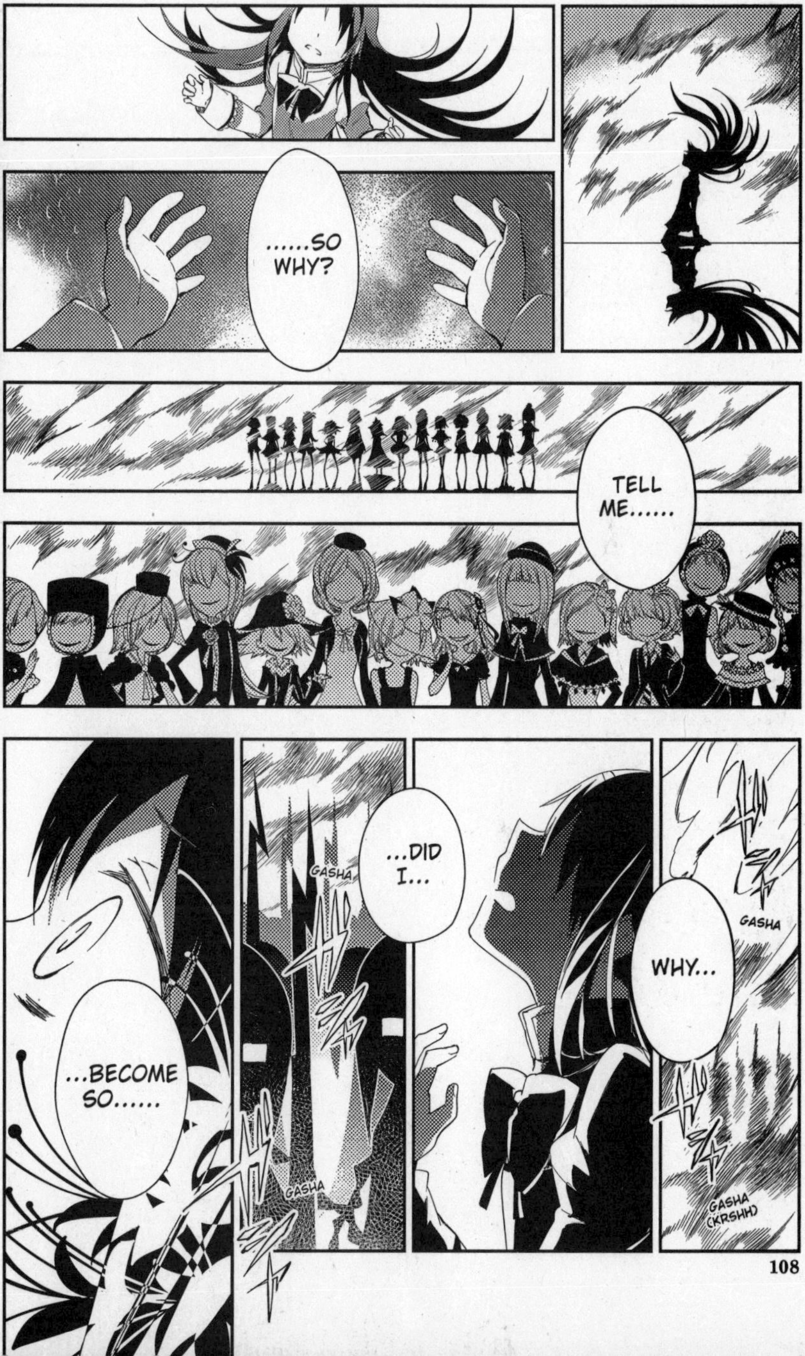

......SO WHY?
TELL ME......
GASHA
WHY...
GASHA (KRSHH)
...DID I...
GASHA
GASHA
...BECOME SO......

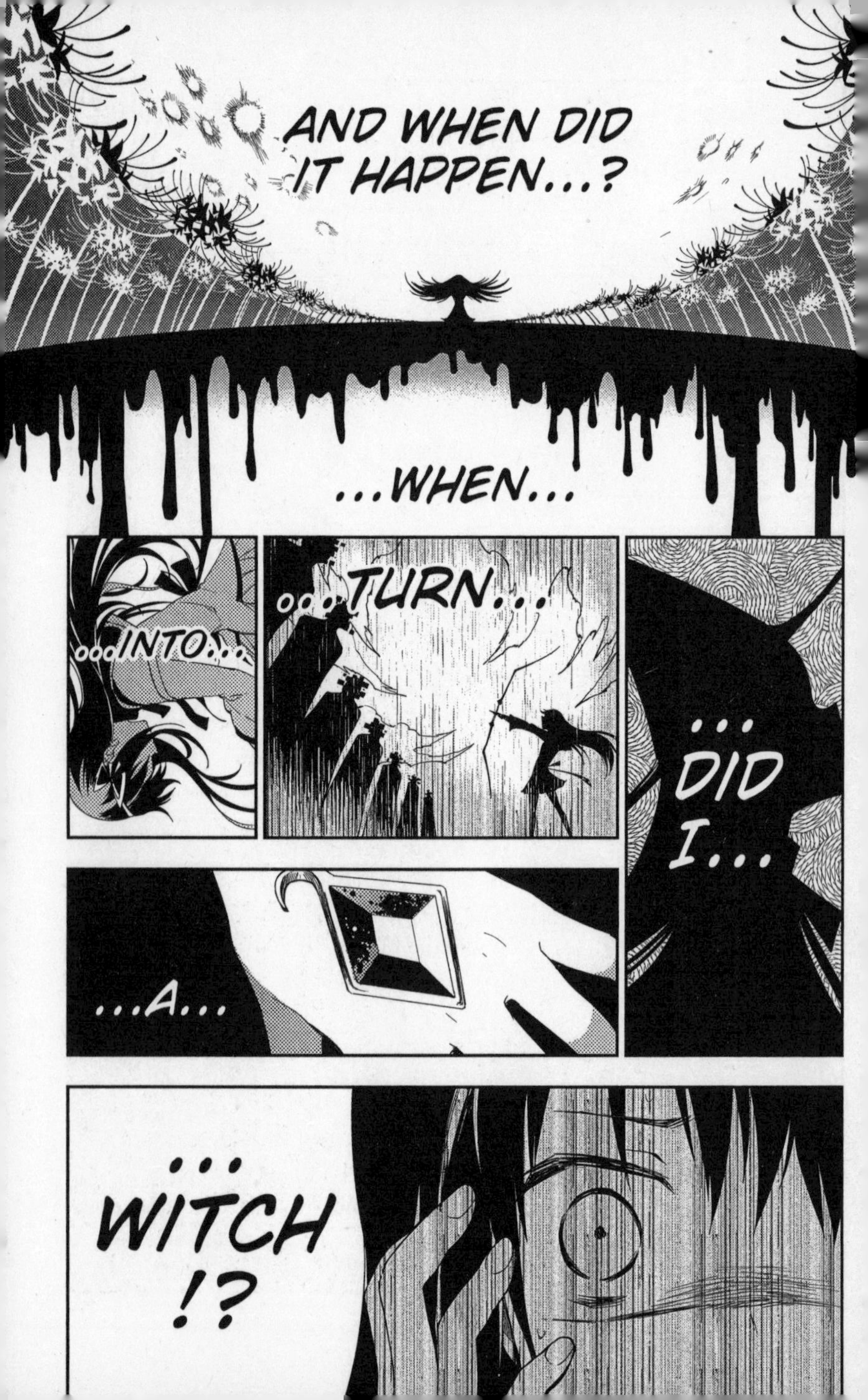
AND WHEN DID IT HAPPEN...?
...WHEN...
... DID I...
...TURN...
...INTO...
...A...
... WITCH !?

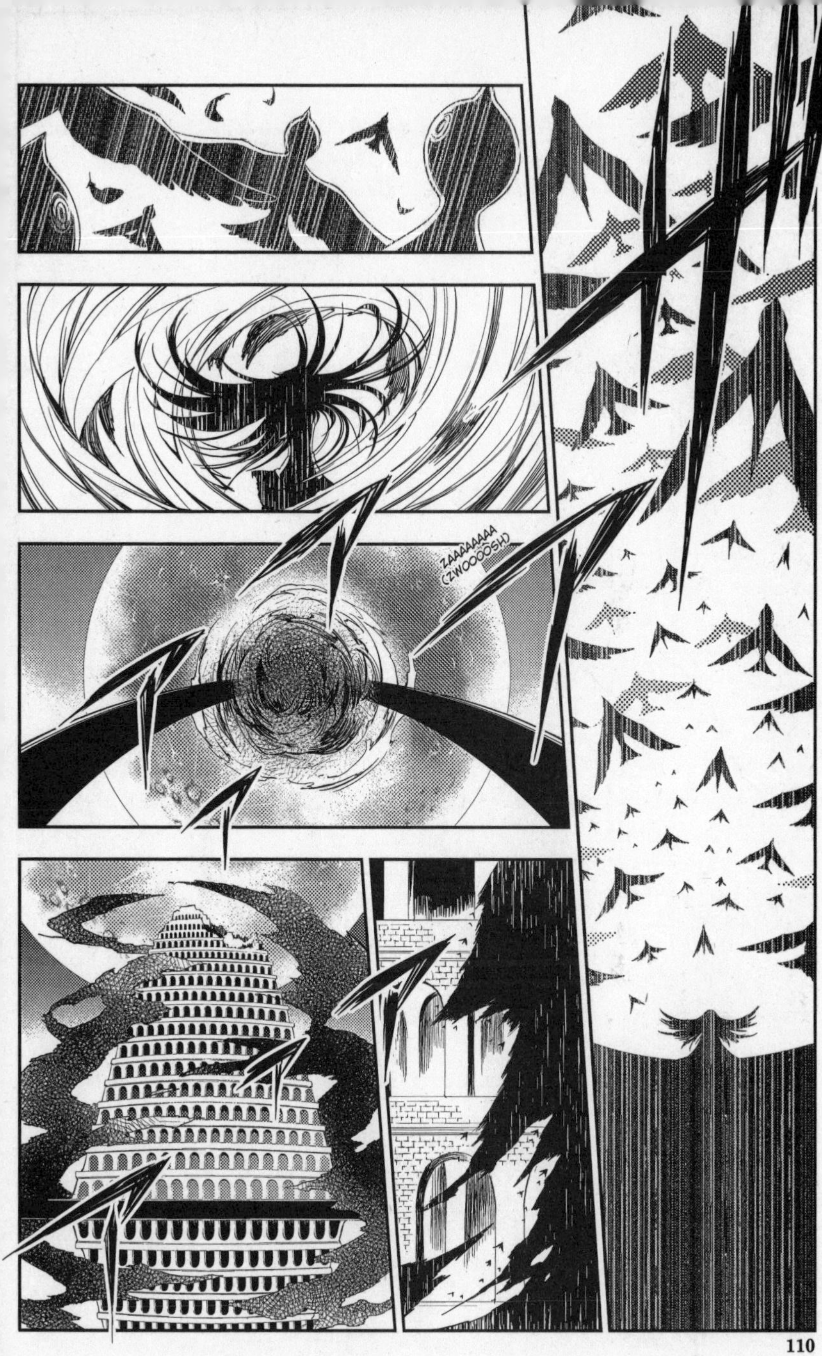
ZAAAAAAAA
(ZWOOOOSH)

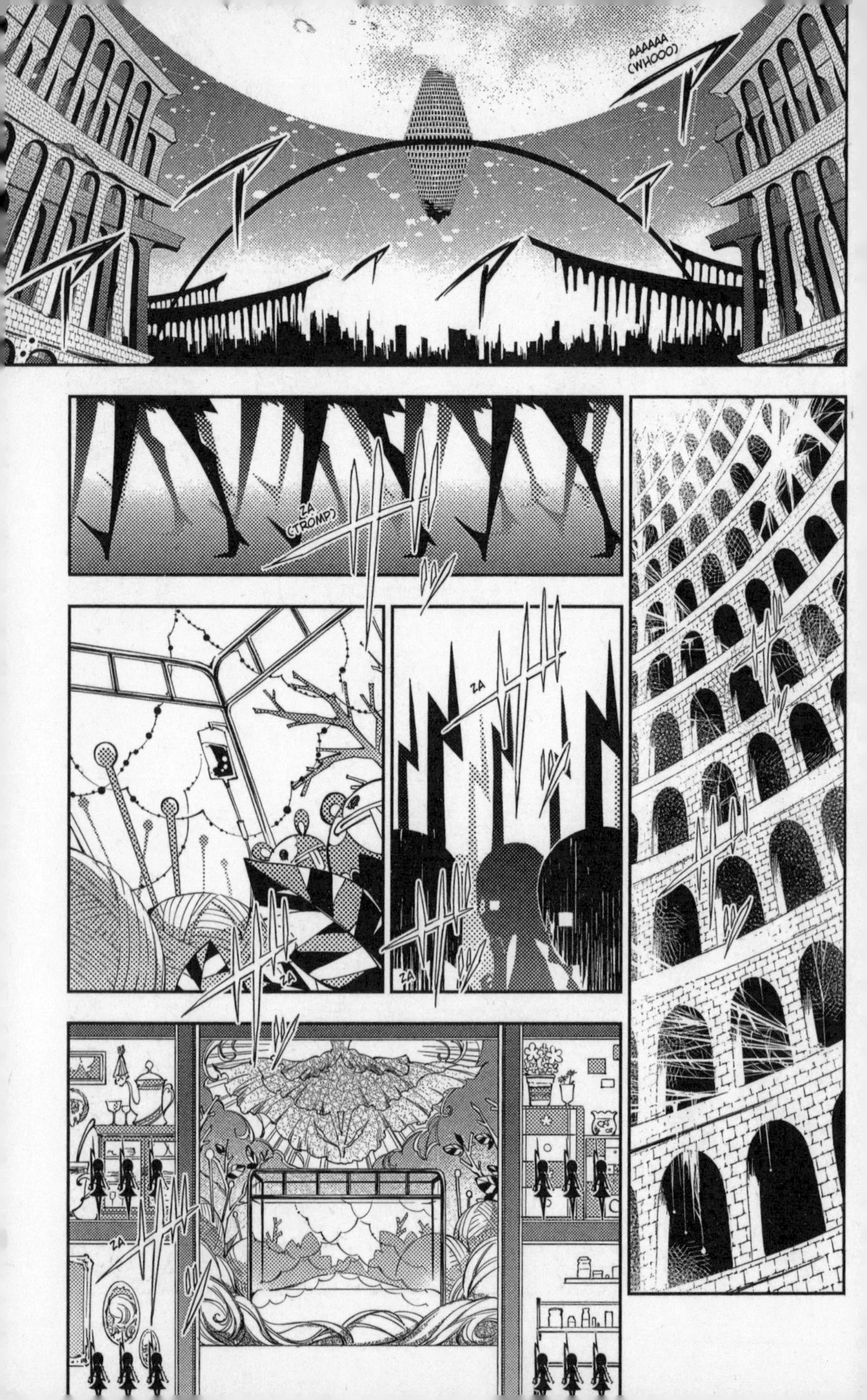
AAAAAA (WHOOO)
ZA (TROMP)
ZA
ZA
ZA
ZA

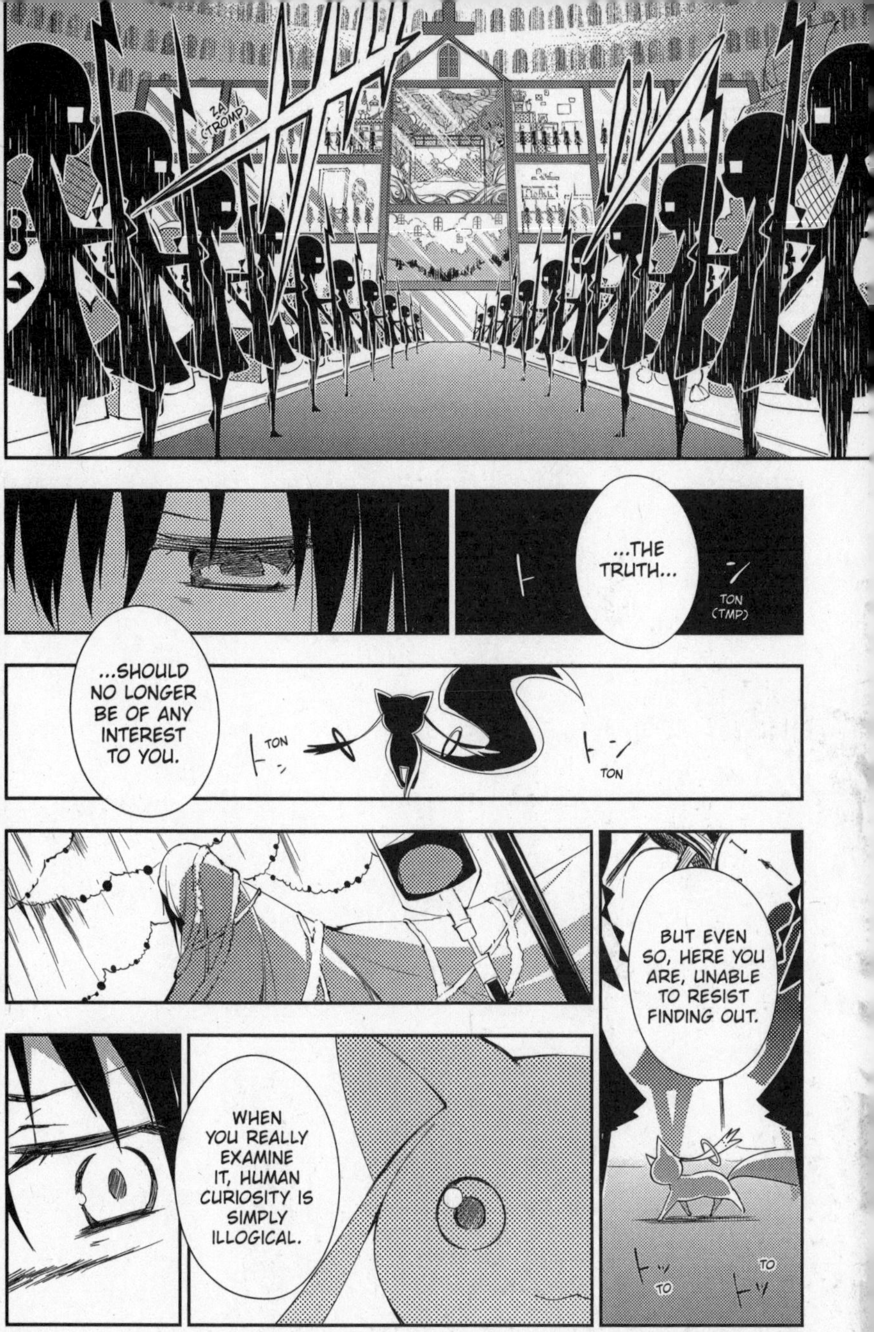
ZA (TROMP)
...THE TRUTH...
TON (TMP)
...SHOULD NO LONGER BE OF ANY INTEREST TO YOU.
TON
TON
BUT EVEN SO, HERE YOU ARE, UNABLE TO RESIST FINDING OUT.
TO
TO
WHEN YOU REALLY EXAMINE IT, HUMAN CURIOSITY IS SIMPLY ILLOGICAL.

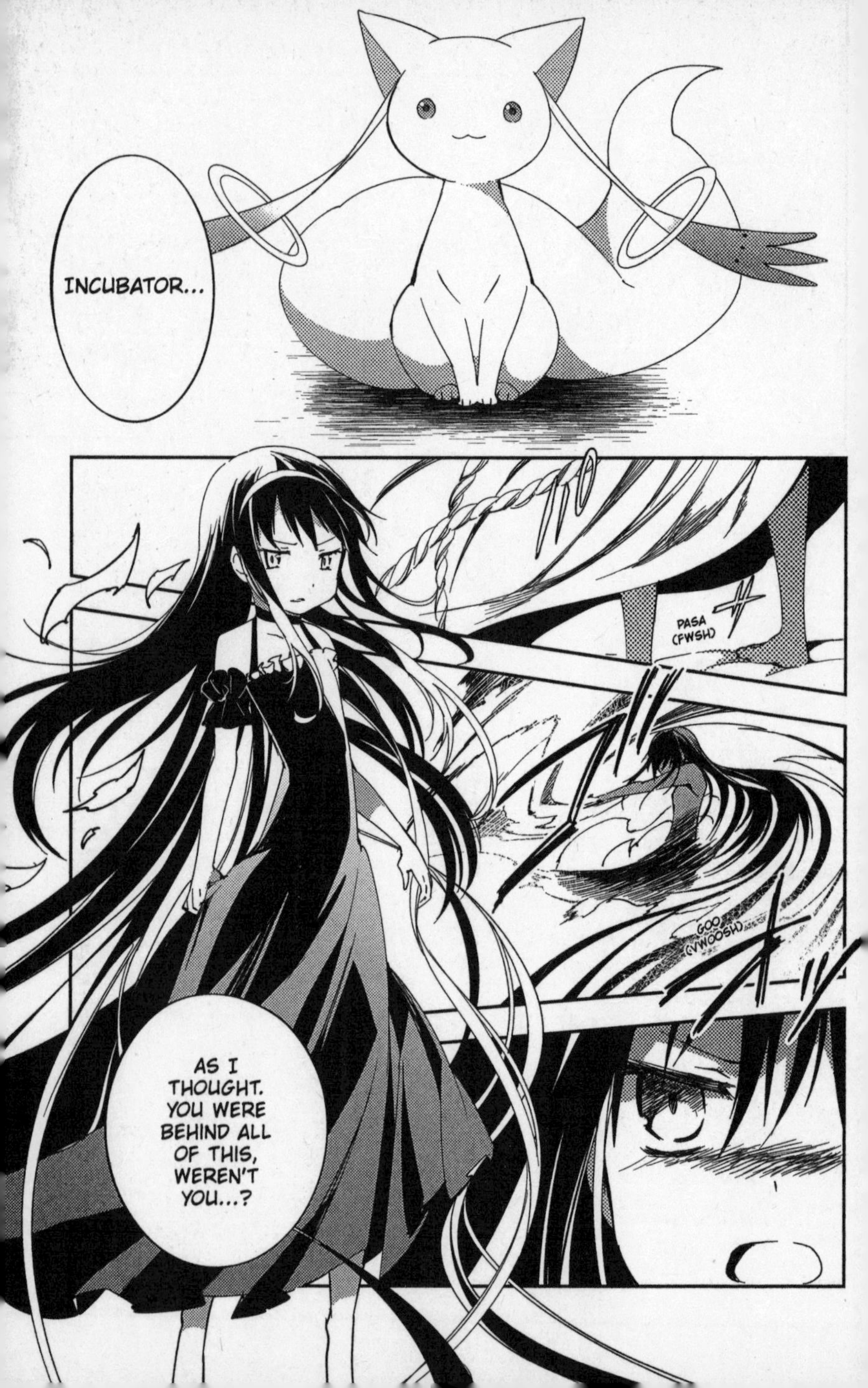
INCUBATOR...
PASA (FWSH)
GOO (VWOOSH)
AS I THOUGHT. YOU WERE BEHIND ALL OF THIS, WEREN'T YOU...?

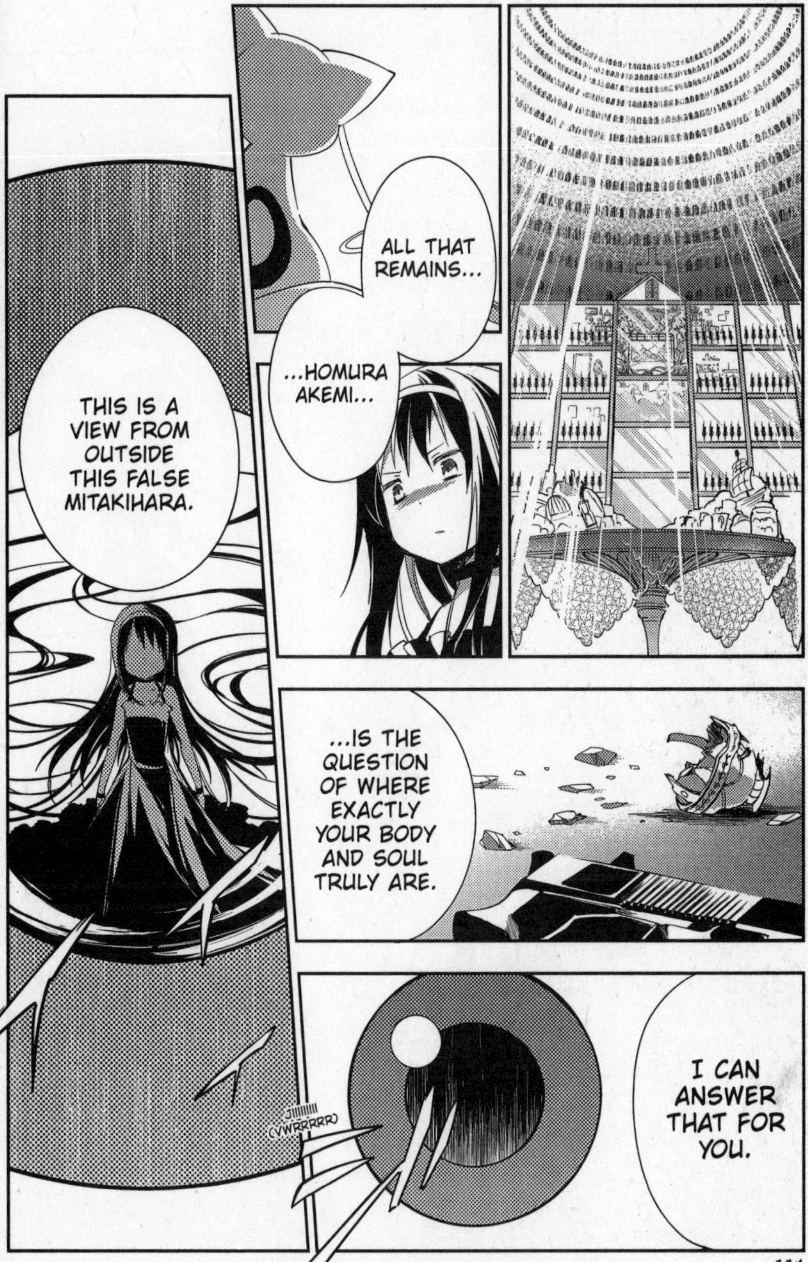
ALL THAT REMAINS...
...HOMURA AKEMI...
...IS THE QUESTION OF WHERE EXACTLY YOUR BODY AND SOUL TRULY ARE.
I CAN ANSWER THAT FOR YOU.
JIIIIIIIIII (VWRRRRR)
THIS IS A VIEW FROM OUTSIDE THIS FALSE MITAKIHARA.

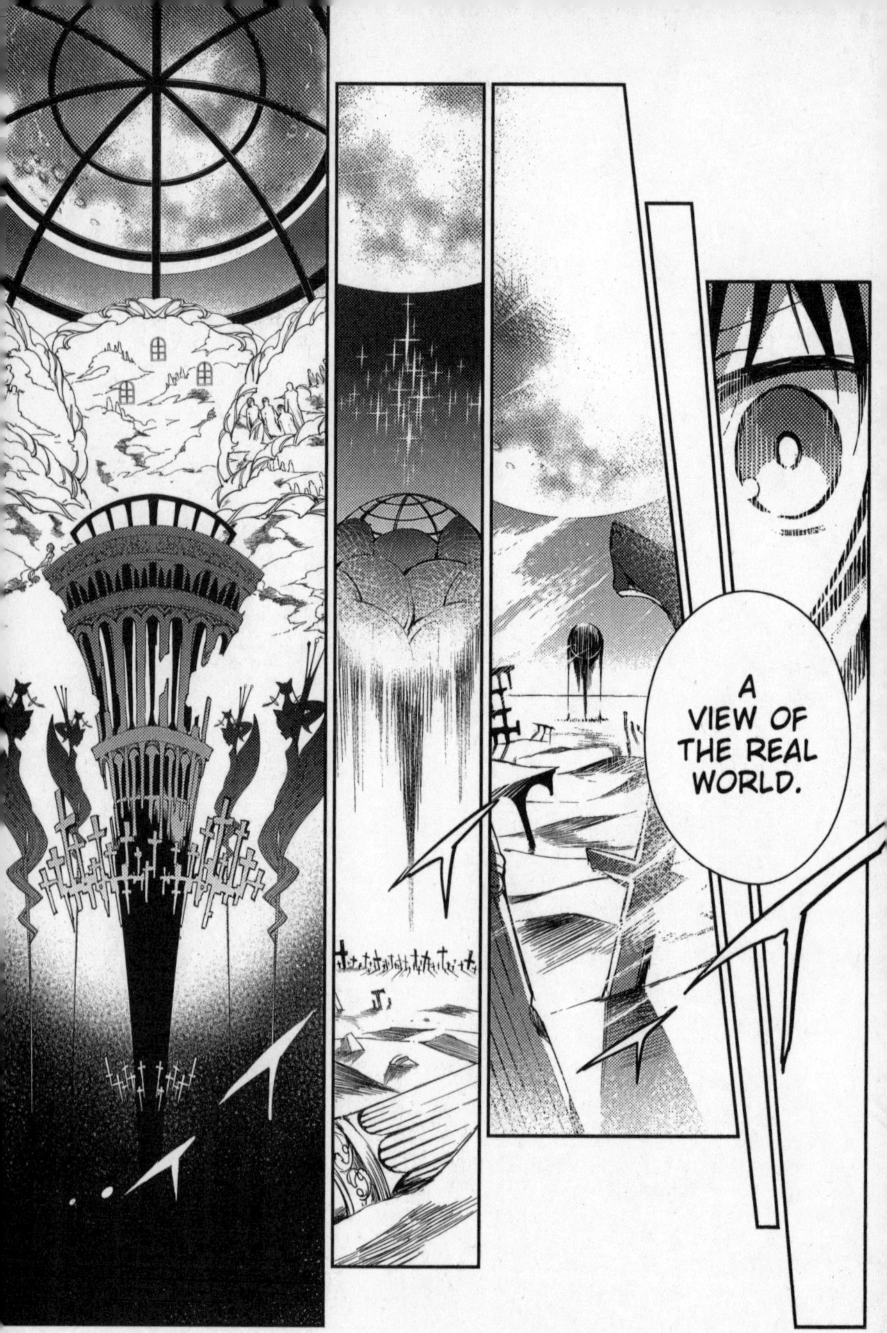
A VIEW OF THE REAL WORLD.

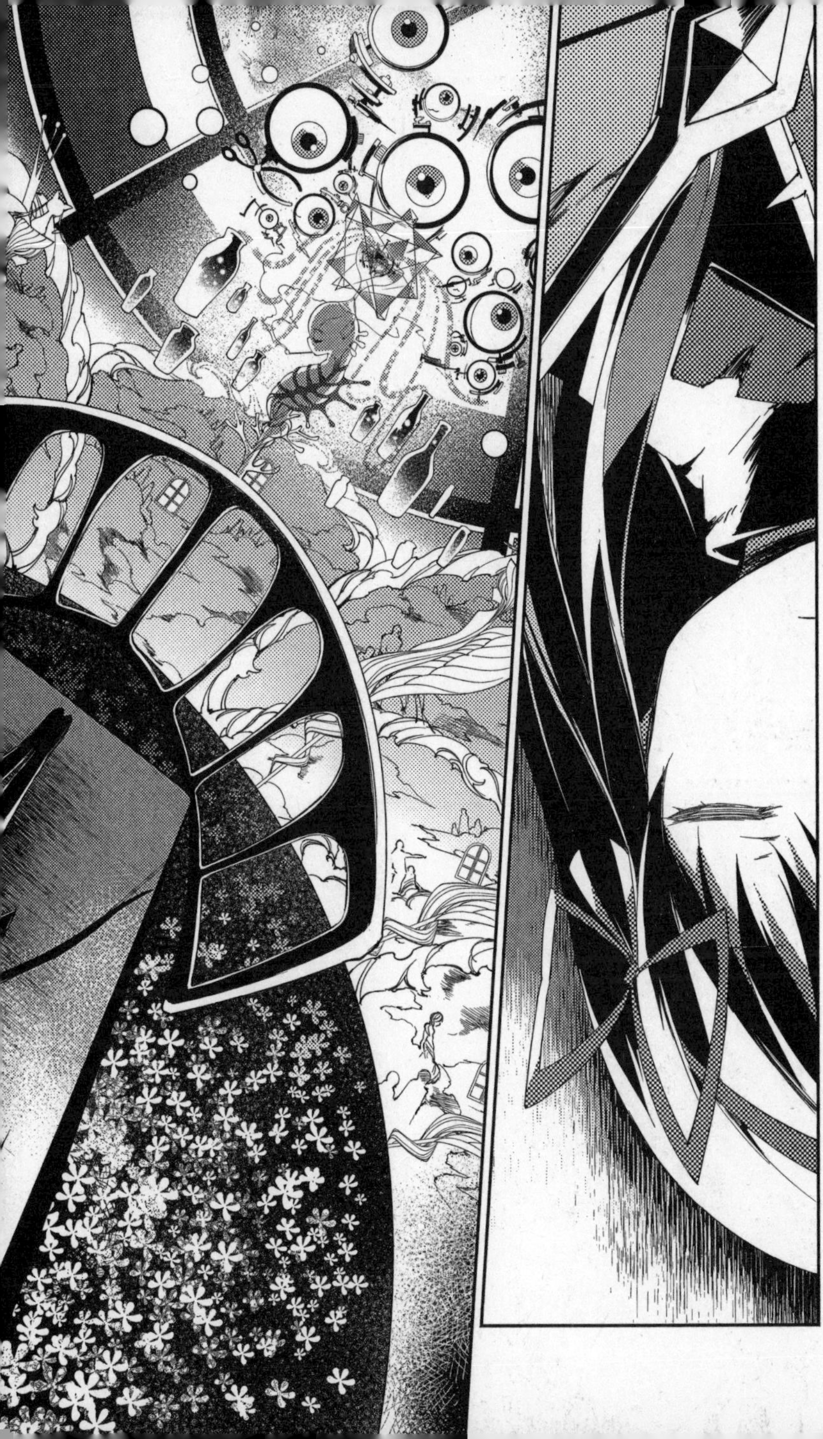

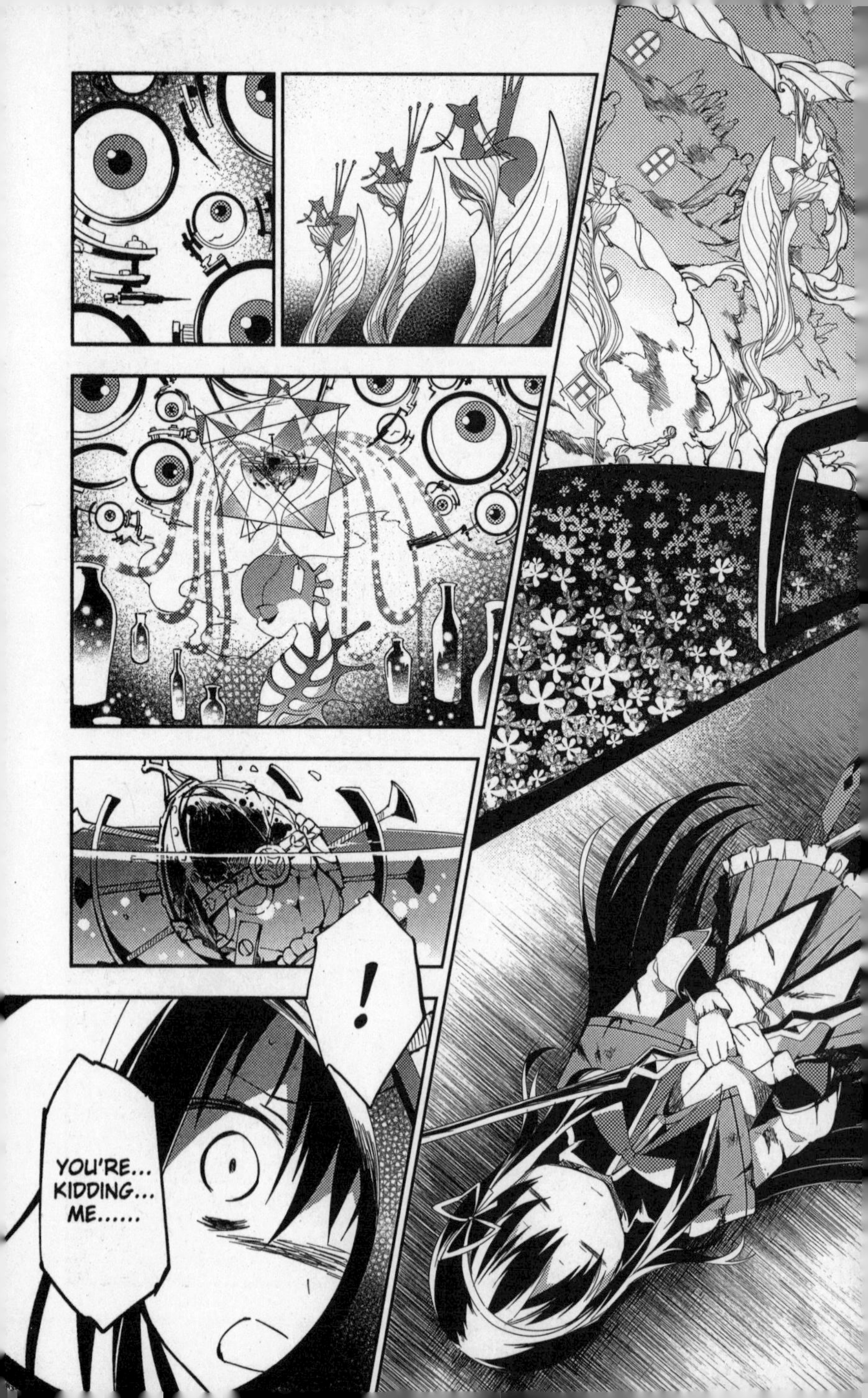
!
YOU'RE... KIDDING... ME......

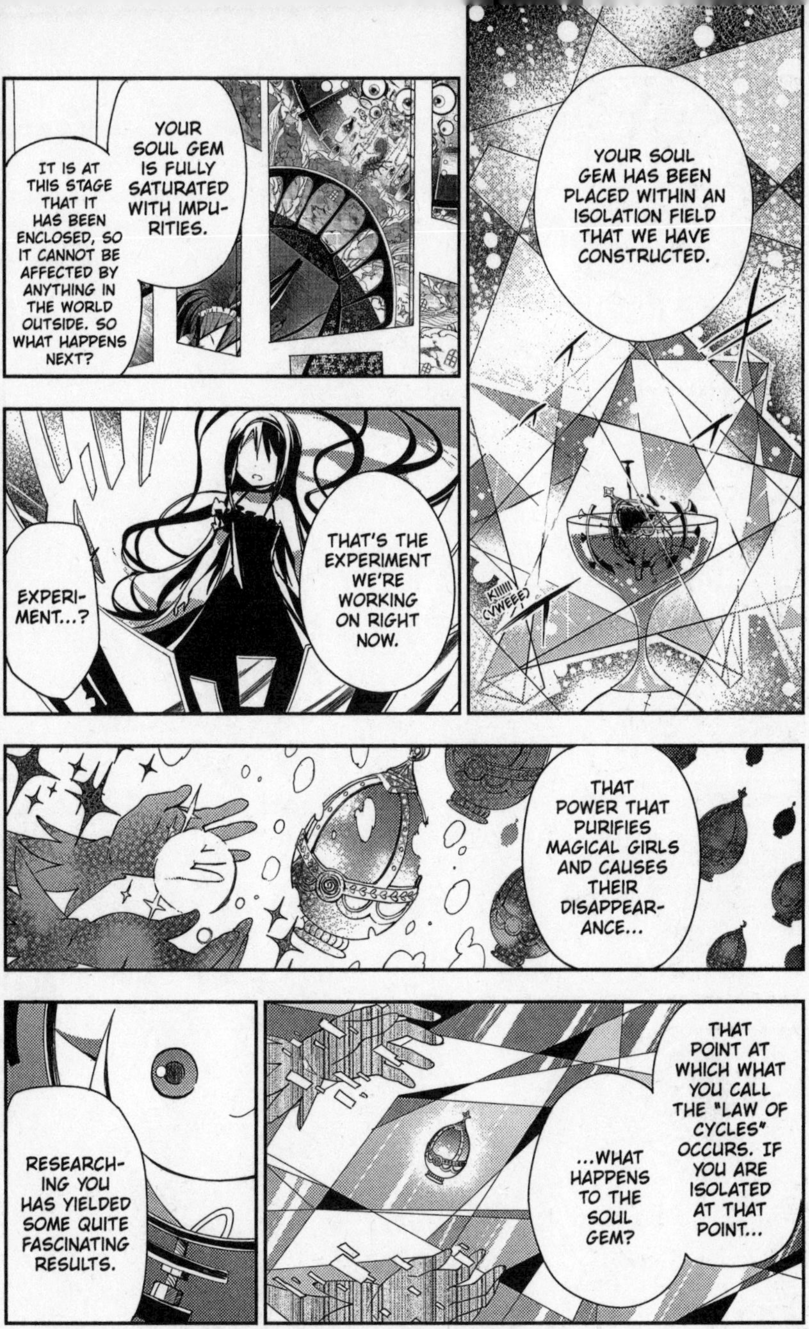
YOUR SOUL GEM HAS BEEN PLACED WITHIN AN ISOLATION FIELD THAT WE HAVE CONSTRUCTED.
KIIIIII (VWEEE)
YOUR SOUL GEM IS FULLY SATURATED WITH IMPURITIES.
IT IS AT THIS STAGE THAT IT HAS BEEN ENCLOSED, SO IT CANNOT BE AFFECTED BY ANYTHING IN THE WORLD OUTSIDE. SO WHAT HAPPENS NEXT?
THAT'S THE EXPERIMENT WE'RE WORKING ON RIGHT NOW.
EXPERIMENT...?
THAT POWER THAT PURIFIES MAGICAL GIRLS AND CAUSES THEIR DISAPPEARANCE...
THAT POINT AT WHICH WHAT YOU CALL THE "LAW OF CYCLES" OCCURS. IF YOU ARE ISOLATED AT THAT POINT...
...WHAT HAPPENS TO THE SOUL GEM?
RESEARCHING YOU HAS YIELDED SOME QUITE FASCINATING RESULTS.

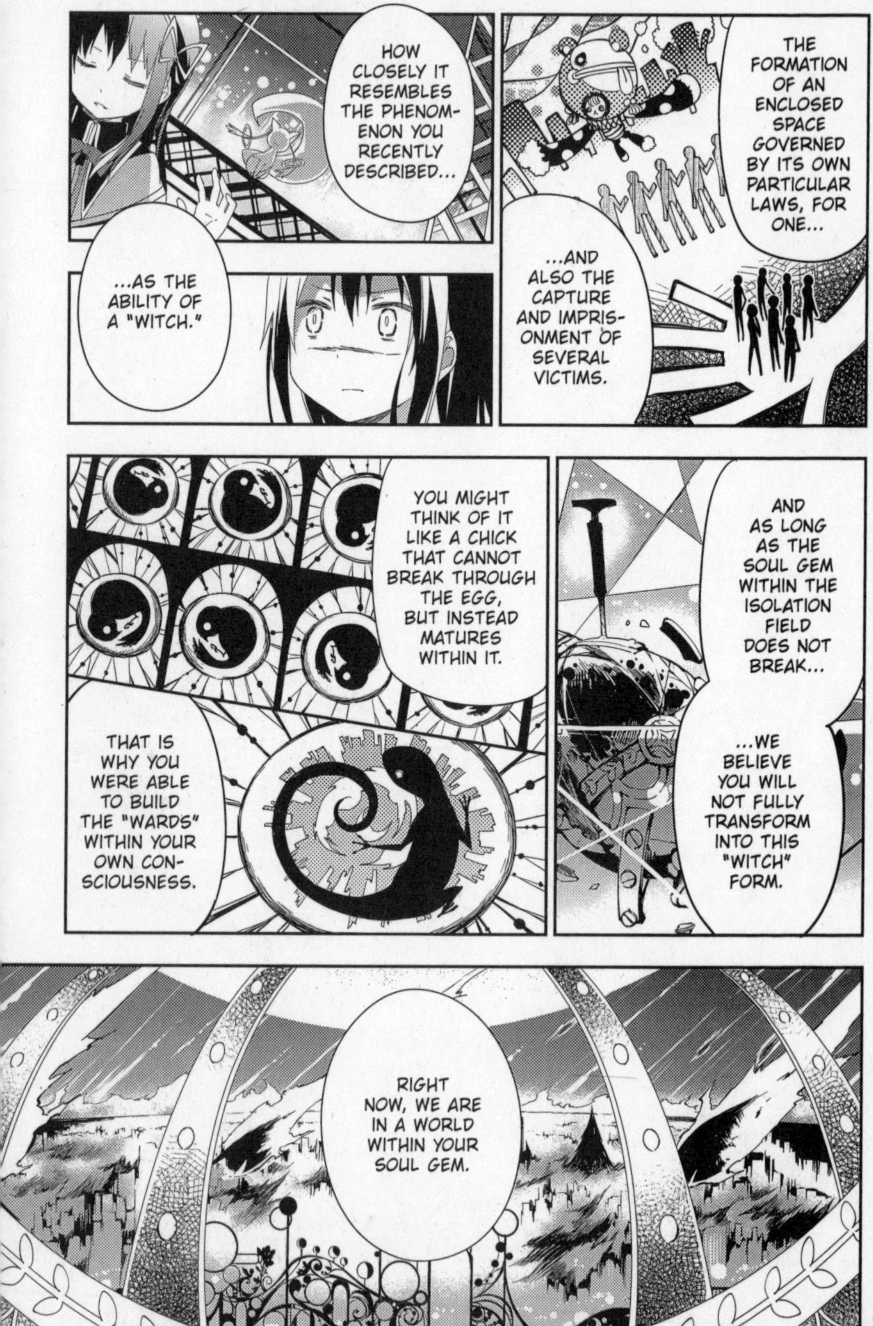
THE FORMATION OF AN ENCLOSED SPACE GOVERNED BY ITS OWN PARTICULAR LAWS, FOR ONE...
...AND ALSO THE CAPTURE AND IMPRISONMENT OF SEVERAL VICTIMS.
HOW CLOSELY IT RESEMBLES THE PHENOMENON YOU RECENTLY DESCRIBED...
...AS THE ABILITY OF A "WITCH."
AND AS LONG AS THE SOUL GEM WITHIN THE ISOLATION FIELD DOES NOT BREAK...
...WE BELIEVE YOU WILL NOT FULLY TRANSFORM INTO THIS "WITCH" FORM.
YOU MIGHT THINK OF IT LIKE A CHICK THAT CANNOT BREAK THROUGH THE EGG, BUT INSTEAD MATURES WITHIN IT.
THAT IS WHY YOU WERE ABLE TO BUILD THE "WARDS" WITHIN YOUR OWN CONSCIOUSNESS.
RIGHT NOW, WE ARE IN A WORLD WITHIN YOUR SOUL GEM.

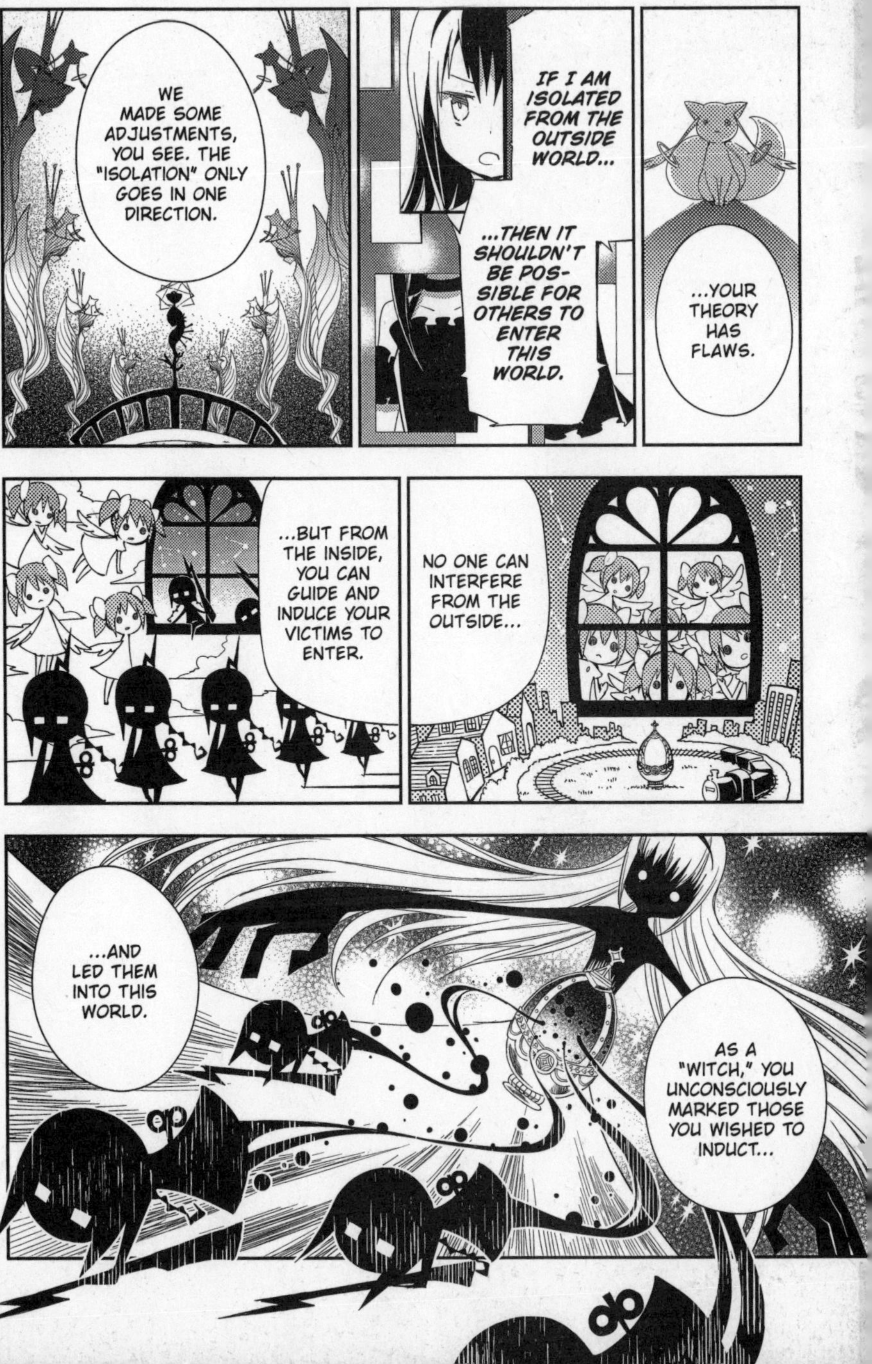
...YOUR THEORY HAS FLAWS.
IF I AM ISOLATED FROM THE OUTSIDE WORLD...
...THEN IT SHOULDN'T BE POS-SIBLE FOR OTHERS TO ENTER THIS WORLD.
WE MADE SOME ADJUSTMENTS, YOU SEE. THE "ISOLATION" ONLY GOES IN ONE DIRECTION.
NO ONE CAN INTERFERE FROM THE OUTSIDE...
...BUT FROM THE INSIDE, YOU CAN GUIDE AND INDUCE YOUR VICTIMS TO ENTER.
AS A "WITCH," YOU UNCONSCIOUSLY MARKED THOSE YOU WISHED TO INDUCT...
...AND LED THEM INTO THIS WORLD.

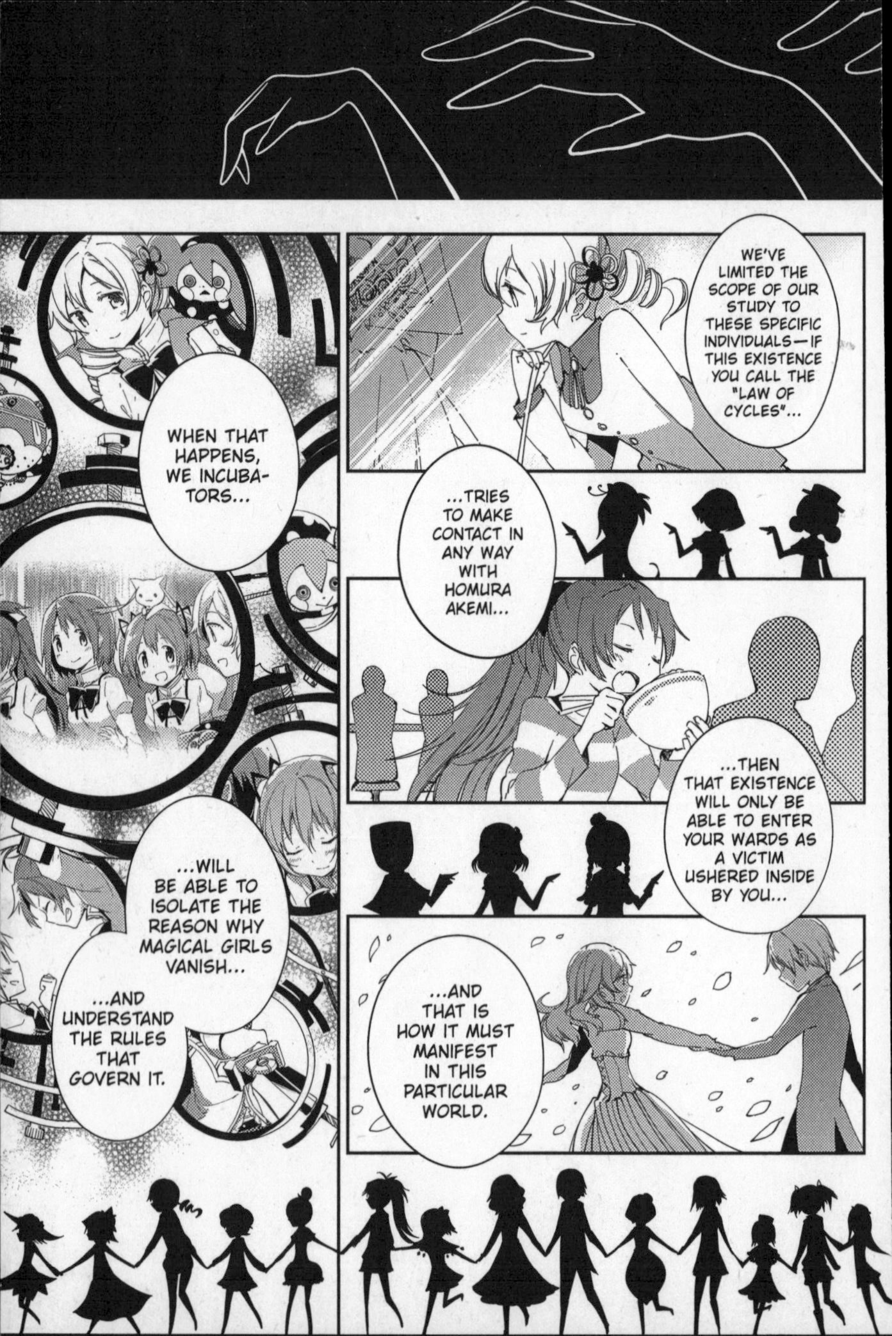
WE'VE LIMITED THE SCOPE OF OUR STUDY TO THESE SPECIFIC INDIVIDUALS—IF THIS EXISTENCE YOU CALL THE "LAW OF CYCLES"...
...TRIES TO MAKE CONTACT IN ANY WAY WITH HOMURA AKEMI...
...THEN THAT EXISTENCE WILL ONLY BE ABLE TO ENTER YOUR WARDS AS A VICTIM USHERED INSIDE BY YOU...
...AND THAT IS HOW IT MUST MANIFEST IN THIS PARTICULAR WORLD.
WHEN THAT HAPPENS, WE INCUBA-TORS...
...WILL BE ABLE TO ISOLATE THE REASON WHY MAGICAL GIRLS VANISH...
...AND UNDERSTAND THE RULES THAT GOVERN IT.

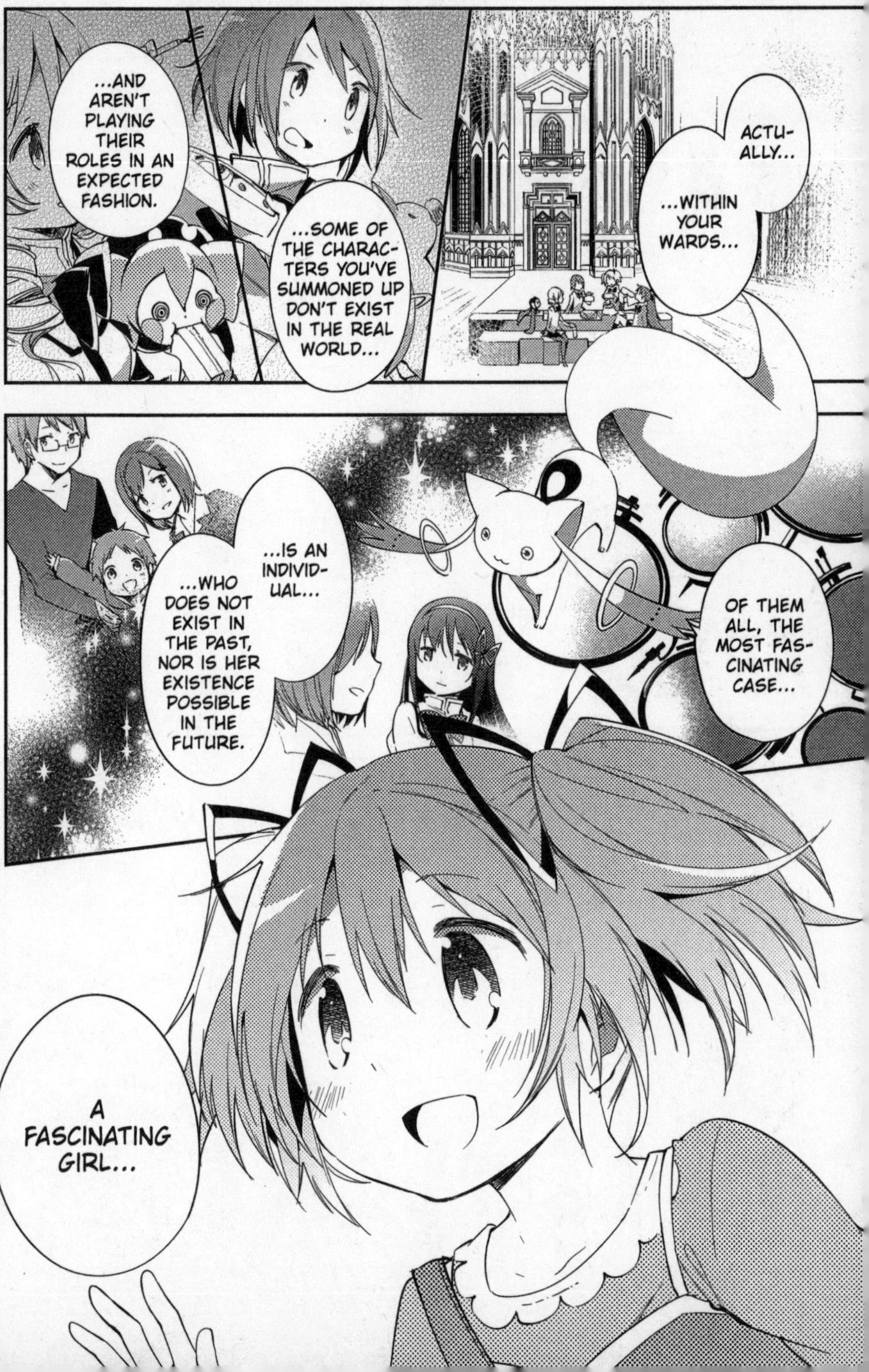
ACTU-ALLY...
...WITHIN YOUR WARDS...
...SOME OF THE CHARAC-TERS YOU'VE SUMMONED UP DON'T EXIST IN THE REAL WORLD...
...AND AREN'T PLAYING THEIR ROLES IN AN EXPECTED FASHION.
OF THEM ALL, THE MOST FAS-CINATING CASE...
...IS AN INDIVID-UAL...
...WHO DOES NOT EXIST IN THE PAST, NOR IS HER EXISTENCE POSSIBLE IN THE FUTURE.
A FASCINATING GIRL...

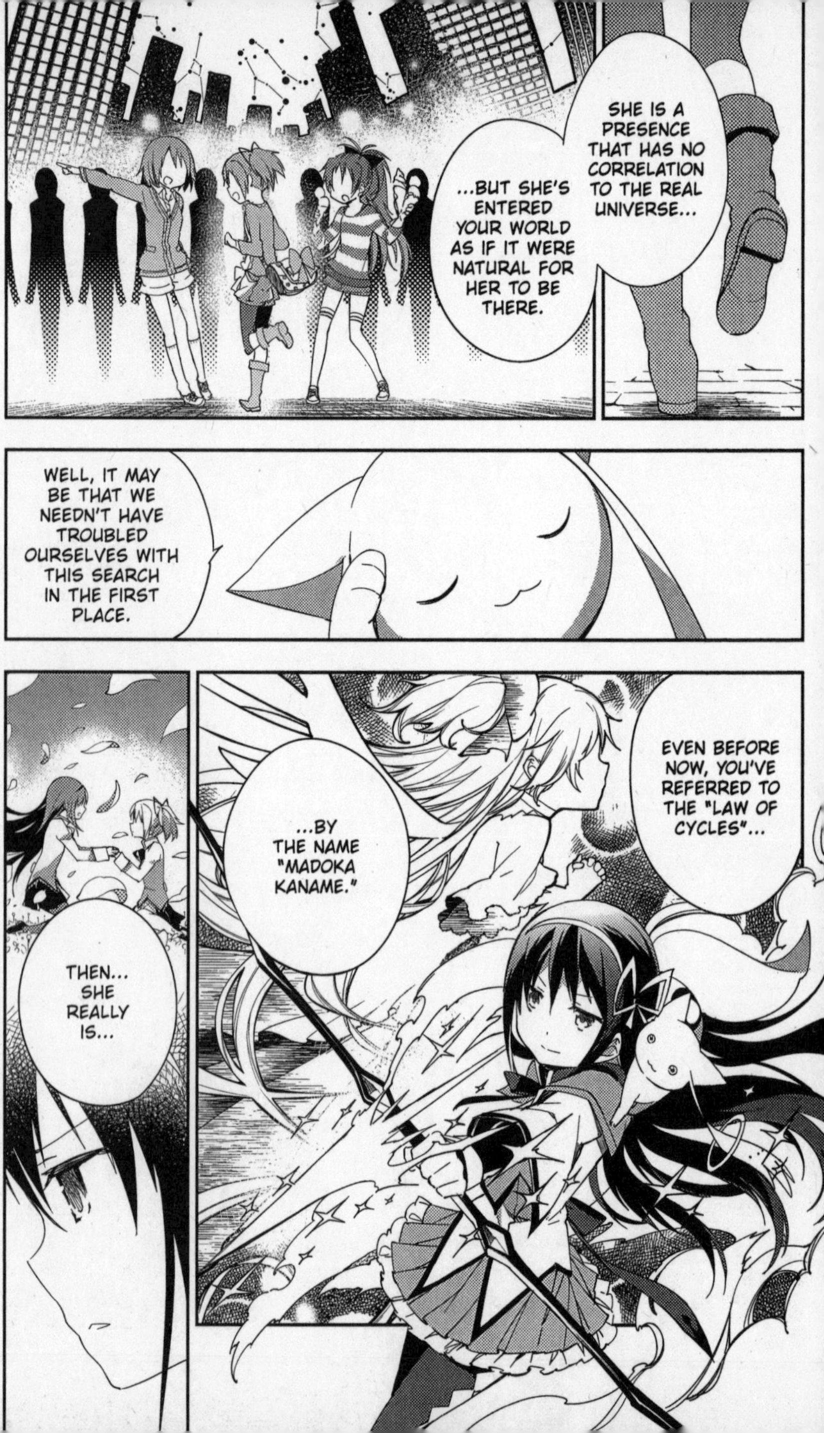
SHE IS A PRESENCE THAT HAS NO CORRELATION TO THE REAL UNIVERSE...
...BUT SHE'S ENTERED YOUR WORLD AS IF IT WERE NATURAL FOR HER TO BE THERE.
WELL, IT MAY BE THAT WE NEEDN'T HAVE TROUBLED OURSELVES WITH THIS SEARCH IN THE FIRST PLACE.
EVEN BEFORE NOW, YOU'VE REFERRED TO THE "LAW OF CYCLES"...
...BY THE NAME "MADOKA KANAME."
THEN... SHE REALLY IS...

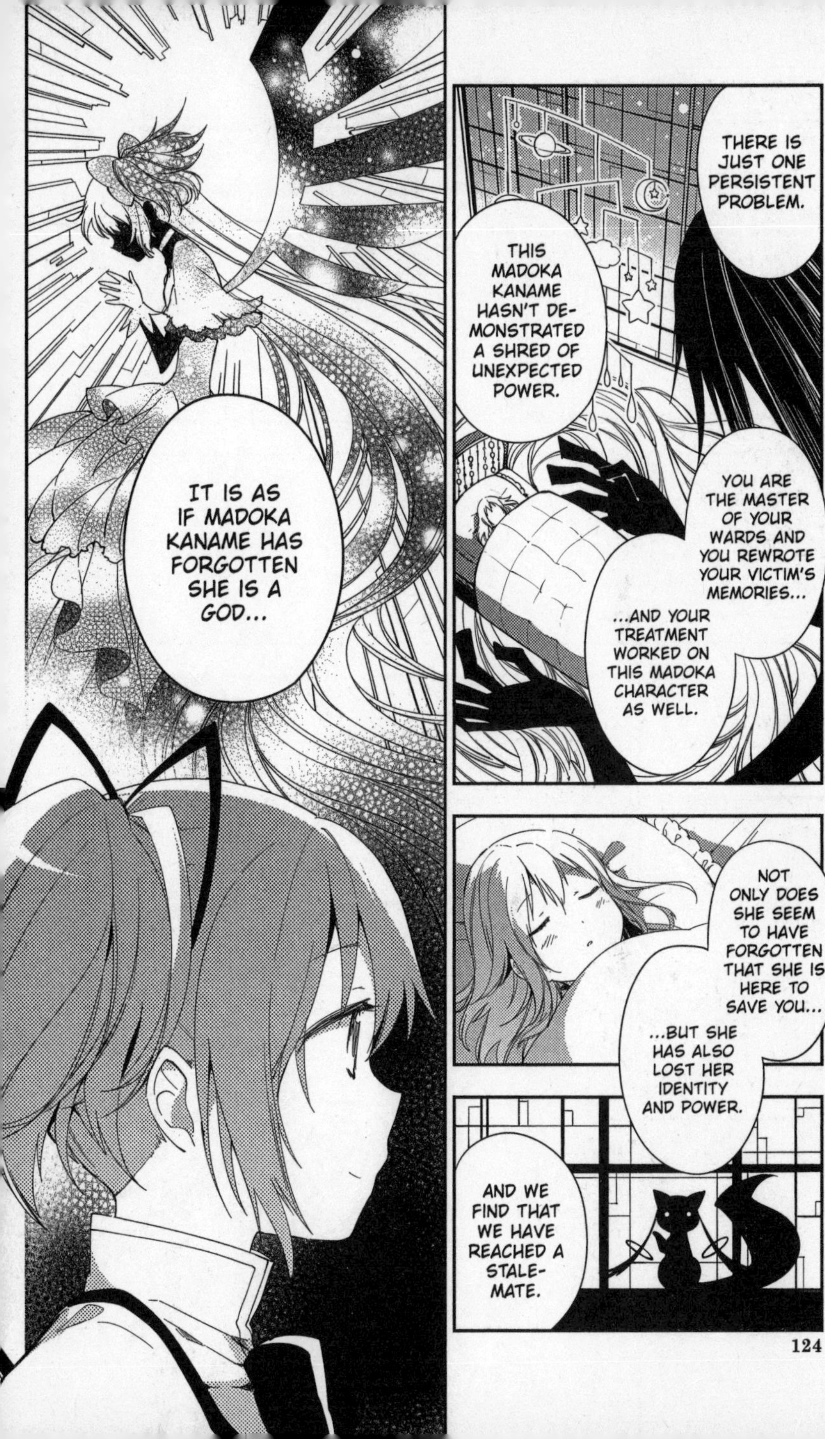
THERE IS JUST ONE PERSISTENT PROBLEM.
THIS MADOKA KANAME HASN'T DE-MONSTRATED A SHRED OF UNEXPECTED POWER.
YOU ARE THE MASTER OF YOUR WARDS AND YOU REWROTE YOUR VICTIM'S MEMORIES...
...AND YOUR TREATMENT WORKED ON THIS MADOKA CHARACTER AS WELL.
NOT ONLY DOES SHE SEEM TO HAVE FORGOTTEN THAT SHE IS HERE TO SAVE YOU...
...BUT SHE HAS ALSO LOST HER IDENTITY AND POWER.
AND WE FIND THAT WE HAVE REACHED A STALE-MATE.
IT IS AS IF MADOKA KANAME HAS FORGOTTEN SHE IS A GOD...

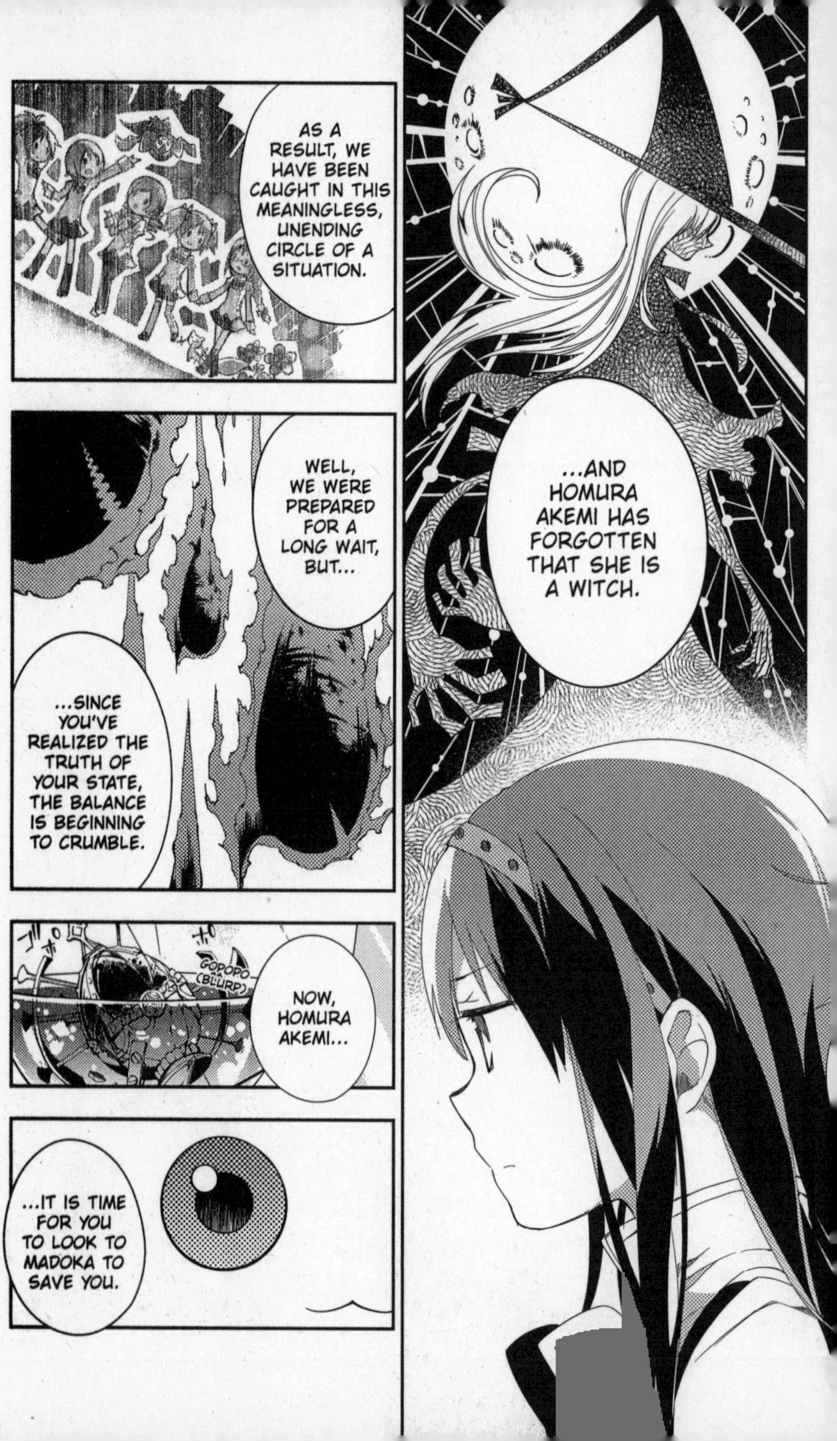
...AND HOMURA AKEMI HAS FORGOTTEN THAT SHE IS A WITCH.
AS A RESULT, WE HAVE BEEN CAUGHT IN THIS MEANINGLESS, UNENDING CIRCLE OF A SITUATION.
WELL, WE WERE PREPARED FOR A LONG WAIT, BUT...
...SINCE YOU'VE REALIZED THE TRUTH OF YOUR STATE, THE BALANCE IS BEGINNING TO CRUMBLE.
GOPOPO (BLURP)
NOW, HOMURA AKEMI...
...IT IS TIME FOR YOU TO LOOK TO MADOKA TO SAVE YOU.

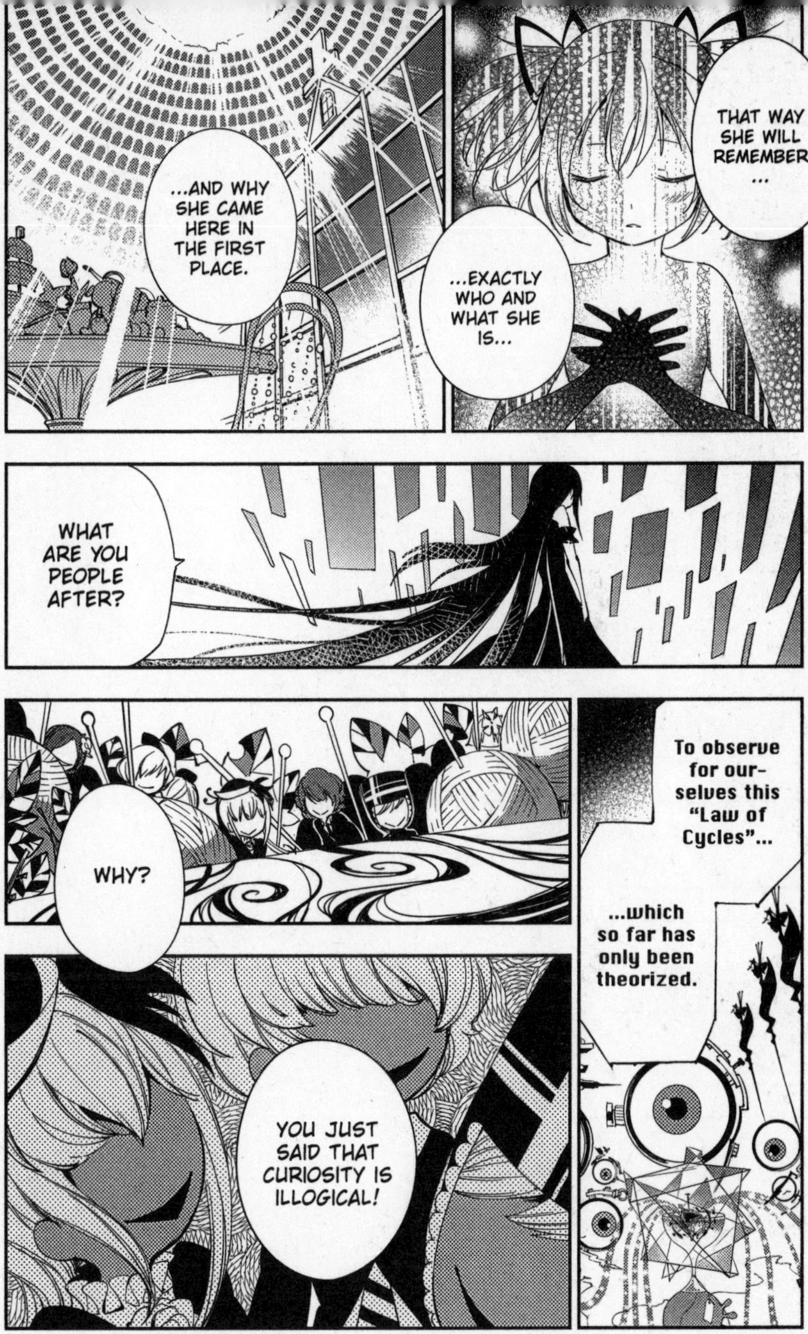
THAT WAY SHE WILL REMEMBER...
...EXACTLY WHO AND WHAT SHE IS...
...AND WHY SHE CAME HERE IN THE FIRST PLACE.
WHAT ARE YOU PEOPLE AFTER?
To observe for ourselves this "Law of Cycles"...
...which so far has only been theorized.
WHY?
YOU JUST SAID THAT CURIOSITY IS ILLOGICAL!

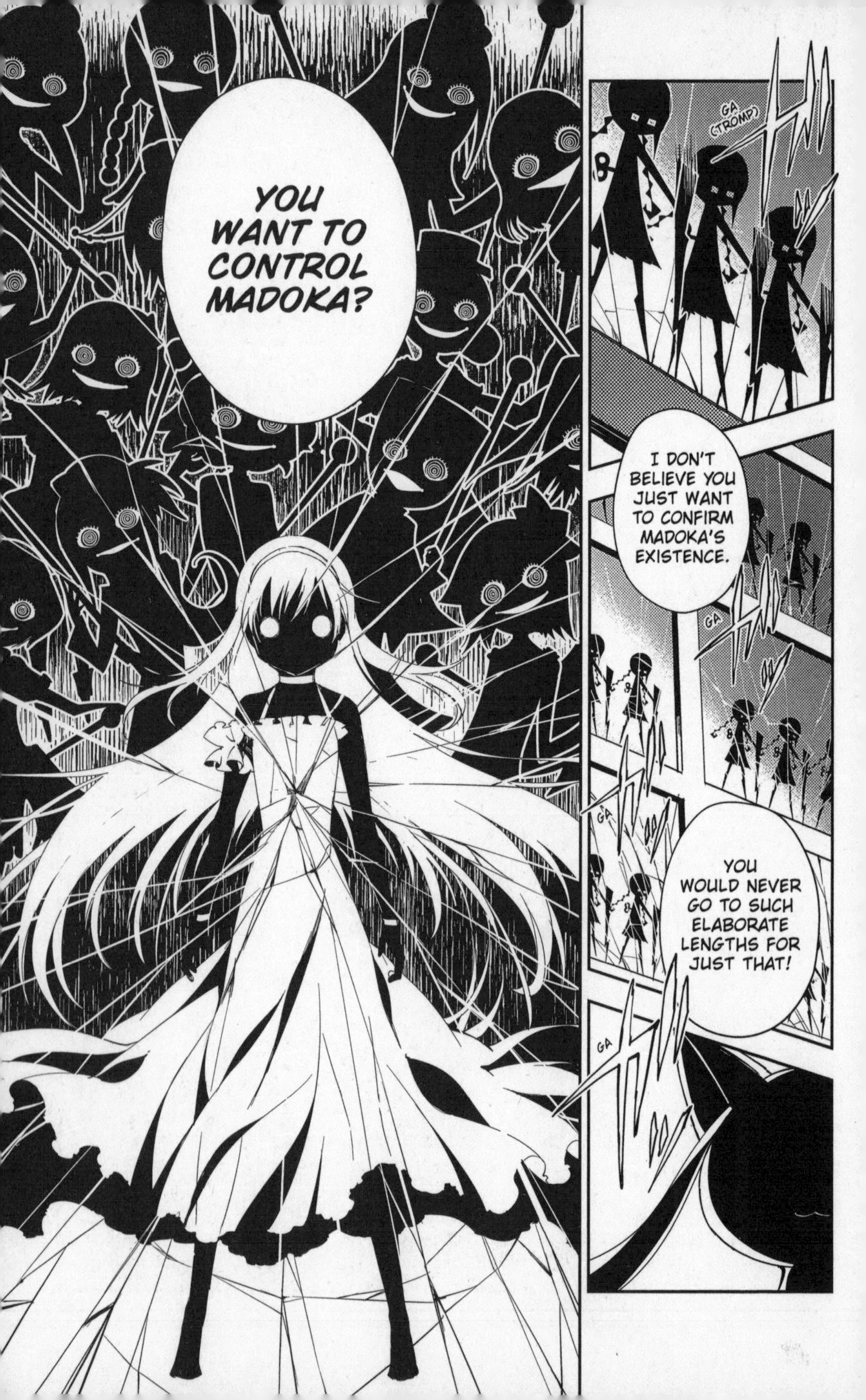
GA (TROMP)
I DON'T BELIEVE YOU JUST WANT TO CONFIRM MADOKA'S EXISTENCE.
GA
GA
YOU WOULD NEVER GO TO SUCH ELABORATE LENGTHS FOR JUST THAT!
GA
YOU WANT TO CONTROL MADOKA?

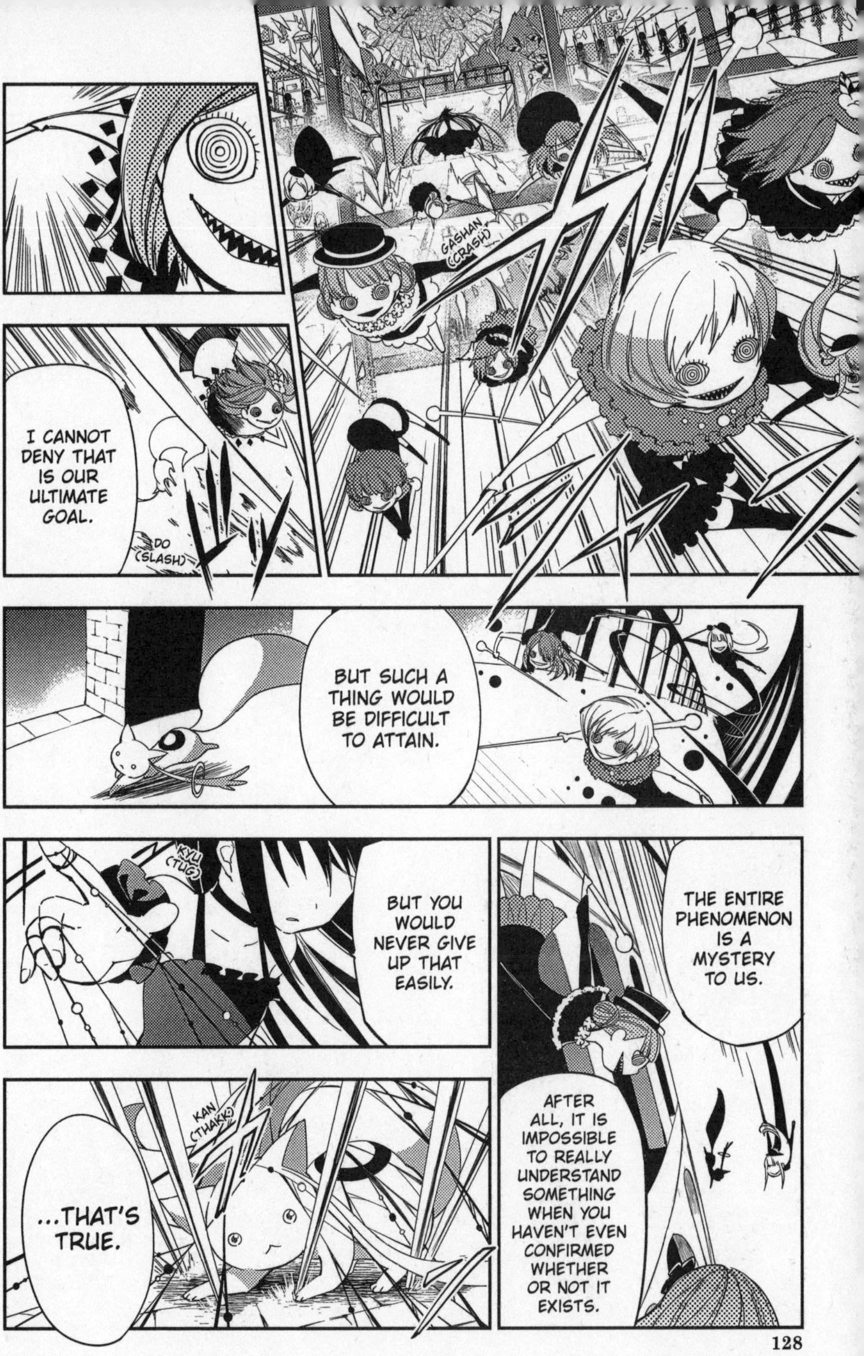
GASHAN (CRASH)
I CANNOT DENY THAT IS OUR ULTIMATE GOAL.
DO (SLASH)
BUT SUCH A THING WOULD BE DIFFICULT TO ATTAIN.
THE ENTIRE PHENOMENON IS A MYSTERY TO US.
AFTER ALL, IT IS IMPOSSIBLE TO REALLY UNDERSTAND SOMETHING WHEN YOU HAVEN'T EVEN CONFIRMED WHETHER OR NOT IT EXISTS.
BUT YOU WOULD NEVER GIVE UP THAT EASILY.
KYU (TUG)
...THAT'S TRUE.
KAN (THAKK)

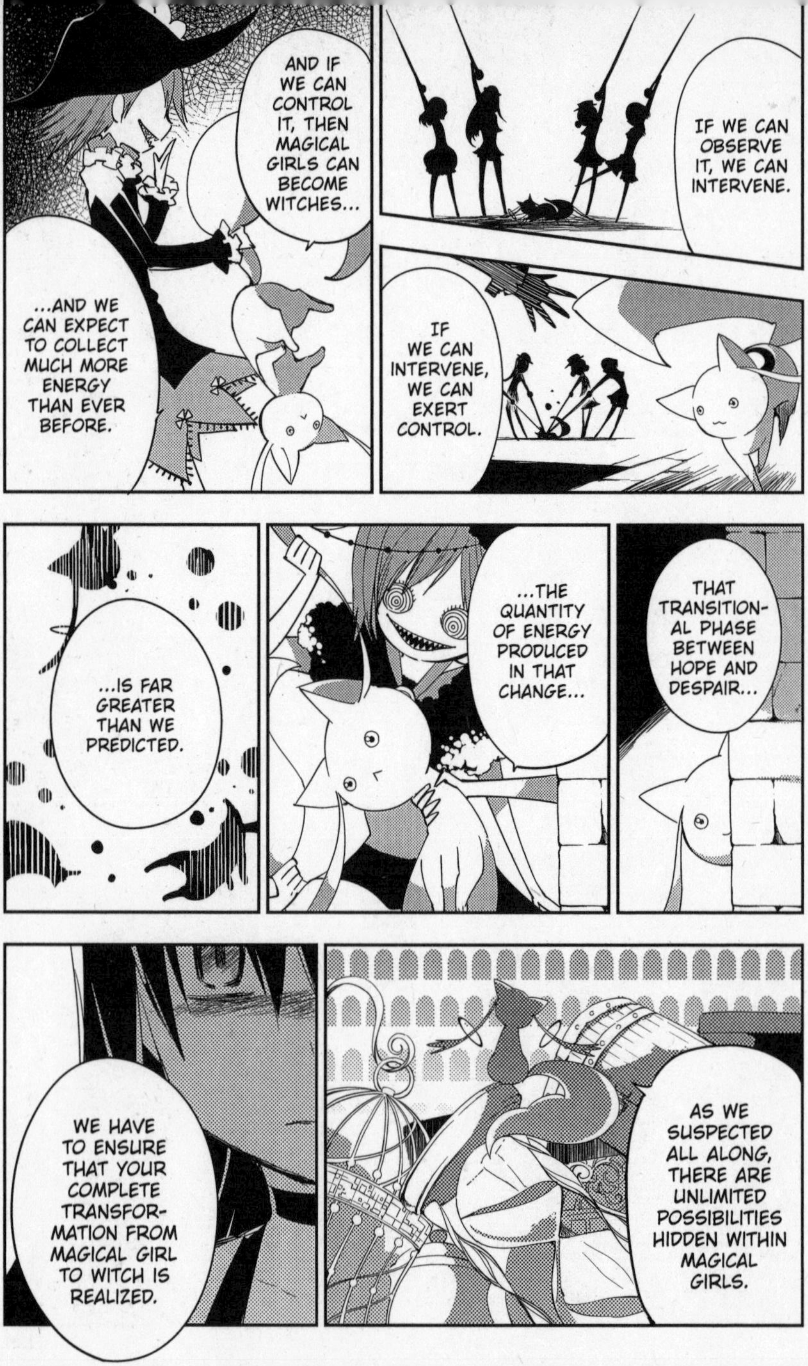
IF WE CAN OBSERVE IT, WE CAN INTERVENE.
IF WE CAN INTERVENE, WE CAN EXERT CONTROL.
AND IF WE CAN CONTROL IT, THEN MAGICAL GIRLS CAN BECOME WITCHES...
...AND WE CAN EXPECT TO COLLECT MUCH MORE ENERGY THAN EVER BEFORE.
THAT TRANSITION-AL PHASE BETWEEN HOPE AND DESPAIR...
...THE QUANTITY OF ENERGY PRODUCED IN THAT CHANGE...
...IS FAR GREATER THAN WE PREDICTED.
AS WE SUSPECTED ALL ALONG, THERE ARE UNLIMITED POSSIBILITIES HIDDEN WITHIN MAGICAL GIRLS.
WE HAVE TO ENSURE THAT YOUR COMPLETE TRANSFOR-MATION FROM MAGICAL GIRL TO WITCH IS REALIZED.

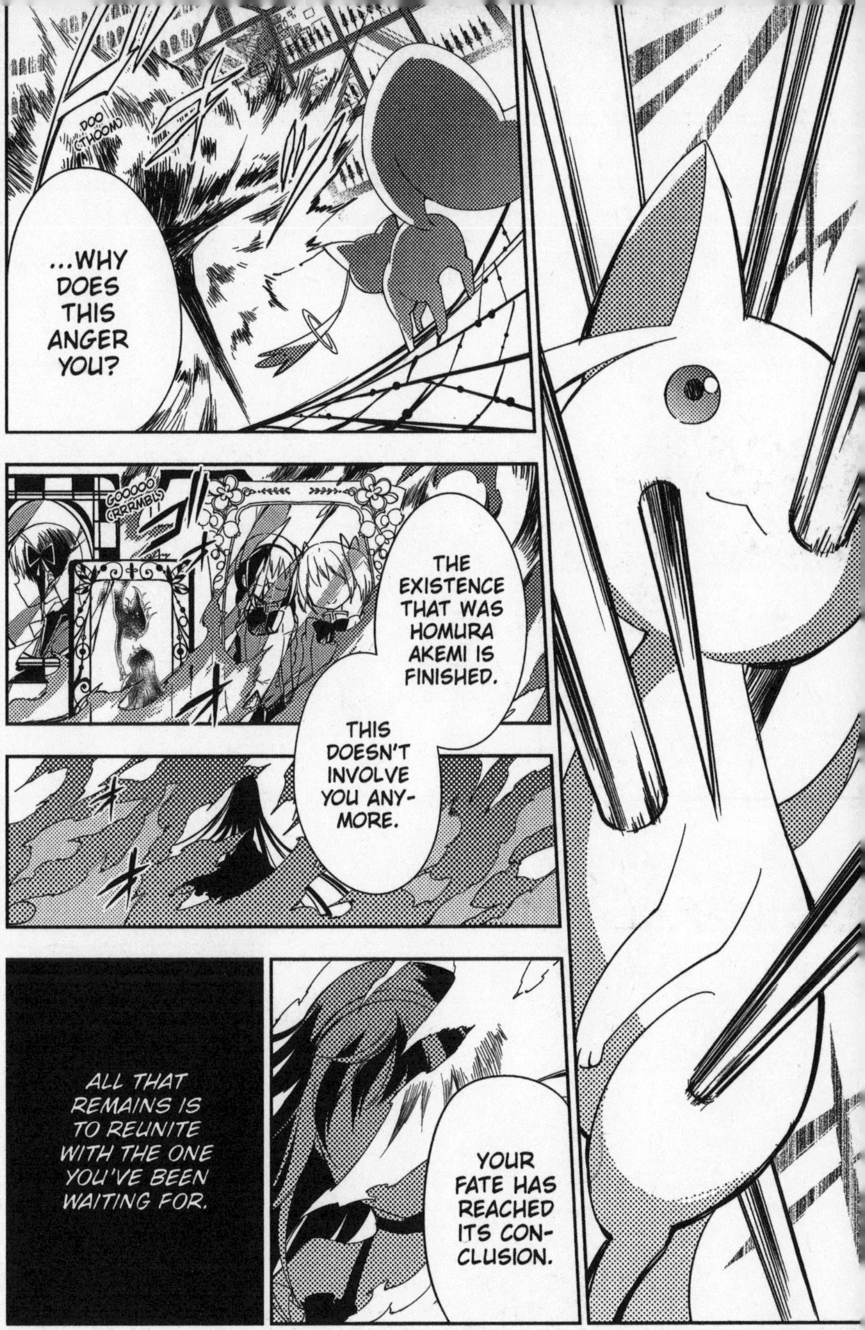
DOO (THOOM)
...WHY DOES THIS ANGER YOU?
GOOOOO (RRRMBL)
THE EXISTENCE THAT WAS HOMURA AKEMI IS FINISHED.
THIS DOESN'T INVOLVE YOU ANY-MORE.
YOUR FATE HAS REACHED ITS CON-CLUSION.
ALL THAT REMAINS IS TO REUNITE WITH THE ONE YOU'VE BEEN WAITING FOR.

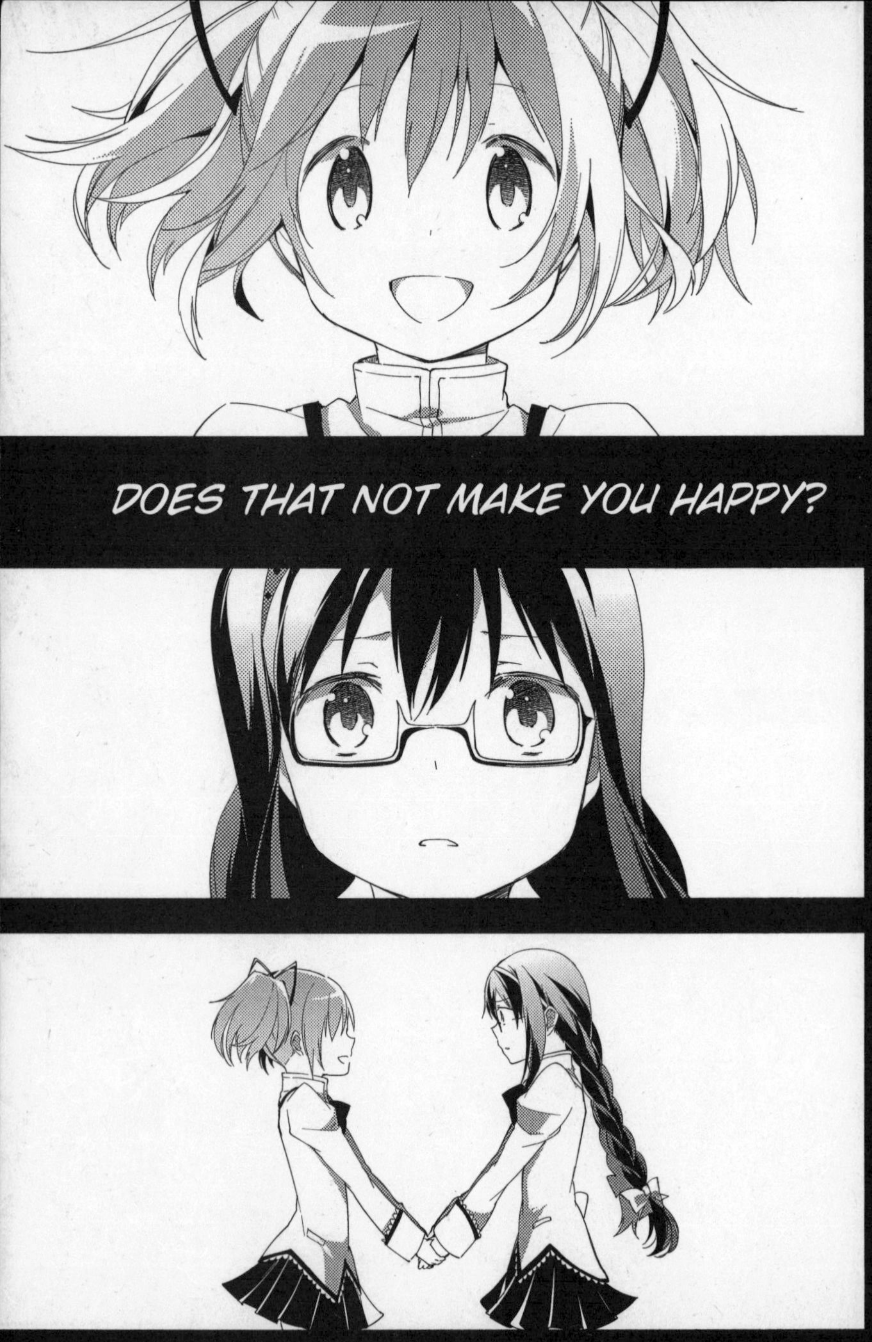
DOES THAT NOT MAKE YOU HAPPY?

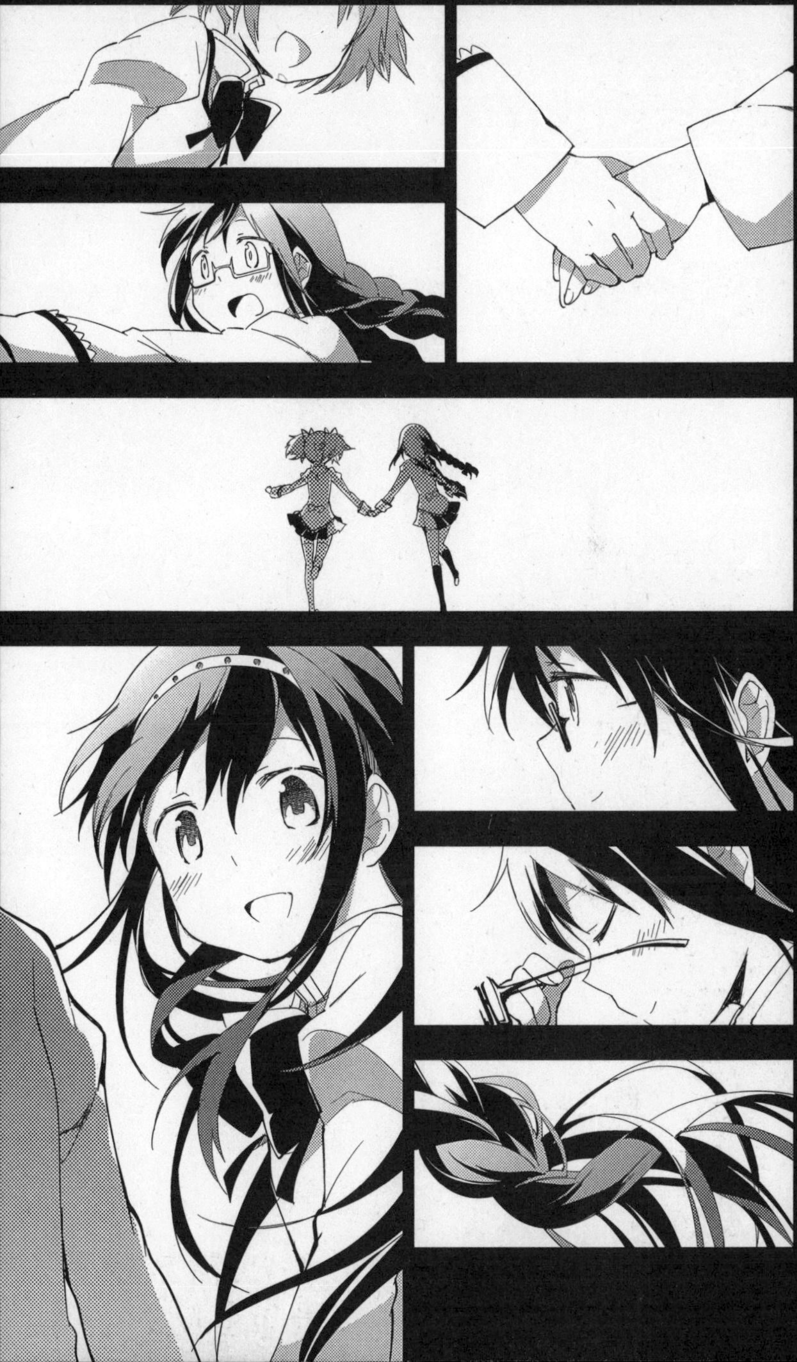

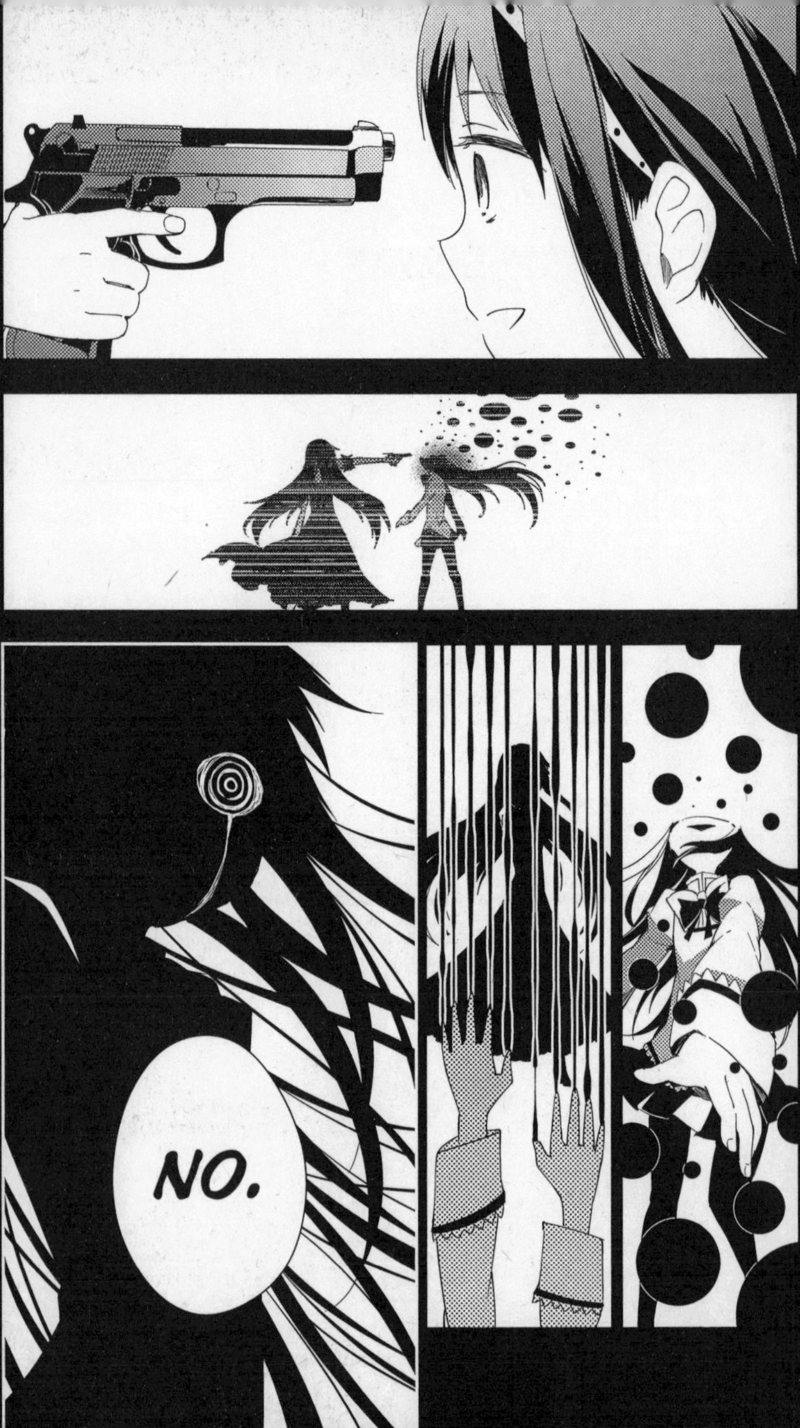
NO.

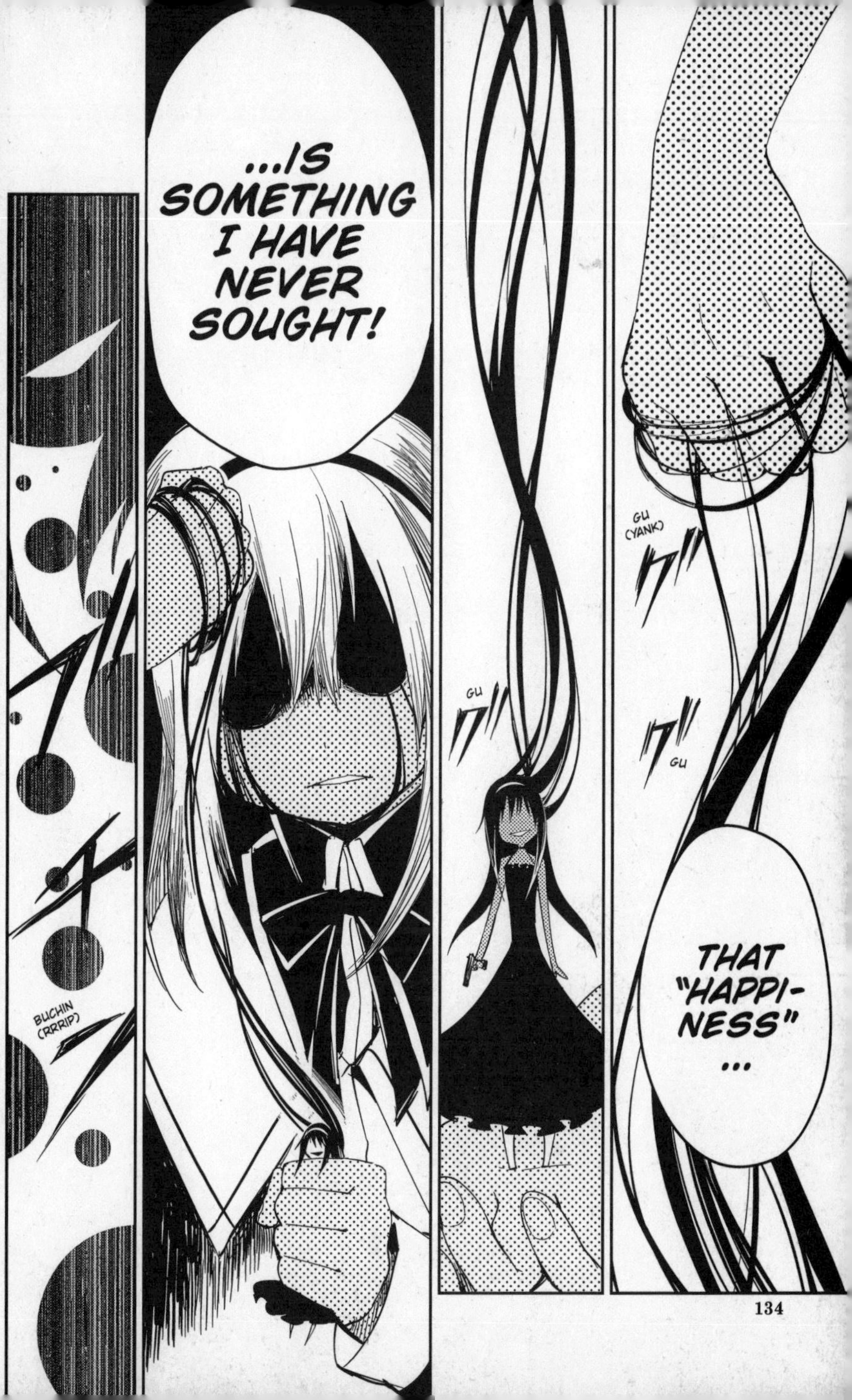
GU (YANK)
GU
THAT "HAPPI-NESS" ...
GU
...IS SOMETHING I HAVE NEVER SOUGHT!
BUCHIN (RRRIP)

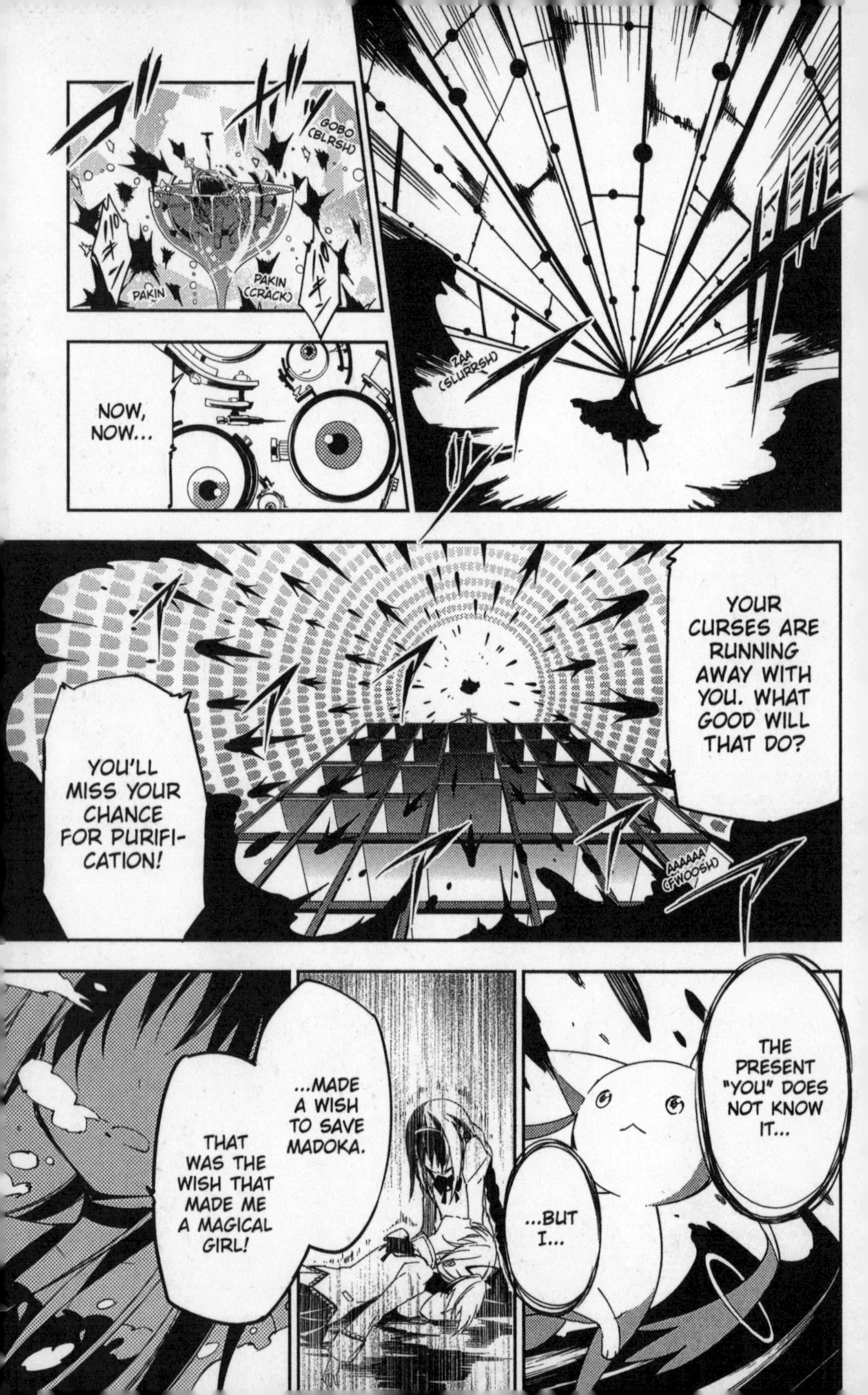
ZAA (SLURRSH)
GOBO (BLRSH)
PAKIN (CRACK)
PAKIN
NOW, NOW...
YOUR CURSES ARE RUNNING AWAY WITH YOU. WHAT GOOD WILL THAT DO?
AAAAAA (FWOOSH)
YOU'LL MISS YOUR CHANCE FOR PURIFI-CATION!
THE PRESENT "YOU" DOES NOT KNOW IT...
...BUT I...
...MADE A WISH TO SAVE MADOKA.
THAT WAS THE WISH THAT MADE ME A MAGICAL GIRL!

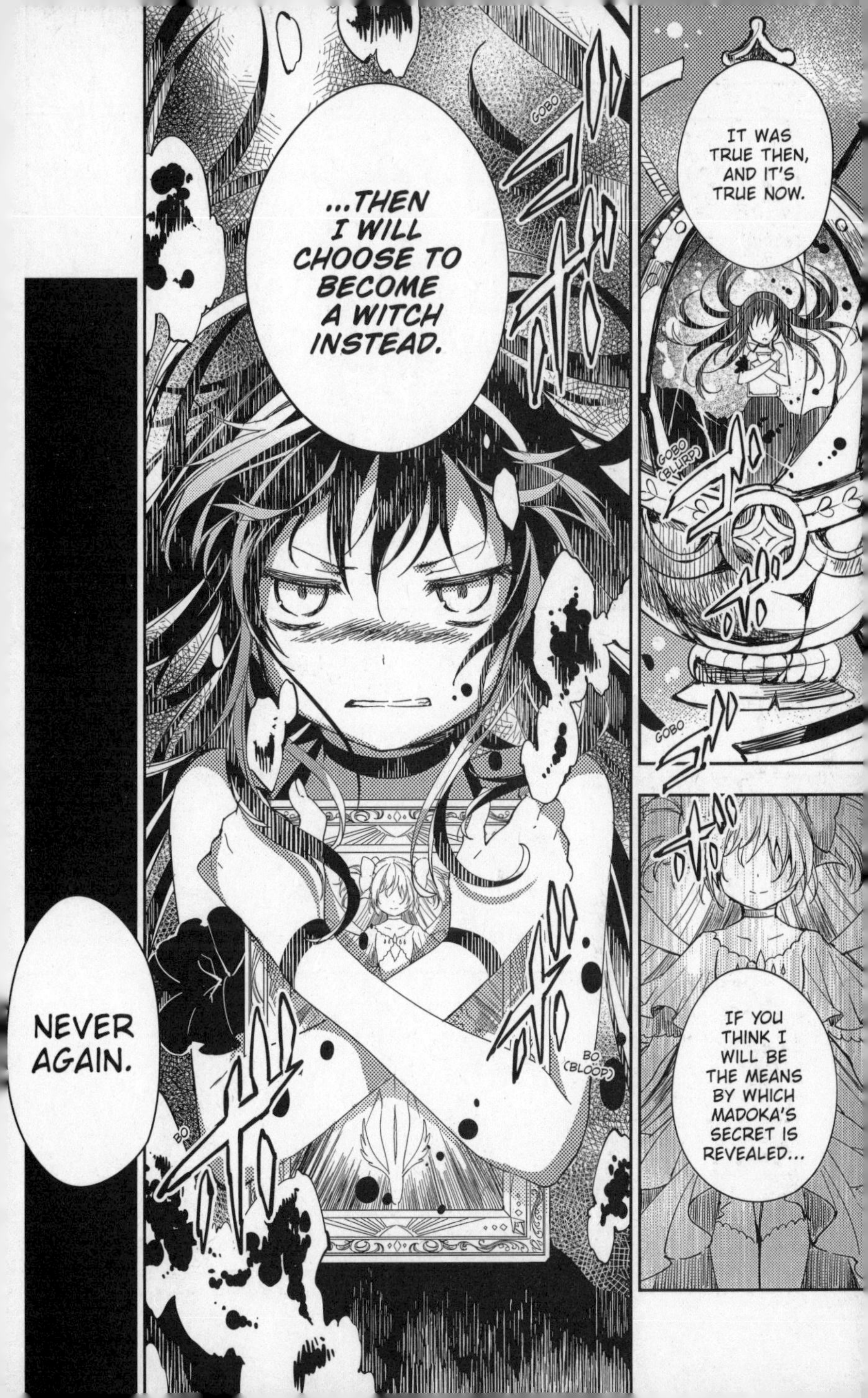
IT WAS TRUE THEN, AND IT'S TRUE NOW.
GOBO (BLURP)
GOBO
IF YOU THINK I WILL BE THE MEANS BY WHICH MADOKA'S SECRET IS REVEALED...
GOBO
...THEN I WILL CHOOSE TO BECOME A WITCH INSTEAD.
BO (BLOOP)
BO
NEVER AGAIN.

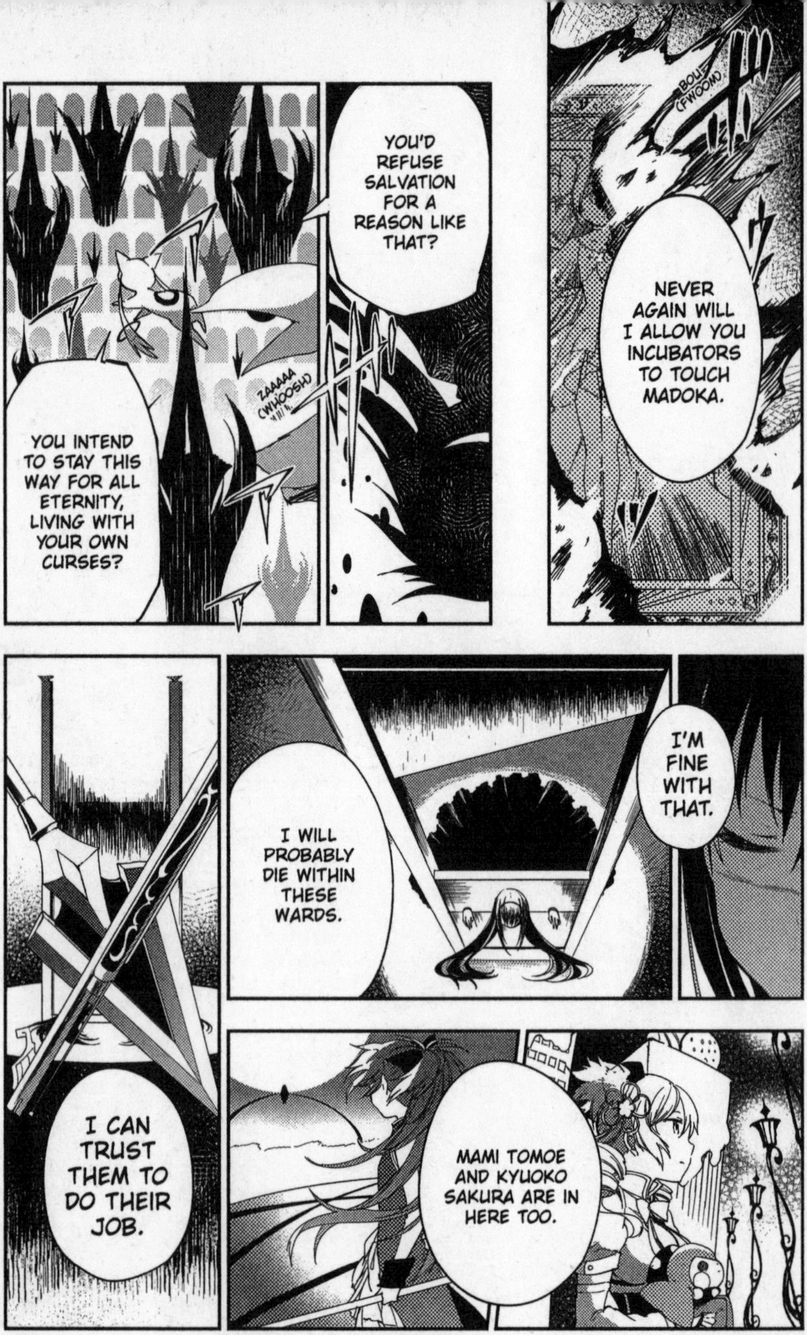
BOU (FWOOM)
NEVER AGAIN WILL I ALLOW YOU INCUBATORS TO TOUCH MADOKA.
YOU'D REFUSE SALVATION FOR A REASON LIKE THAT?
ZAAAAA (WHOOSH)
YOU INTEND TO STAY THIS WAY FOR ALL ETERNITY, LIVING WITH YOUR OWN CURSES?
I'M FINE WITH THAT.
I WILL PROBABLY DIE WITHIN THESE WARDS.
MAMI TOMOE AND KYUOKO SAKURA ARE IN HERE TOO.
I CAN TRUST THEM TO DO THEIR JOB.

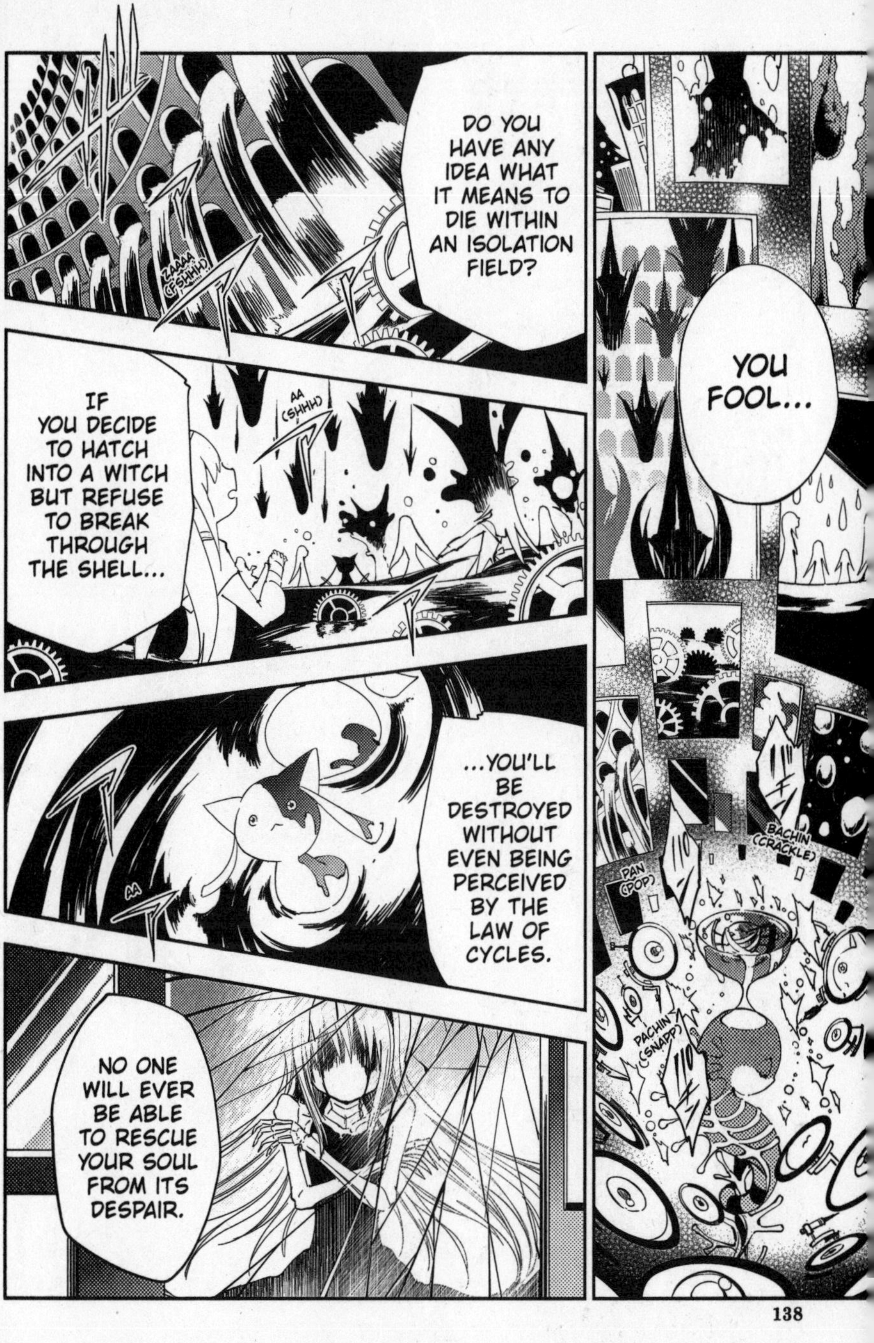
YOU FOOL...
BACHIN (CRACKLE)
PAN (POP)
PACHIN (SNAPP)
DO YOU HAVE ANY IDEA WHAT IT MEANS TO DIE WITHIN AN ISOLATION FIELD?
ZAAAA (FSHHH)
AA (SHHH)
IF YOU DECIDE TO HATCH INTO A WITCH BUT REFUSE TO BREAK THROUGH THE SHELL...
...YOU'LL BE DESTROYED WITHOUT EVEN BEING PERCEIVED BY THE LAW OF CYCLES.
AA
NO ONE WILL EVER BE ABLE TO RESCUE YOUR SOUL FROM ITS DESPAIR.

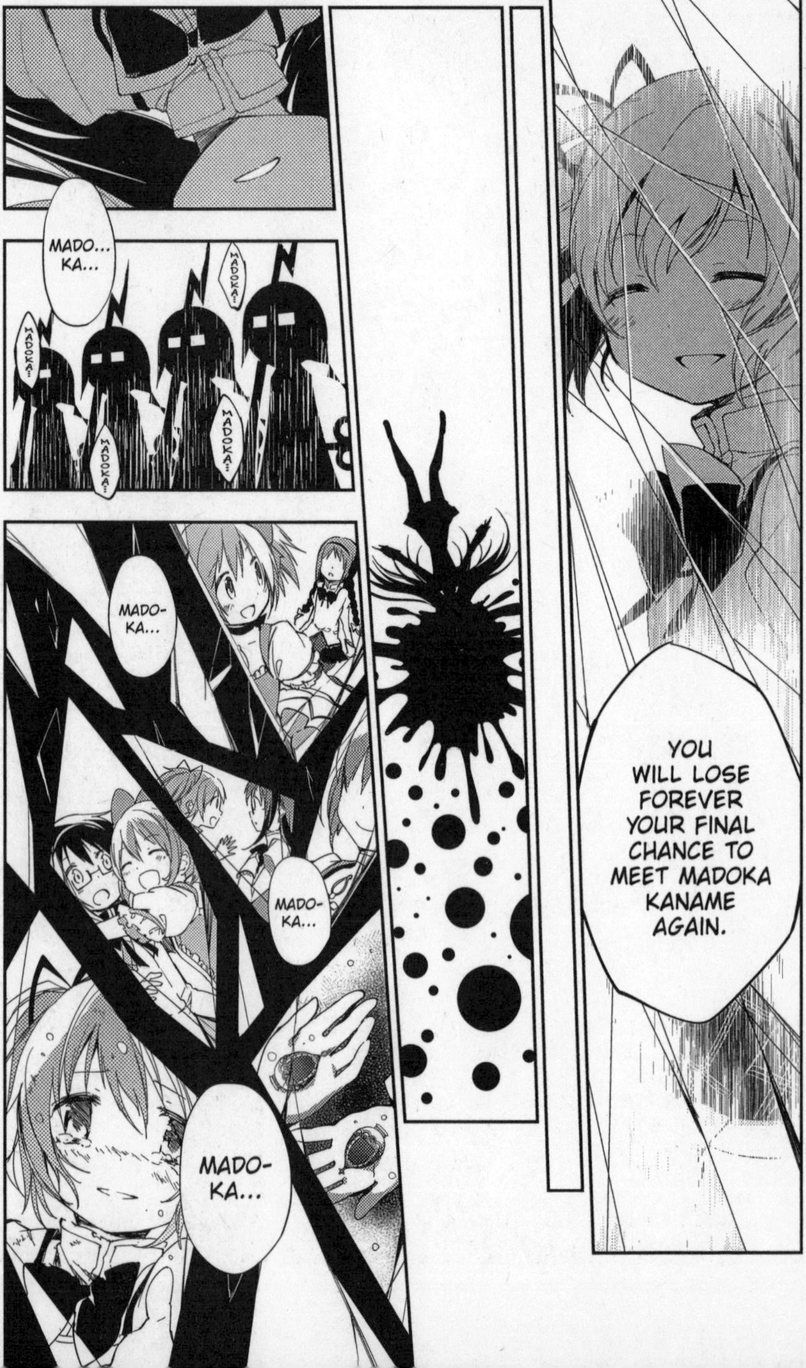

YOU WILL LOSE FOREVER YOUR FINAL CHANCE TO MEET MADOKA KANAME AGAIN.
MADOKA...
MADO... KA...
MADOKA...
MADOKA...
MADOKA...
MADO-KA...
MADO-KA...
MADO-KA...

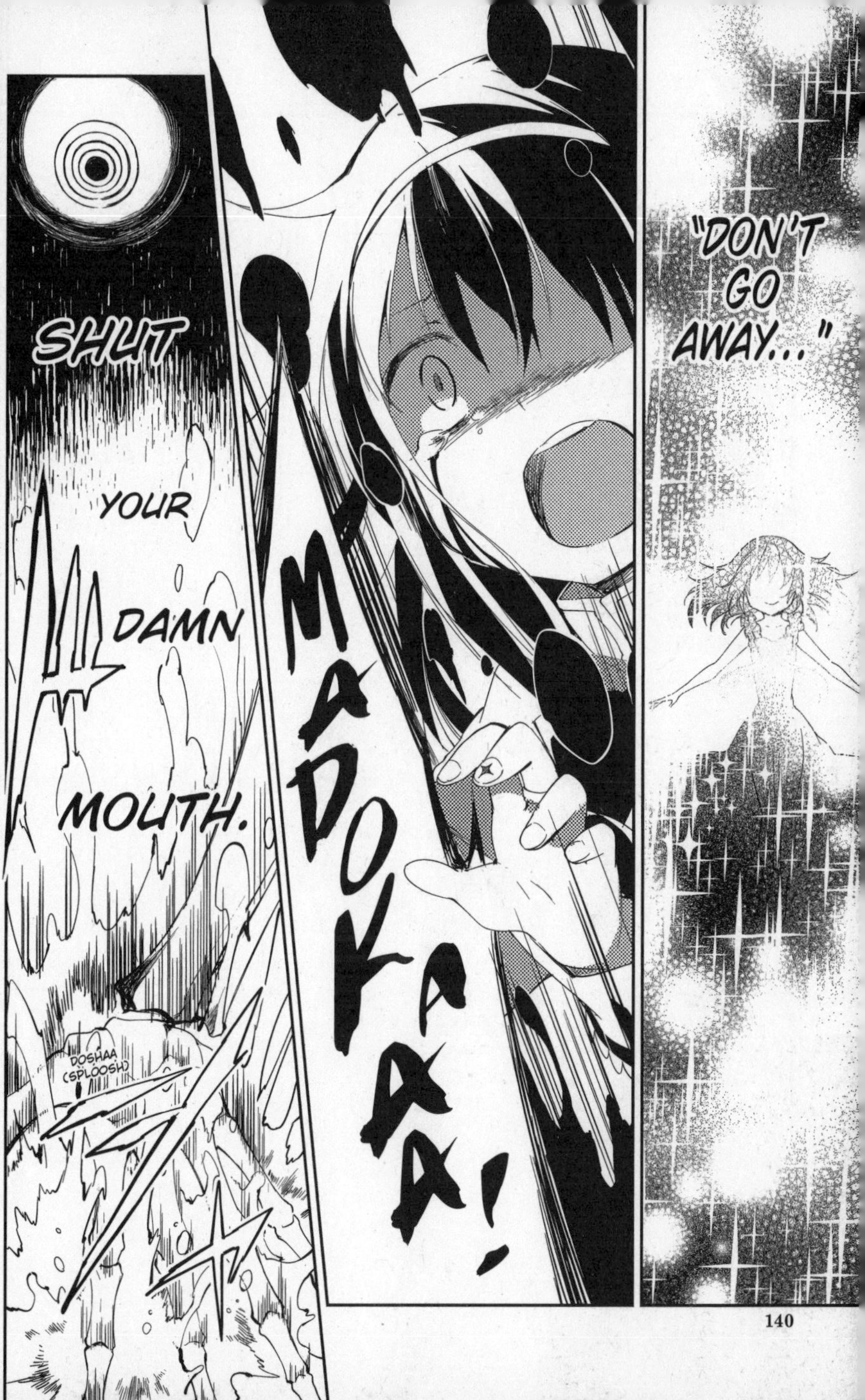
"DON'T GO AWAY..."
MADOKAAAA!
SHUT YOUR DAMN MOUTH.
DOSHAA (SPLOOSH)

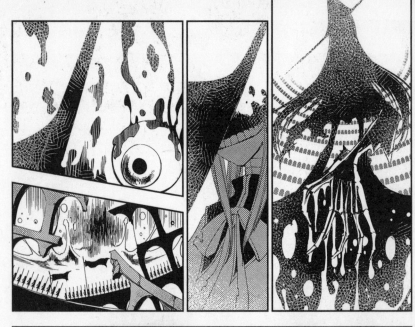

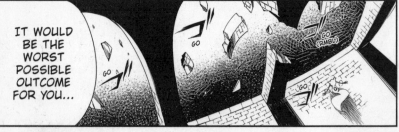

IT WOULD BE THE WORST POSSIBLE OUTCOME FOR YOU...

GO

GO

GO (RMBL)

GO

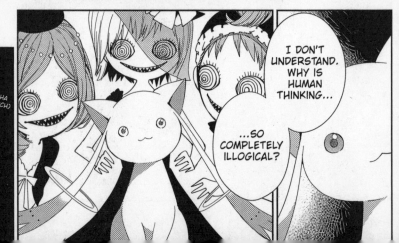

GUSHA (GLURCH)

グシャ

I DON'T UNDERSTAND. WHY IS HUMAN THINKING...

...SO COMPLETELY ILLOGICAL?

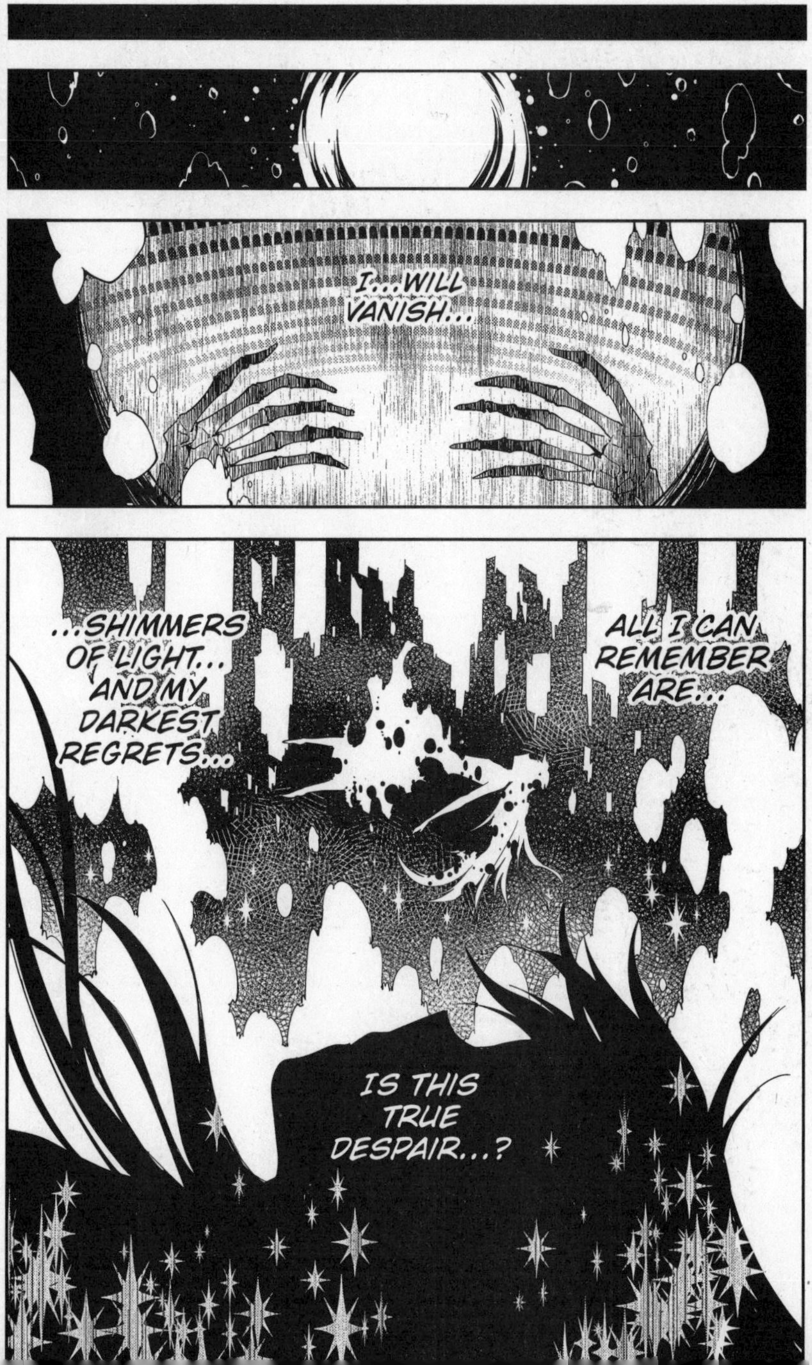
I...WILL VANISH...
ALL I CAN REMEMBER ARE...
...SHIMMERS OF LIGHT... AND MY DARKEST REGRETS...
IS THIS TRUE DESPAIR...?

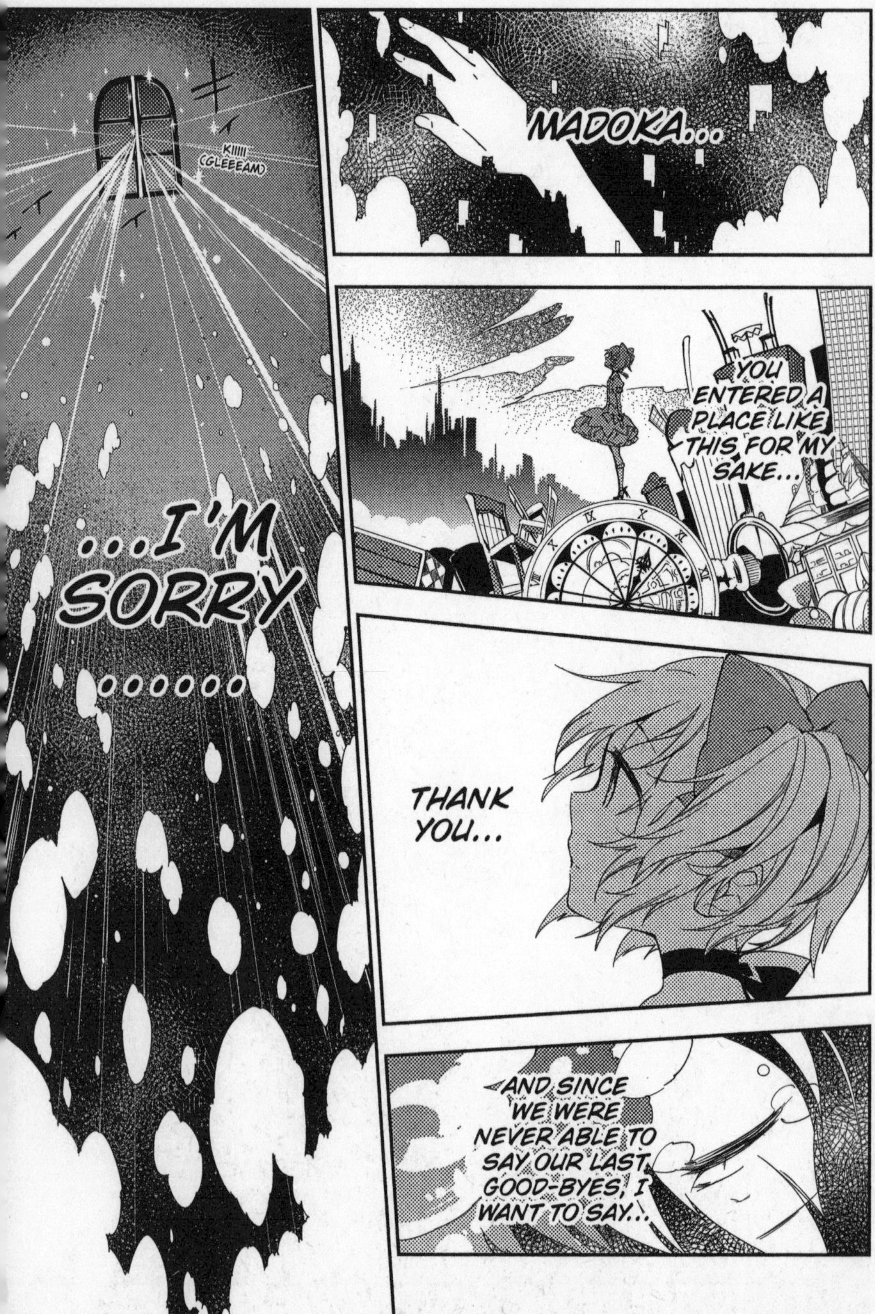
MADOKA...
YOU ENTERED A PLACE LIKE THIS FOR MY SAKE...
THANK YOU...
AND SINCE WE WERE NEVER ABLE TO SAY OUR LAST GOOD-BYES, I WANT TO SAY...
KIIIII (GLEEEAM)
...I'M SORRY
OOOOOOO

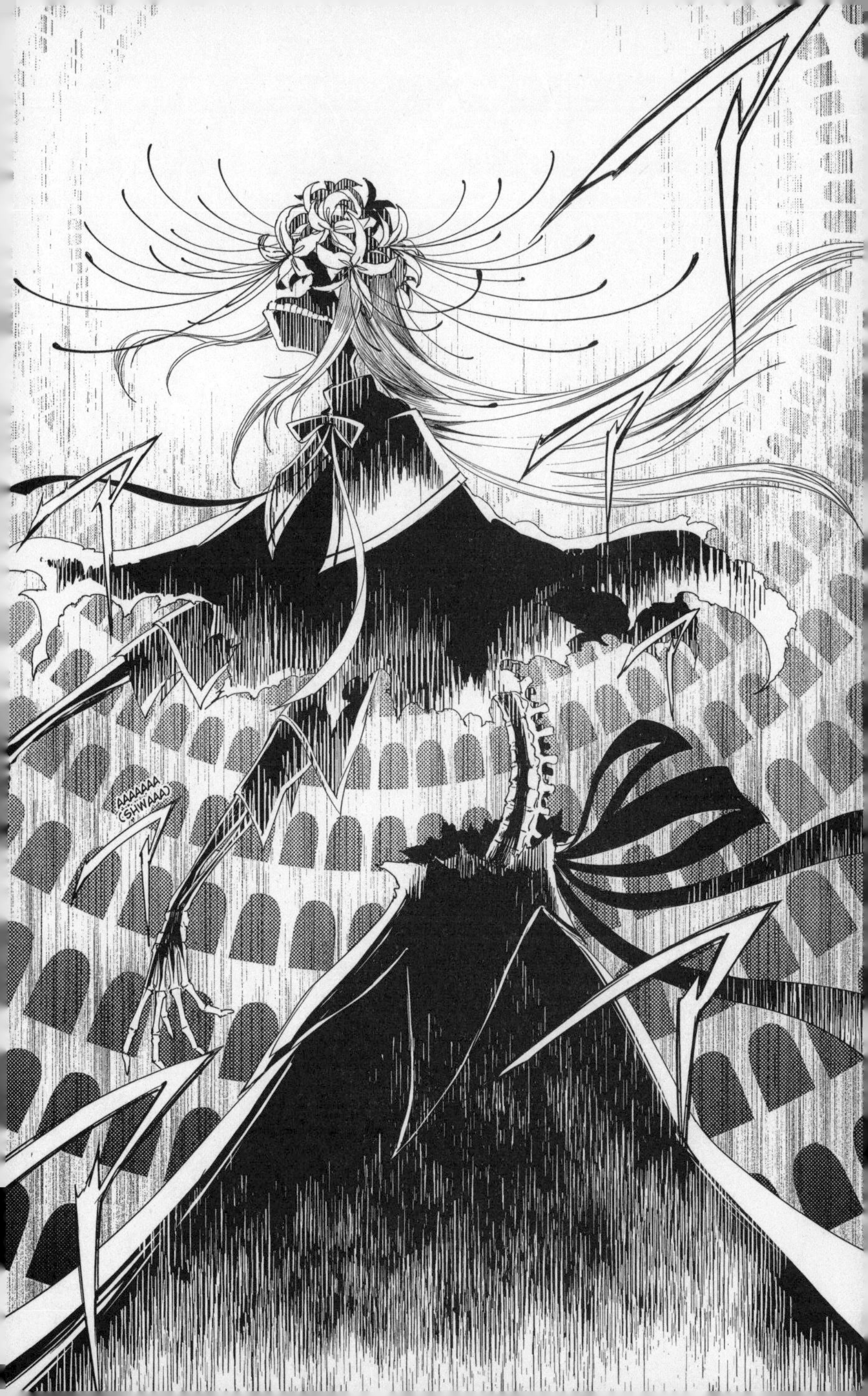
AAAAAAA
(SHWAAA)

PUELLA MAGI
MADOKA★MAGICA
THE MOVIE -REBELLION-

PUELLA MAGI
MADOKA☆
THE MOVIE

HANOKAGE

Translation: William Flanagan • Lettering: Abigail Blackman

This book is a work of fiction. Names, characters, places, and incidents are the product of the author's imagination or are used fictitiously. Any resemblance to actual events, locales, or persons, living or dead, is coincidental.

GEKIJYOUBAN MAHO SHOJO MADOKA☆MAGICA [SHINPEN] HANGYAKU NO MONOGATARI VOL. 2
© 2013 Magica Quartet / Aniplex, Madoka Movie Project Rebellion All rights reserved. First published in Japan in 2013 by HOUBUNSHA CO., LTD., Tokyo. English translation rights in United States, Canada, and United Kingdom arranged with HOUBUNSHA CO., LTD. through Tuttle-Mori Agency, Inc., Tokyo.

Translation © 2015 by Hachette Book Group, Inc.

Yen Press
Hachette Book Group
1290 Avenue of the Americas
New York, NY 10104

www.HachetteBookGroup.com
www.YenPress.com

Yen Press is an imprint of Hachette Book Group, Inc. The Yen Press name and logo are trademarks of Hachette Book Group, Inc.

The publisher is not responsible for websites (or their content) that are not owned by the publisher.

First Yen Press Edition: January 2016

Library of Congress Control Number: 2015952588

ISBN: 978-0-316-30939-4

10 9 8 7 6 5 4 3 2 1

BVG

Printed in the United States of America